The Four Seasons

with

Mark Allen Ballard

Printed in the U.S.A. by
Cookbooks by Morris Press
P. O. Box 2110 • Kearney, NE 68848

The Four Seasons

Spring

Shortly after the dormant chill of winter
Sheds its woolen blanket of white snow,
The precious gift of Spring gently comes to us
With its profusion of color, fragrance, rebirth and cheer,
Sprinkling Hope and Blessings on all that is near.

Summer

As the majestic Sun warms the Earth and Air,
And the gentle Rain waters the precious and fertile Soil,
Summer yields a bounty of flora, fruit and fun piled high,
As beautiful painted butterfly wings
Flit playfully against the cobalt blue Sky.

Fall

A brisk air slowly blows Summer into the past,
Changing its green leaves and fragile flowers
Into dormant symbols of much needed rest,
Carefully arranging a colorful cornucopia
Of a time with no complaints,
Gently preparing us for a season
To harvest, pause and give thanks!

Winter

The fragile Earth seems to close its eyes as if to sleep,
Under the frozen blanket that Winter almost always brings.
Only the evergreens, hollies, berries and cones,
Give us hope and dot the landscape with signs that life exists,
Because we know that after this much needed time of rest,
We will appreciate more the colors and all the Seasons' best!

Mark Ballard

Dedication

For being "raised right" as a child in a sometimes confusing and unsettled world. . .

For giving me the precious gift to develop my personality and allowing me to be myself. . .

For being able to learn to cook while making a horrible mess in the kitchen . . .

For showing me to appreciate beauty and how to plant and care for the Earth . . .

For being taught to be thankful for each and every gift and blessing that comes my way. . .

For giving me the courage to go out and create something beautiful in the world around me. . .

I sincerely and from the bottom of my heart, dedicate this book to the memories of my dear grandparents, Charlie and Clyde Allen, and my wonderful parents, Raymond and Jo Ballard, without whom I would not be the adult I am today.

Special Thanks To

.....my wife and business partner, Debra, who helps me coordinate my wildest ideas into some semblance of order. Without her organization and editing skills, my books would never come together.

....my children, Courtney and Blake, who have grown into wonderful adults and good cooks since the last book. Their support and love mean the world to me.

....family members, friends and scores of fans who shared their favorite recipes for this book.

....Jo Ann Stephens, a great friend and cook who assisted in proofreading and clarifying the recipes.

....you, for purchasing The Four Seasons!

Welcome to The Four Seasons

Some of my fondest memories of growing up in the South pertain to food. As a child, food always invited me to come closer and then enveloped me with an overwhelming comfort much like an old friend waiting at the front door with a pleasant smile and arms opened wide. As long as a spoon or fork was in my month, I was happy. I could, and still can, almost hear it call my name with that gleeful, smug voice of someone who is about to win the battle. "Mark, don't you want something sweet?" or "Mark, one more will not make a difference. Go ahead, have another!" And have another, I did!

It's funny how much of our lives revolve around the preparation and eating of food. The changing of seasons, special occasions, birthday celebrations, holidays and even plain get-togethers offer the perfect backdrop for a tasty feast. In fact, we don't even need a reason to celebrate; just fire up that oven or grill. Quite simply, we Southerners are known by the food we prepare, eat and share with others.

Life was so much simpler in "the good ole' days." We were unaware of all the unhealthy repercussions of our transgressions with food. Helping by helping we piled our plates so as not to miss out on one single taste sensation. In fact, if we became too skinny, we were forced to eat a little extra. And then there were all those people who were starving overseas. I never understood how cleaning my plate in Macon, Georgia would help someone be less hungry in Ethiopia. I still don't!

I, to this day, am mesmerized by a kitchen that is full of simmering pots, baking and bubbling casseroles, people in colorful aprons, and hands patting out biscuits with flour flying around like a tornado about to touch down. That, when accompanied by the mixing and mingling of the fragrant and wonderful aromas of food, is almost more than this mere mortal can bear.

I came from a family of cooks. Not trained chefs, but simple cooks. My grandmother didn't even know what a quiche was, but she sure could whip up some mashed potatoes with butter and sour cream. My mother and daddy taught my sister and me how to cook at a really early age. This training left us far more advanced than the other kids in our neighborhood. While they were making a peanut butter and jelly sandwich, we were preparing an entire meal from scratch. We thought all children were cooks until we stayed at out best friends' houses. Their mothers did everything for them, including cleaning their bedrooms. What was that about? Not ours, she wanted us to not only be self- sufficient, but also to lend her a helping hand. Since she worked, it was often our responsibility to cook supper and maintain some sort of semblance to our home.

We did it on our time, however. During the summer when we could go swimming, what we were cooking for supper became less important. We swam until the very last moment, and then, racing at record speeds back to our house, tried to throw something together so that it appeared we had been cooking all afternoon. This feat took amazing concentration and absolute determination and allowed my sister and me to work together in harmony for a common goal. Today, I realize my mother was a genius. She got us to clean our house and prepare our meals, while teaching us an important lesson that we both use to this day.

The television show called Bewitched was popular during our growing up years. I always dreamed of a way to get the magical powers Samantha had. Look how much longer we could have swam, if, with the twitch of our noses, we could have speeded up the process. Sometimes it definitely needed speeding up. A frozen pack of ground beef comes to mind. Why didn't we take it out of the freezer before we left to go swimming? You would think we would have learned our lesson after so many times. I became a pro at thawing out a pound of ground beef. I'd throw the frozen block of pinkish ground beef squarely into the bottom of a cast iron pan, making sure that it made a sound loud enough to wake the dead. Then I'd turn on the burner to a very low temperature and wait for a few minutes. When I thought it had been long enough, I would flip it over, scrape off the browned part and repeat this process until all that was left was a tiny, hard, frozen piece of meat that refused to give in to the heat. That's when my plan of attack was activated. Using a wooden spoon as a weapon, I chopped in forceful, slow and calculated motions until that last little frozen nub surrendered to my force and the heat of the frying pan. My sister then retrieved the browned meat.

Sometimes it ended up being tacos, sometimes spaghetti, but most of the time it was stirred into what would become a one-dish casserole. I still love a casserole. It's easy, quick and contains the whole meal in one dish with the help of a tried and true can of cream of chicken soup. You can't have a truly good casserole without that soup, and a cup or two of cheese!

It's funny that both my sister and I now make a living with food. What a gift we were given at such an early age. We have been destined to have food around us along with the weight problems it always unselfishly brings.

While I was in the process of deciding how I wanted to approach my second cookbook, I, being a theme oriented guy who is always in tune to the different seasons and holidays, decided to present this cookbook with that in mind. I have grouped these fabulous recipes into the times of the year I felt they would be appropriate. No, that certainly does not mean it's the only time you can prepare them, but by organizing them in this fashion, it allows us to take a year-long journey with food. And what else could we possibly ask for?

I hope you will enjoy reading and cooking from my new book. It contains wonderfully tasty recipes, some of my favorite short stories and poetry. Sit back, choose a recipe, and fire up the oven or grill. You are only minutes away from a craving!

Until we cook again,

Mark Allen Ballard

Table of Contents

Mark's Special Stories and Patterns

Spring

One of my favorite seasons of the year, Spring quietly steals in on the wings of chirping birds and delicate flower petals. It is as if a gigantic paint brush reaches down from the sky and paints our winter landscape with pastel colors and multiple shades of green. Flowers pop out of nowhere and the bees begin to buzz. It is truly a time for celebration. Everything becomes alive with a freshness that is guaranteed to rejuvenate us all. Easter is a big holiday that is celebrated during this season, and with it comes new spring clothes, decorated eggs and, less we forget, the Easter Bunny. Our friends south of the border throw a big party on May 5 to celebrate the ideals of liberty and freedom. And, then it's time to honor a most important person - our mother - on her special day. So, sit back and enjoy this beautiful and fresh season we adoringly call Spring!

Easter

Chirping Birds and Edible Nests

Easter always brings with it wonderful memories of my childhood. The collage includes crowded worship services, pristine white lilies, fresh new outfits and hats, hopping Easter bunnies, competitive egg hunts, chirping birds, chocolate and brightly colored eggs. Nestled deep within my memory banks, these images surround me with a feeling of rebirth and new beginnings. Spring is truly a magical time of year where nature shoves away the dull and ushers in a bright, new season. For some reason this takes me back to kindergarten. Talk about rebirth. Why is it the older we get the more we remember our youth?

When I think of my days in kindergarten, my mind vividly conjures up a fun room filled with smells of new and old books, sweaty youngsters hard at play, bluish-purple mimeographed handouts and thick paste. I can still see my teacher, Miss Betty, as she was known to us, commanding attention as the ruler of our class. She was a pleasant woman with a wonderful smile. I loved her. I especially loved the creative sessions of the day. This is where I first learned to "go out and create something beautiful."

Our little playhouse sat high atop a hill and really reminded me of a cottage from a fairy tale. Every morning when we were dropped off for our day of learning and fun, Miss Betty eagerly awaited us with open and caring arms. We thought this class was made just for us kids to have fun, but since I have had kids of my own, I realize that it was for our parents as much as ourselves. Parents certainly need a break!

Our playroom had three large tables with little children's chairs neatly placed around them. The tables were named – the

Papa Bear Table, the Mama Bear Table, and the Baby Bear Table. Clever and inventive, don't you think? Miss Betty had named them for a very important reason. You sat at the table that represented how you behaved that particular day. A seat at the Baby Bear Table meant that you were not well behaved. Being raised right, even then, I made it my goal to never sit there.

One Easter, Miss Betty cooked us a very special surprise. She made us edible bird nests filled with little candy eggs. They were delicate and beautiful. I was amazed! I still remember saving my nest the whole day, on a grease-stained napkin, to show my mother when she picked me up that afternoon. I knew we had to make some of our own.

Mother asked Miss Betty for the recipe the next day. We made nests for everyone we knew that Easter. When I got ready to compile my first cookbook a few years ago, I knew I had to include those edible bird nests. I dug through my mother's stained and old recipes until I came upon the one that read "Miss Betty's Nests." I was transported, at the speed of light, right back to being a child. It was a wonderful feeling. But what made it so special was that it was written in Mother's handwriting on the original envelope. Now that she is gone, the nest recipe is even more special!

Take a few extra minutes to make some of these nests with your children this Easter. Who knows, they may have the same memories one day!

MISS BETTY'S MACAROON BIRD NESTS

5 ½ to 6 ½ oz. Sweetened Angel Flake Coconut*
1 T. cornstarch
2 egg whites
½ tsp. vanilla flavoring
¼ cup sugar
Pinch of salt

* The amount of coconut will vary depending on the size of egg whites you use. Begin with 6 ounces unless egg whites are small.

Grease a baking sheet and dust with flour. Mix coconut thoroughly with cornstarch and sugar and set aside. Whip egg whites until frothy. Add salt and beat until stiff. Stir in vanilla. Gradually stir in the coconut mixture, adding enough to give a crumbly, not wet, texture. Shape into nests, placing on the cookie sheet. Bake approximately 20 minutes in moderate oven or until golden brown.

ASPARAGUS ROLLS

Cele Minshew

1 loaf crustless bread
1 stick butter
2 14-oz. cans asparagus
1½ c. pimento cheese spread

Roll each slice of bread flat using a glass or rolling pin. Spread pimento cheese over each flattened slice. Place an asparagus spear on top of cheese and roll up. Place on a cookie sheet. Melt butter and drizzle over all the rolled spears. Broil until brown on top.

SPINACH AND ARTICHOKE DIP

Dallas Chambers

1 lb. spinach leaves, stemmed and washed
¼ c. unsalted butter
½ c. onion, finely chopped
1 tsp. minced garlic
⅓ c. all-purpose flour
1 c. chicken broth
1 c. heavy cream
¾ c. milk
½ c. shredded part-skim mozzarella cheese
½ c. grated Parmesan cheese
½ c. sour cream
1 tsp. red hot pepper sauce
½ tsp. salt
¼ tsp. black pepper
9 oz. frozen artichoke hearts, thawed and chopped

In a Dutch oven, cook wet spinach, covered for 3 minutes, tossing once, until wilted. Drain, let cool and then chop. In a saucepan, melt butter. Add onion and saute until softened, about 2 minutes. Add garlic and cook 30 seconds. In a bowl, mix flour and broth. Add to pan with cream and milk. Simmer 5 minutes to thicken. Stir in mozzarella and Parmesan cheeses, sour cream, hot sauce, salt and pepper. Cook, stirring until cheese melts. Do not let boil. Add spinach and artichokes. Simmer for 5 minutes, stirring. Pour into serving bowl and serve with tortilla chips. Serves 8+.

EVER-SO-EASY DEVILED EGGS

Mark Ballard

6 hard-cooked eggs
⅓ c. (2.66-oz.) reduced-fat sour cream
⅓ c. (1.33-oz.) reduced-fat shredded cheese
3 T. minced green onions with tops
Additional minced green onion, optional
pimento strips or parsley leaves, optional

Cut eggs in half lengthwise. Remove yolks. Set whites aside. Mash yolks with fork. Stir in sour cream, cheese and 3 tablespoons of onions. Refill whites, using 1 heaping tablespoon of yolk mixture for each egg half. Garnish with additional onions and pimento, if desired. Chill to blend flavors.

YOGURT DEVILED EGGS

Mark Ballard

6 hard-cooked eggs
¼ c. plain, low-fat yogurt
1 tsp. minced onion
1 tsp. parsley flakes or freeze-dried chives
1 tsp. lemon juice or dry vermouth
¾ tsp. prepared mustard
¼ tsp. salt, optional
¼ tsp. Worcestershire sauce
⅛ tsp. pepper
dash of paprika

Cut eggs in half lengthwise. Remove yolks and set whites aside. In small bowl, mash yolks with fork. Stir in yogurt, onion, parsley, juice, mustard, salt (if desired), Worcestershire sauce, pepper and paprika. With spoon or pastry bag, refill whites using about 1 tablespoon yolk mixture for each egg half. Or place yolks in food-storage bag. Add remaining ingredients, except egg whites, to the bag. Close. Knead until everything is well-blended and smooth. Push the contents toward the corner. Snip about ½-inch off the corner of the bag. Squeezing the bag gently, fill the whites with the yolk mixture. Chill to blend flavors.

ONION CHEESE BISCUITS

Mark Ballard

3 T. butter for sauteing onions
1 stick butter, softened
1 3-oz. pkg. cream cheese, softened
¼ tsp. salt
paprika
1 med. onion, chopped
¼ lb. cheese, softened
1 tsp. Worcestershire sauce
1 c. flour
¼ med. Vidalia onion, chopped

Saute onions in 3 T. butter. Blend stick of butter and cheese until smooth. Add Worcestershire Sauce. Add all other ingredients and shape into balls. Place in preheated 350° oven for 20 minutes or until done. Sprinkle with paprika if desired.

SOUR CREAM BISCUITS

Mark Ballard

1 c. sour cream
2 sticks butter, melted
2 c. self-rising flour

Melt butter, stir in sour cream. Add flour. Mix well. Grease muffin pans. Fill half-full. Bake at 350°. Cook from 12 to 15 minutes or until done.

DALLAS' BUTTERMILK WAFFLES

Dallas Chambers

1 stick unsalted butter, melted
2 c. all-purpose flour
¼ c. light brown sugar, packed
1 tsp. baking soda
1½ tsp. baking powder
½ tsp. ground cinnamon
½ tsp. salt
3 lg. eggs, separated, at room temperature
2 c. buttermilk, at room temperature
1 tsp. pure vanilla extract

Spray waffle iron with non-stick cooking spray and begin to slowly heat. In a large bowl, sift together the flour, sugar, baking soda, baking powder, cinnamon and salt. In a separate bowl, whisk together the egg yolks, buttermilk, melted butter and vanilla. Pour into the dry mixture and mix well. In a medium bowl, beat egg whites until stiff but not dry. Fold egg whites into the batter. Ladle batter into the heated waffle iron and spread almost to the edges. Close lid, cook for 3 to 5 minutes, until no steam emerges form the waffle iron. Transfer cooked waffles to a baking sheet and place in a 200 degree oven to keep warm while cooking the remaining waffles.

7-UP SALAD

Rita Misinco

2 pkg. lemon gelatin
1 c. hot water
1 can 7-UP, not chilled
1 pkg. (8-oz.) cream cheese
1 lg. can crushed pineapple, drained
½ c. chopped nuts

Beat cream cheese in mixer. Combine hot water, gelatin and 7-UP. Add pineapple and nuts. Blend well. Add green food coloring if desired. Pour into mold and if desired cover top with tiny marshmallows. Chill until firm before serving.

DEBRA'S FAVORITE BROCCOLI SALAD

Gayle Fox

1 bunch broccoli, chopped so that you have mini florets
1 c. golden raisins
1 lb. bacon (fried and crumbled)
1 sm. onion, chopped finely
1 c. walnuts, finely chopped
Prepare the ingredients (chopping and crumbling) and place in a bowl large enough to stir in.

Dressing:
1 c. mayonnaise
½ c. sugar
2 T. rice vinegar

Mix dressing in separate bowl. Pour over the ingredients in larger bowl and stir well to coat. Refrigerate at least overnight. This salad gets better with age and lasts up to a week in the refrigerator.

My wife Debra says that if she had to take just one dish to a desert island, this would be the one.

BROCCOLI SALAD

Betty Jones

1 head fresh broccoli, chopped
½ to 1 head fresh cauliflower, chopped (optional)
1 c. shredded cheddar cheese
8 strips bacon, crisp crumbled
1 purple onion, chopped (may use only ½ if desired)

Dressing:
½ c. mayonnaise
1 T. red wine vinegar
¼ c. sugar

Toss first 5 ingredients together. Mix dressing ingredients thoroughly and pour first mixture. Toss again. Best if refrigerated overnight to blend flavors.

FRESH BROCCOLI SALAD

Virginia Avery

1 bunch of fresh broccoli, chopped
1 can B & B mushrooms, chopped
⅔ c. black olives, chopped
4 hard boiled eggs, chopped
1 c. mayonnaise
2 T. lemon juice
⅔ c. chopped onions
salt and pepper to taste

Mix all ingredients well and chill overnight.

MACARONI SALAD

Edith Sullivan

1 lb. (sm.) box macaroni shells, cooked and drained
1 grated carrot
3 ribs celery, cut small
1 green bell pepper, cut small
1 c. grated med. cheddar cheese
2 c. salad dressing or mayonnaise
1 pkg. ranch dressing mix
1 jar salad olives (6 or 7-oz.), do not drain

Cook macaroni according to box directions. Drain and cool. Mix salad dressing/mayonnaise, ranch dressing mix and salad olives. Add other vegetables and macaroni. Mix well. May add salt and/or pepper to taste. Refrigerate. Serves 24. May add onions, cooked ham, bacon or anything you wish.

MANDARIN ORANGE FRUIT SALAD

Barbara Rouse

1 (3-oz.) pkg. orange Jell-O
1 (3-oz.) pkg. lemon Jello-O
1 c. boiling water
3 (11-oz.) can Mandarin oranges with juice
1 lg. can crushed pineapple with juice
1 (10-oz.) pkg. mini marshmallows
1 (9-oz.) Cool Whip
1 c. mayonnaise
1 c. grated cheese

Dissolve Jell-O in boiling water. Add oranges and pineapples with juice. Spread marshmallows on top and push down into mixture lightly. Put in refrigerator and let mixture congeal. Mix Cool Whip and mayonnaise and spread over congealed mixture. Sprinkle cheese over top.

BROCCOLI CASSEROLE

Virginia Avery

2 bunches of broccoli
1 can cream of mushroom soup
¼ sm. onion (chopped fine)
1 T. mayonnaise
1 c. shredded American cheese
4 slices of bacon (fried and diced)
salt and pepper to taste

Cook broccoli until it is aldente and drain the water off. Mix soup, onion, mayonnaise and broccoli in casserole dish. Sprinkle the cheese and bacon on top. Place in oven and bake 375° until golden brown on top.

BROCCOLI-CAULIFLOWER CASSEROLE

Gladys Aaron

2 pkg. broccoli spears
2 pkg. cauliflower
1 can cream of celery soup
1 can cream of chicken soup
1 sm. jar Cheese Whiz
1 sm. can French Onion Rings

Boil broccoli and cauliflower until tender. In another pan mix both soups together and Cheese Whiz. Stir this together and heat until blended well. Spray the bottom of a casserole dish with Pam. Next, lay the broccoli and cauliflower in the dish. Now, pour the soup over the broccoli and cauliflower. Bake for 30 minutes at 350 degrees or until bubbly. Take it out and put onion rings on top. Put back in oven and bake for 5 more minutes.

POTATOES IN SALT CRUST

Cele Minshew

2 cloves garlic, peeled and halved
extra-virgin olive oil
2 T. fresh rosemary
3 lbs. yellow finn or fingerling potatoes, scrubbed
1½ lbs. Kosher or course salt
¼ c. all-purpose flour
½ c. water
1 c. sour cream

Heat oven to 450 degrees. Rub garlic over the bottom and sides of an iron skillet. Brush a thin layer of olive oil over the pan. Sprinkle the rosemary over the bottom of the pan and place the potatoes in a snug layer on top. In a large bowl, whisk together the salt and flour. Slowly stir in water until thoroughly combined. Pour the salt mixture over the potatoes in an even layer, making sure to fill in any gaps between the potatoes. Roast potatoes in oven for 1 hour and 15 minutes. Remove pan from oven and allow potatoes to cool for 5 minutes. Invert pan onto a large serving platter or cookie sheet. Crack open the salt crust and remove potatoes. Drizzle the potatoes with olive oil and serve with sour cream. (The salt seals the potatoes, giving them a wonderful velvety texture.)

ASPARAGUS SOUFFLE

Cele Minshew

1 14-oz. can asparagus
1½ c. grated cheddar cheese
1 c. mayonnaise
1 can cream of mushroom soup
4 eggs

Blend all ingredients until mixed well. Pour into a greased 1½-quart casserole dish. Bake at 350 degrees for 1 hour.

CARROT SOUFFLÉ

Beverly Futch

1 lb. carrots
½ c. melted butter
3 eggs
1 tsp. vanilla
1 T. plain flour
1 tsp. baking powder
1 c. sugar

Cook carrots until tender in lightly salted water. Combine carrots and butter in blender or food processor until smooth. Add remaining ingredients and blend. Bake in 1 quart casserole at 350°, 45 minutes. Dust top with powdered sugar.

ROASTED PORK LOIN WITH PEACH PUREE

Mark Ballard

Pork tenderloin weighing approximately 3½ lbs.
1 15-oz. can sliced peaches pureed in blender (or one junior size jar of baby food peaches)
1 10-oz. bottle Heinz 57 sauce or A-1 sauce
2 T. brown sugar
1 lg. pod garlic cleaned and separated into cloves
1 T. rosemary
2 tsp. salt
2 tsp. pepper
1 or 2 T. flour as needed

Marinate tenderloin for 24 hours prior to preparation in first five ingredients (inserting cloves of garlic in meat). Bring to room temperature before cooking. Preheat oven to 400°. Drain tenderloin and save marinade. Rub salt and pepper over meat and cook ten minutes. Reduce heat to 350° and continue to cook 15 minutes to a pound or until meat thermometer indicates the meat is cooked thoroughly. Baste every ten minutes with marinade adding remainder of marinade last ten minutes. Do not overcook. Remove tenderloin from pan and add flour to thicken sauce. Serve with sauce over tenderloin. Serves 4 to 6.

RAISIN SAUCE FOR HAM OR FRESH PORK

Mary Jean Moore

1 box dark brown sugar
1 box raisins
1 qt. water
dash vinegar

Combine all ingredients. Simmer. Serve over sliced ham or fresh pork.

CHEESE CAKE

Nell Lamb Holland

1½ c. swieback crumbs (available on cookie aisle)
3 T. butter, melted

Combine ingredients and press into bottom of 9-inch spring form pan. Bake 5 minutes at 350°.

Layer #1:
2 8-oz. pkg. cream cheese
¾ c. sugar
4 egg yolks
1 T. lemon juice
2 tsp. vanilla extract
4 egg whites

Combine cream cheese and sugar. Add egg yolk, lemon juice and vanilla extract. Beat egg whites until stiff and fold into other mixture. Bake 30-45 minutes at 350° until lightly brown.

Layer #2:
1 c. sour cream
2 T. sugar
1 tsp. vanilla

Spread over layer #1 and bake 15 minutes longer. Refrigerate overnight. Serves 10.

DELI LANE'S CARROT CAKE

Deli Lane

2 c. all-purpose flour
1 tsp. baking soda
1 tsp. cinnamon
½ tsp. salt
2 c. sugar
3 eggs
¾ c. buttermilk
¾ c. vegetable oil
1 tsp. vanilla
1 c. fresh pineapple, diced
1 c. med.-grated carrots
1 c. fine-grated coconut
1 c. chopped walnuts

For the cake:
Place flour, baking soda, cinnamon and salt in a bowl and mix with a wire whisk. Beat sugar, eggs, buttermilk, oil and vanilla into the flour mixture. Combine pineapple, carrots, coconut and walnuts; fold into the batter. Grease and flour a 10-inch springform pan. Add batter to the pan. Place on cookie sheet in preheated 250° oven for about 1 hour and 15 minutes, or until golden brown and a toothpick inserted in center comes out clean. Let cool completely on a wire rack before removing from pan.

Frosting:
1 stick butter, softened
1 8-oz. pkg. cream cheese, softened
½ tsp. vanilla
1 c. confectioners' sugar

For the frosting: Beat butter and cream cheese with an electric mixer until creamy and fluffy. Add vanilla and confectioners' sugar. Start mixer slowly and mix until well-blended.

CHERRY CRUMB CAKE

Mark Ballard

1 c. Crisco (white works best)
1 c. Miracle Whip (or any whipped) margarine
2¾ c. sugar
5 eggs
3 c. cake flour
1 c. milk
2 tsp. vanilla
1 T. butter flavoring

Cream first three ingredients together well. Then add eggs one at a time. Alternate adding 1 cup flour at a time and milk. Add flavorings. Mix well. Makes four layers. Set aside to cool completely before icing.

Icing:
Beat 4 egg whites until stiff
¾ cup Crisco (white works best)
1 box 10x confectioners sugar
1 tablespoon pure lemon extract
2 6-oz. packages of frozen coconut (slightly thawed)
8 oz. jar cherries (drained and chopped)

Mix Crisco and sugar together, adding egg whites along. Add remainder, stir well and ice cake.

LEMON CHEESE ICING

Gloria Sikes

1½ c. sugar
4 T. self-rising flour
2 T. grated lemon rind
⅔ c. lemon juice
2 eggs, beaten
2 T. oleo

Mix sugar and flour thoroughly. Add remaining ingredients and blend well. Cook in double boiler over boiling water, stir constantly until thickened. Cool. Frost 3 layer cake.

WHIPPED CREAM POUND CAKE

Mark Ballard

½ lb. butter (no substitute)
2½ c. sugar
6 lg. eggs
1 c. whipping cream (not whipped)
3 c. sifted cake flour
1 tsp. *each*: vanilla, almond, lemon flavorings

Cream butter that is room temperature with sugar. Beat in eggs one at a time. Add whipping cream alternately with flour. Add your choice of 2 flavorings. Bake at 325° for 1½ hours. Start in a cold oven. Use a 10 cup tube pan. Serves 12 to 15.

Cinco de Mayo

May 5 is not Mexican Independence Day as many people assume. And, it's not an American holiday - but it should be. Cinco de Mayo is one big party that celebrates freedom and liberty, ideals that both Mexicans and Americans have fought shoulder-to-shoulder to protect ever since May 5, 1962.

My entire family loves Mexican food - the spicier the better. Enjoy and Ole!

ARMADILLO BITES

Judy Harris

1 lb. grated Cheddar
1 lb. ground pork sausage
2 c. baking mix
(10-oz.) jar jalapeño pepper slices original
Shake-n-Bake coating mixture

Mix cheese and sausage until well blended. Add baking mix and mix well. Remove about 50 jalapeño slices from jar, shake off liquid, and lay on paper towels to absorb excess liquid. Take a chunk of dough mixture about the size of a walnut. Pat into flat patty, lay slice of pepper on it, and fold up edges around pepper and seal well. Roll into a ball between your hands, pressing firmly. After mix has been used up, pour Shake-n-Bake into small bowl. Rolls balls in this and place on a cookie sheet, about an inch part. Bake at 325° for 20-25 minutes until they are cooked through and golden brown. Drain on paper towels. Can be frozen and cooked later. Add 5 extra minutes baking time if frozen.

ROASTED RED PEPPER SALSA

Mark Ballard

2 (15-oz.) cans black beans, rinsed and drained
1 (12-oz.) jar roasted red peppers, drained and diced
1½ c. frozen corn kernels, cooked and drained
1½ c. thick and chunky salsa
1 c. canned tomato sauce
½ c. chopped green onions
½ c. chopped cilantro, optional
salt and freshly ground pepper to taste

Combine all ingredients in a large bowl. Stir well. Refrigerate several hours or up to 3 days before serving. Serve with corn chips and sour cream. Also delicious over grilled fish, shrimp or chicken.

FIESTA SALSA

Mark Ballard

2 avocados, peeled and chopped
1 pt. cherry tomatoes, quartered or halved
1 c. frozen corn, thawed
3 T. chopped green chilies, drained
3 T. lime juice
½ tsp. sugar
salt and pepper to taste

Carefully toss avocados, tomatoes, corn, green chilies, green onions, lime juice, sugar, and salt and pepper together.

GUACAMOLE

Mark Ballard

1 Haas avocado
1 tsp. chopped jalapeño chiles
1½ tsp. chopped cilantro
Juice of one lime
3 T. chopped onions
½ tsp. salt
2 T. chopped tomato (discard seeds & juice)

Using the back of wooden spoon, thoroughly mash 1 T. chopped onion, ½ tsp. chopped jalapeño chiles, ½ tsp. chopped cilantro and ½ tsp salt. Holding the avocado in the cup of the hand, split the avocado in half lengthwise and remove the seed. Scoop the avocado out of the skin with a spoon and add it to the paste, mixing together. Then fold in tomatoes and lime juice. Add more jalapeño chiles and salt to taste.

This recipe is from Zarela, our favorite Mexican restaurant in New York City. It is fabulous!

HOT CHEESE IN A JAR

Betty Jones

2 lb. Velveeta cheese (do not substitute)
1 med. onion, grated
1 (5.33-oz.) evaporated milk
1 pt. Miracle Whip Salad dressing (do not substitute)
1 (8-oz.) can seeded, de-veined jalapeño peppers, chopped fine (cut off stems)

Melt cheese in top of double boiler. Add onion, milk, Miracle Whip and peppers to melted cheese and mix well. Pour into 6 (8 ounces) jelly jars. Cool, screw on caps and refrigerate. May be used as a spread or let stand about 20 minutes and use as a dip.

MEXICORN DIP

Vicki Brantley

2 12-oz. cans Mexicorn
1 c. sour cream
8-oz. cheddar cheese, shredded
1 4-oz. can chopped green chilies, drained
1 sm. onion, chopped
1 c. mayonnaise
½ tsp. red pepper (cayenne)
chopped jalapeño peppers - to taste
garlic salt - to taste

Mix all ingredients in bowl. Serve with corn chips. Dip is even better when allowed to chill overnight.

NACHO SAUSAGE DIP

Judy Harris

2 lb. pork sausage/ one hot, one mild
2 cans cream of mushroom condensed soup
5-oz. evaporated milk, undiluted
2 lb. processed American cheese
2 4-oz. cans chopped chilies
1 4-oz. jar pimentos
1 8-oz. jar taco sauce, mild or hot
tortilla chips

Cook sausage in large skillet, crumbling into ½-inch pieces. Drain and place in crockpot. Add remaining ingredients and cook on high until cheese is melted and ingredients are combined, stirring often. Turn to low heat and serve with tortilla chips.

TACO DIP APPETIZER

Jo Ann Stephens

1 pt. sour cream
1 8-oz. pkg. cream cheese, softened
1 pkg. taco seasoning mix
shredded lettuce
chopped tomatoes
shredded cheese

Mix sour cream, cream cheese and taco seasoning together until smooth. Spread in a 9 x 13-inch dish. Top with shredded lettuce, chopped tomatoes and spread shredded cheese on top. Refrigerate and serve with chips.

TORTILLA SPINACH ROLL

Vicki Brantley

1 c. sour cream
8-oz. cream cheese, softened
3 10-oz. pkg. frozen chopped spinach, thawed and drained
1 env. ranch salad dressing mix
3 green onions, finely chopped
½ tsp. dillweed
garlic powder to taste
4 slices of crisp bacon, crumbled
1 10-count pkg. large flour tortilla

Beat cream cheese and sour cream until light and fluffy. Add spinach and mix well. Add salad dressing mix, green onions, dillweed, garlic powder, and bacon. Mix well. Cut edges from tortillas to make them square. Spread mixture over tortillas. Roll and wrap individually in waxed paper. Chill or freeze until serving time. Cut into ½-inch to 1-inch pieces. Serve chilled or warm in the microwave for a few seconds.

CO-JITO

Debra Ballard

3 c. fresh mint leaves
¾ c. sugar
8-oz. freshly squeezed lime juice
24-oz. Malibu rum
4 limes cut into thin slices to garnish

Add the mint, sugar, and lime juice to a pitcher, and muddle with a wooden spoon to crush the mint leaves. Stir in the rum, making sure the sugar has dissolved, then add 4 cups of ice. Garnish each tall glass with lime slices.

SANGRIA ROSA

Marianne Lokey

1 bottle dry red wine
6-oz. Ciroc grape vodka
3-oz. Cointreau or Triple Sec
2-oz. white grape juice
2-oz. lemon juice
2-oz. simple syrup
3-oz. pomegrante juice
3-oz. strained orange juice
club soda
blackberries, raspberries, or huckleberries

Simple syrup:
1 c. granulated sugar
1 c. water

Add the first 8 ingredients and a few berries to a large pitcher half filled with ice, and stir briefly. The mixture should be very light pink. Pour into long-stem white-wine glasses over a small amount of fresh ice, and top off each glass with about ½ ounce of club soda. Garnish with a berry or two. Serves 8.

Simple syrup:
Combine 1 cup granulated sugar and 1 cup water in a saucepan. Bring the mixture to a boil for a few seconds. Set aside to cool.

JALAPENO & FRESH CORN CORNBREAD

Mark Ballard

½ c. hot water
¼ c. sun-dried tomato bits
1 c. all-purpose flour
1 c. yellow cornmeal
2 T. sugar
1 tsp. baking soda
¾ tsp. salt
1 c. nonfat buttermilk
2 T. vegetable oil
2 egg whites, lightly beaten
1 egg, lightly beaten
1 c. fresh corn cut from cob (about 2 ears)
½ c. sliced green onions
3 T. minced jalepeño pepper
1 clove garlic, minced
vegetable cooking spray

Combine hot water and tomato bits in a bowl; cover and let stand 10 minutes. Drain and set aside. Combine flour and next 4 ingredients in a large bowl; make a well in center of mixture. Combine buttermilk and next 3 ingredients; stir well. Add tomato bits, corn and next 3 ingredients to buttermilk mixture; stir well. Add to dry ingredients, stirring just until moistened. Spoon batter into a 9-inch square baking pan coated with cooking spray. Bake at 375° for 30 minutes or until a wooden pick inserted in center comes out clean. Cool 10 minutes in pan on a wire rack. Yield 16 servings.

HUEVOS RANCHEROS, SOUTHERN STYLE

Mark Ballard

1 T. olive oil
1 c. chopped onion
2 cloves garlic, minced
1 c. tomato sauce
1 c. thick and chunky picante salsa
4 c. water
1 tsp. salt
1 c. quick-cooking grits
4 lg. eggs
2 T. cilantro, chopped
1 c. Cheddar cheese, shredded
cilantro springs, to garnish

Heat olive oil in a heavy large skillet over medium heat. Add onion and garlic; cook, stirring constantly, for 3 minutes. Add tomato sauce and picante sauce; simmer, uncovered for 5 minutes. In a heavy saucepan, bring water and salt to boil. Slowly stir in grits. Cook, uncovered, stirring occasionally, 3-5 minutes, or until thickened. With back of spoon, make four indentations in red sauce. Slip an egg into each indentation. Cover and cook over medium heat until eggs reach desired degree of doneness, about 5-7 minutes. Spoon grits evenly in the center of four dinner plates. Carefully lift eggs from skillet and place in the center of grits. Stir chopped cilantro into sauce; spoon sauce around eggs. Top eggs with cheese. Garnish with cilantro springs, if desired.

JALAPENO CHEESE GRITS

Debra Ballard

3 c. boiling water
¾ c. grits
½ stick margarine
½ lb. grated cheddar cheese (sharp)
½ tsp. salt
2 beaten eggs
¼ c. milk
2 tablespoons chopped jalapenos (pickled)

Cook grits in boiling water 10-15 minutes until done. Remove from heat and add margarine, cheese, salt, milk and jalapenos. Mix well. Cool slightly. Beat eggs and add to mixture when cooled enough not cook eggs. Pour in casserole dish and bake at 300° for 1½ hours. This can be made ahead and refrigerated until time to cook.

CALICO BLACK BEAN SALAD

Jim Fobel

½ c. olive oil
2 lg. garlic cloves, minced or crushed through a press
1 or 2 fresh jalapeño chiles, minced
2 tsp. ground cumin
1 tsp. dried oregano, crumbled
3 c. fresh or frozen corn kernels
1 tsp. salt
1½ c. shelled fresh or frozen green peas
2 16-oz. cans black beans, drained or 3 c. cooked black beans
2 med. tomatoes, cut into ½-inch dice
½ c. sliced whole scallions or chopped purple onion
½ c. chopped fresh cilantro
1 T. Dijon mustard
½ tsp. black pepper
¼ c. fresh lime or lemon juice

Spoon 2 tablespoons of the olive oil into a large heavy skillet set over moderate heat. Add the garlic, jalapeño, cumin, and oregano and saute until fragrant, about 30 seconds. Add the corn, toss, increase the heat to moderately high, and saute for 2 minutes. Pour in ½ cup water, cover, and cook for 2 minutes. Turn the mixture into a large bowl and add the salt. Toss and set aside to cool to room temperature. Drop the peas into a small pot of lightly salted boiling water and cook until tender, 3 to 5 minutes for fresh, 2 minutes for frozen. Rinse under cold water. Add the peas to the salad, along with the black beans, tomatoes, scallions, and cilantro. Make a dressing by stirring together the mustard, pepper, and lime juice. Gradually whisk in the remaining ¼ cup plus 2 tablespoons olive oil. Pour over the salad and toss thoroughly. Cover and chill for at least 1 hour. Serve cold.

GAZPACHO

Debra Ballard

4-6 ripe tomatoes
1 bell pepper, cored
2 peeled cucumbers
2 stalks celery
1-2 Vidalia onions
¼ c. Balsamic vinegar
¼ c. olive oil
2-3 T. cumin
Any of your favorite garden fresh veggies
banana or jalepeño pepper to taste

Add ¼ cup Balsamic vinegar, ¼ cup olive oil, pinch of dried or fresh basil, and vegetables in blender and blend well. Let set in refrigerator for 1-4 days before serving. Garnish with a dollop of sour cream, fresh cilantro and small slices of green pepper. Can also use fresh crab or shrimp to garnish. Try squeezing fresh lime juice into bowl prior to serving. Delicious!

SANTA FE CHICKEN SALAD

Mark Ballard

1 head of lettuce (iceberg, romaine, any type you like)
1 can whole kernel corn
1 can of Goya black beans
2 boneless, skinless chicken breasts
juice of 4-5 limes
cilantro, chopped
1 lg. red onion, chopped
ripe tomato, chopped
peanut dressing (may be found in Kroger in the gourmet section)
peanuts
corn chips

Clean chicken removing any fat. Place in shallow dish. Squeeze 3 limes over chicken and place limes in dish. Chop cilantro and sprinkle over chicken, making sure underneath chicken as well. Salt and pepper lightly. Cover and marinate for several hours or overnight in refrigerator. Bake in 400° degree oven until done, making sure that it does not dry out or, if time permits, grill the chicken. Cool chicken. Tear lettuce into large bowl. Drain corn and beans and add to lettuce. Chop cilantro to taste into bowl. Chop onion into bowl. Chop tomato into bowl. Squeeze juice from remaining limes over mixture. Add peanuts. Cut chicken into small pieces and add. Toss well. At last minute, pour dressing over entire mixture and crunch corn chips over top. Serve with more chips.

TACO SOUP

Alice Graham

2 lbs. ground beef
4 (16-oz.) cans tomatoes
1 (16-oz.) can pinto beans
1 pkg. ranch dressing mix
tabasco sauce to taste
1 lg. onion (chopped)
1 lb. can whole kernel corn (drained)
1 (16-oz.) can red beans
1 pkg. taco seasoning mix

Brown ground beef and onion together. Drain. Add other ingredients to beef mixture. Simmer for one hour. Serve topped with sour cream or grated cheese.

RIO FRESH SALAD

Mildred Gossett

1 red, green and orange bell pepper
1 purple onion **1 can of sweet yellow corn, drained**
1 jicama (Mexican root vegetable)
1 bunch of cilantro **1 can of pinto beans (optional)**
1 bottle of "Old Dutch" Sweet-N-Sour dressing

Dice the bell peppers and put into a large bowl. Chop the purple onion (you can use either ½ or the whole onion). Dump the corn into the bowl. Peel and dice the jicama. Chop about ⅓ cup of cilantro and add to the other vegetables. Drain and rinse the pinto beans and add. Pour the whole bottle of dressing over the salad. Allow to refrigerate 8 hours.

JALAPENO CORN CASSEROLE

Barbara Rouse

½ c. uncooked white rice
½ med. chopped onion
½ med. chopped bell pepper
½ c. chopped celery
¼ melted butter
½ T. sugar
2 jalapeño peppers, finely chopped
½ c. sharp cheese
1 can (17-oz.) cream corn

Cook rice according the package. Set aside. Saute onion, bell pepper and celery in butter until tender. Combine rice and vegetables with next 4 ingredients. Stir well. Spoon mixture into lightly greased 9 x 12 dish. Bake 325° for 30-45 minutes.

BLACK BEAN ENCHILADA BAKE

Mark Ballard

1½ c. dried black beans
6 c. water
2 c. chopped unpeeled tomatoes
1¾ c. chopped onion
2 T. chili powder
2 T. chopped jalapeño pepper
1½ tsp. ground cumin
½ tsp. dried whole oregano
¼ tsp. salt
2 lg. cloves garlic, crushed
1 8-oz. can no-salt added tomato sauce
10 (6-inch) corn tortillas
vegetable cooking spray
Mexican Cheese sauce (recipe follows)

Place beans in a Dutch oven. Cover with water 2 inches above beans, and bring to a boil; cook 2 minutes. Remove from heat; cover and let stand 1 hour. Drain beans. Combine beans and 6 cups water; bring to a boil. Partially cover, reduce heat, and simmer 1 hour. Add tomato and next 8 ingredients; cook, uncovered, over medium heat 40 minutes or until liquid evaporates and bean mixture is very thick, stirring frequently. Wrap tortillas in damp paper towels and then in aluminum foil. Bake at 350° for 10 minutes or until softened. Spread half of bean mixture in a 13 x 9 x 2-inch baking dish coated with cooking spray. Arrange half of tortillas over bean mixture; top with remaining mixture. Arrange remaining tortillas over mixture; spread Mexican Cheese Sauce over tortillas. Cover and bake at 350° for 15 minutes. Uncover, and bake 15 minutes or until thoroughly heated. Let stand 5 minutes. Yield: 10 servings.

Mexican Cheese Sauce:

vegetable cooking spray
¾ c. finely chopped bell pepper
1 T. finely chopped jalapeño pepper
1 c. frozen whole kernel corn
¾ tsp. ground cumin
1 c. tomato juice
1 T. all purpose flour
1 tsp. cornstarch
¼ c. skim milk
4-oz. shredded reduced-fat sharp Cheddar cheese
2-oz. shredded reduced-fat Monterey Jack cheese

Coat saucepan with cooking spray, and place over medium heat until hot. Add peppers, and saute 3 minutes. Add corn, cumin, and tomato juice, and simmer 5 minutes. Place flour and cornstarch in a bowl. Gradually add milk, blending with a wire whisk; add to corn mixture. Bring to a boil, and cook 1 minute or until thickened, stirring constantly. Remove from heat, and stir in cheeses. Yield: 2¾ cups.

CARAMELIZED VIDALIA ONION QUESADILLAS

Mark Ballard

Quesadillas:
3 Vidalia onions, halved with skins removed
1 T. safflower oil (or other mild vegetable oil)
1 tsp. apple cider vinegar
4 (8-inch) soft flour tortillas
1 c. grated Mexican Queso Blanco (Mozzarella can be substituted)

Pico de Gallo:
4 ripe plum tomatoes
½ Vidalia onion
juice of ½ lime
½ jalapeño
¼ c. chopped fresh cilantro
¼ tsp. salt

Caramelized Onions:
Note: Caramelizing the onions takes approximately 1 hour. This part can be done up 2 days ahead of time if caramelized onions are kept refrigerated.

Slice onions into very thin half-moon slices. In a heavy gauged, 2-quart saucepan with a tight fitting lid, heat the oil on medium high. Add the onions. Once the onions start to steam, stir once, lower heat to medium and replace cover. Allow to cook for 45 minutes, stirring occasionally. Begin preparing the Pico de Gallo. Remove lid and continue to cook another 15 minutes. As the onions begin to caramelize, stir more frequently. Add the vinegar and remove from the heat.

Pico de Gallo:
Dice tomatoes and onion into ¼-inch dice. Remove the seeds and white veins from the jalepeño and mince. (Use gloves if your hands are at all sensitive and be sure to wash hands after handling chiles.) Combine all ingredients and set aside at room temperature until ready to serve.

Quesadilla:
Spread ¼ of the caramelized onions evenly over ½ of each tortilla. Put ¼ cup of the cheese on each tortilla and fold in half. Place quesadillas in a hot dry skillet (medium-high) and cook until golden brown (about 1-1½ minutes) on each side. Remove from skillet; cut into quarters and serve immediately with the Pico de Gallo.

CHEESY CHIPOTLE ENCHILADAS

Mark Ballard

1 pkg. refrigerated flour tortillas, room temperature
12-oz. (3 c.) shredded Mexican blend cheese, divided

Sauce:
1-1½ lb. ground round
1 med. onion, diced
1 env. enchilada sauce mix
1 jar chipotle marinara OR
1 (lg. can) enchilada sauce plus 1 tsp. dried chipotle flakes
1 (14.5-oz.) can diced tomatoes
1 (14.5-oz.) can tomato sauce
1 c. water

Preheat oven to 350°. Generously grease 9 x 13 x 2-inch baking pan or suitable casserole. Prepare sauce. In Dutch oven over medium-high heat, brown beef and onions. Drain well. Stir in remaining ingredients until all ingredients are well incorporated. Spoon a portion of sauce in prepared baking dish, using just enough to barely cover bottom. Spoon a bit of sauce down center of a tortilla. Sprinkle with cheese. Roll up and place in baking dish. Repeat and fill casserole in a single layer. Sprinkle cheese over filled tortillas. Spoon remaining sauce over all, ensuring good coverage. Cover with parchment or wax paper, then cover tightly with foil. Bake 30-40 minutes. Remove from oven. Remove foil. Let stand 5-10 minutes before serving.

CROCK POT FAJITAS

Sharon Freeman

3 to 4 lb. boneless, lean roast
chili powder
cumin
garlic salt
black pepper
1 c. dry pinto beans, washed but not soaked
1 onion, sliced or chopped
1 can green chilies, undrained
1 can cream of mushroom soup
2 cans diced rotel tomatoes, undrained
1 can water

Spray crock pot with non-stick cooking spray. Rub roast with spices. Place the following in crock pot in this order: roast, pinto beans, onions, green chilies, soup (spread around without disturbing ingredients already in crock pot), Rotel tomatoes and water. Do NOT mix. Cover and cook on slowest setting for 16 hours. Do NOT peek. Serve with flour tortillas and any other south of the border condiments (cheese, guacamole, sour cream....)

CHICKEN ENCHILADAS

Bettye Cox

1 sm. to med. onion, chopped
1 sm. green pepper, chopped
1 sm. can chopped green chiles
3 to 4 c. chopped, cooked chicken
10 lg. flour tortillas
8-oz. cream cheese
1 can cream of chicken soup
8-oz. sour cream
1 to 2 c. shredded cheddar cheese

Brown onion, pepper and chiles in large skillet in 2 tablespoons butter or margarine. Add chicken and cream cheese, and mix thoroughly. Spoon 1/10th of mixture on each tortilla, roll and place side by side, seam side down in 13 x 5-inch baking dish or pan. Mix sour cream and chicken soup. Pour over tortillas. Cover with cheese and bake at 350° 30 to 35 minutes.

CHICKEN ROTEL

Mildred Gossett

3 lb. chicken
1 can. Rotel tomatoes
1 lb. Velveeta cheese
1 green pepper, chopped
1 onion, chopped
2 ribs of celery
1 stick oleo
16-oz. pkg. vermicelli noodles
1 can. mushroom soup
1 sm. can English peas

Boil chicken in salted water. Cool; pick off bone. Cook noodles in chicken broth. Saute onion, pepper and celery in oleo. Add mushroom soup, cheese and Rotel tomatoes. Heat until cheese melts. Add to noodles. Add chicken. Put in casserole. Heat to bubbly at 350°. Will freeze.

EL PASO PILAF

Mark Ballard

½ c. chopped onions
2 tsp. olive oil
1 can (15-oz) red kidney beans, rinsed and drained
1¾ c. reduced-fat chicken broth
1 c. long-grain white rice
1 c. corn
1 c. chunky salsa
¼ c. lentils
¼ c. chopped red bell peppers
½ tsp. chili powder
4 lg. tomatoes, hollowed

In a 3-quart saucepan over medium heat, cook onion in oil until tender but not brown, about 5 minutes. Add beans, broth, rice, corn, salsa, lentils, peppers, and chili powder. Bring to a boil, then reduce to a simmer. Cover and cook until rice and lentils are tender and most of liquid has been absorbed, 20 to 25 minutes. Stuff pilaf into hollowed tomatoes. Serve extra pilaf on the side. Serves 4.

QUICK CHICKEN TOSTADAS

Mark Ballard

6 (6-inch) flour tortillas
2 T. butter, melted
4 grilled chicken breast halves, chopped
2 tomatoes, chopped
1 (4.5-oz.) can chopped green chiles
½ c. (2-oz.) shredded Monterey Jack cheese
½ c. (2-oz.) shredded Cheddar cheese
3 green onions, chopped
paprika, (optional)
sour cream

Place tortillas in a single layer on baking sheets; brush with butter. Bake at 400° for 4 to 5 minutes or until lightly browned. Combine chicken, tomato, and chiles; spoon evenly onto tortillas. Top evenly with cheeses and green onions; sprinkle with paprika, if desired. Bake 3 to 4 more minutes or until cheeses melt. Serve with sour cream. Yield: 6 servings.

TURKEY OR CHICKEN ENCHILADAS

Mary Ballard

1 16-oz. ctn. plain nonfat yogurt
¾ c. chopped green bell pepper
½ c. chopped onion
¼ c. all-purpose flour
¾ tsp. ground coriander
¼ tsp. salt and a dash of pepper
Chicken Broth (reserved or canned)
2½ c. chopped turkey or chicken
¼ c. commercial medium salsa
6 (6-inch) flour tortillas

Place a small colander in a 2-quart glass measure or medium bowl. Line colander with 4 layers of cheesecloth, allowing cheesecloth to extend over outside edges. Spoon yogurt into colander. Cover colander loosely with plastic wrap; let stand at room temperature 2 hours. Spoon yogurt cheese into a bowl; discard liquid. Set yogurt cheese aside. Coat a medium saucepan with cooking spray, and place over medium heat; add bell pepper and onion. Saute 3 minutes or until tender. Combine flour and next 3 ingredients; gradually add broth, stirring with a wire whisk. Add to saucepan, bring to a boil, and cook 3 minutes or until thickened, stirring frequently. Remove from heat; stir in Monterey Jack cheese. Let stand 10 minutes. Gradually stir in yogurt cheese. Combine 1 cup cheese mixture, turkey, and salsa in a bowl; stir well, and set aside. Brush one side of each tortilla with water. Stack tortillas; wrap in wax paper. Microwave at HIGH 30 to 45 seconds. Spread ½ cup turkey mixture down center of each tortilla; roll up. Place in a 13 x 9 x 2-inch baking dish coated with cooking spray. Pour remaining cheese mixture over tortillas. Bake, uncovered, 25 minutes or until bubbly.

VEGETABLE BURRITOS

Mark Ballard

1 (16-oz.) can light red kidney beans, drained
1 T. chili powder
½ tsp. garlic powder
½ c. frozen whole kernel corn, thawed
6 (7-inch) flour tortillas
vegetable spray
1 c. thinly sliced onion
½ c. thinly sliced green bell pepper rings
½ c. thinly sliced red bell pepper rings
1½ T. lemon juice
⅓ c. commercial mild salsa
1 (14½-oz.) can no-salt-added whole tomatoes, drained and chopped

Drain beans, reserving ¼ cup liquid. Position knife blade in food processor bowl; add beans, reserved bean liquid, chili powder, and garlic powder. Process until smooth. Spoon bean mixture into a bowl; stir in corn. Set aside. Stack tortillas; wrap stack in damp paper towels and microwave at HIGH for 20 seconds. Spread ¼ cup bean mixture down center of each tortilla; roll up. Place, seam side down, in an 8-inch square baking dish coated with cooking spray. Cover and bake 350° for 30 minutes or until heated. Set aside; keep warm. Coat a large nonstick skillet with cooking spray; place over medium-high heat until hot. Add onion and next 3 ingredients; saute 5 minutes or until crisp-tender. Reduce heat to medium. Add salsa and tomatoes; simmer 1 minute. Serve over burritos. Yield: 6 servings.

CHICKEN FAJITAS

Mark Ballard

1½ lbs. boneless, skinless chicken breast halves, cut into ¾-inch strips
5 T. plus 1 tsp. olive oil, separate from each other
1½ tsp. ground cumin
Juice of one lime (2 to 3 T.)
½ tsp. cayenne pepper
¾ tsp. kosher salt
½ tsp. freshly ground black pepper
3 med. mixed sweet or hot peppers (about 1 lb.) stemmed, seeded and cut into ¾-inch strips
1 lg. yellow onion (about ½ lb.) cut in half and then into ¼-inch thick slices
1 pkg. fajita-size flour tortillas (one doz.)
slices of avocado, cilantro leaves and lime wedges, for garnish

Combine 5 tablespoons olive oil, cumin, lime, cayenne, salt and black pepper. Pour the marinade ingredients over chicken-breast strips. In a well-seasoned cast-iron pan, heat 1 teaspoon of olive oil until very hot, but not smoking. Place the pepper strips into the pan, and cook over very high heat, stirring and tossing often until charred and softened, about 10 minutes. Remove the peppers, and set aside. Add the onions to the pan and cook in the same manner until brown and soft, about 5 minutes. Set aside with the peppers. Place the chicken on the grill, and grill for about 3 minutes per side. (5-8 minutes total). Meanwhile heat the tortillas one by one in the cast-iron pan or over the grill for a few seconds per side, to soften. Serve family-style, so everyone can build their own fajitas.

STEAK FAJITAS

Mark Ballard

2 boneless ribeye steaks, or steaks of choice, about 10 to 12-oz.
2 lg. Vidalia onions, cut into strips
1 bell pepper, cut into strips
garlic salt, to taste
soft tortillas

Cut steaks into strips. In a nonstick pan, stir-fry meat until browned. Add onion and pepper strips and stir-fry until tender. Serve tortillas. Note: Top tortillas with cheese, sour cream, salsa or your favorite toppings. (If using chicken instead of steak, add 1 envelope of taco seasoning mix when you add the onions and peppers, stirring well.) Serves 4.

CREAMY CARAMEL FLAN

Mark Ballard

¾ c. sugar
4 eggs
1¾ c. water
1 14-oz. can sweetened condensed milk (not evaporated milk)
1 tsp. vanilla extract
⅛ tsp. salt
Sugar garnish, optional (recipe follows)

Preheat oven to 350 degrees. In heavy skillet, over medium heat, cook and stir sugar until melted and caramel-colored. Pour into 8 ungreased 6-oz. custard cups, tilting to coat bottoms. In a bowl, beat eggs with mixer or wire whisk; stir in remaining ingredients until well blended. Pour into prepared custard cups. Set cups in large shallow pan. Fill pan with 1 inch hot water. Bake 25 minutes or until knife inserted near center comes out clean. Cool. Chill. To serve, invert flans onto individual serving plates. Garnish as desired.

Sugar Garnish: Fill a medium-sized metal bowl half-full of ice. Combine 1 cup sugar with ¼ cup water in saucepan. Stir; cover and bring to a boil. Cook over high heat until amber in color. Immediately put pan in ice for one minute. Using spoon, carefully drizzle sugar decoratively over aluminum foil. Cool; peel from foil just before ready to serve. Place artistically on plate with flan.

FROZEN MARGARITA MOUSSE

Mark Ballard

Crust:
3 c. coarsely crushed salted pretzels
¾ c. butter, melted
½ c. sugar

Filling:
1 can sweetened condensed milk
8-oz. cream cheese
12-oz. frozen whipped topping, thawed
1 6-oz. frozen limeade concentrate, thawed
¼ c. tequila, optional
3-5 drops green food coloring, optional

Preheat oven to 350°. Combine pretzels, butter and sugar and mix well. Press firmly into bottom of 9x13x2-inch baking pan. Bake 10-12 minutes. Cool. Beat together sweetened condensed milk and cream cheese until smooth. Blend in remaining ingredients. Pour into cooled crust, spreading to level filling. Cover with foil and refrigerate several hours until firm. Serve frozen or slightly thawed. Makes 15 servings.

Mother's Day

A Bouquet for Mother

Whether I skinned my knee, made a boo-boo on my finger or just needed an unconditional hug, my mother was always there with arms wide open and a loving smile on her face. It wasn't until she died almost nine years ago, that I realized what an impact mothers have on our lives.

From the moment we are born, they are angels on loan to us for a time when we need their help the most. They guide us through the good, bad and ugly and serve up compassion just as easily as a healthy meal. They cheer us on when we're about to give up and car pool us around with all our friends. They are there to rock us, to teach us manners and to be sweet!

But, before we can truly appreciate their role, the years pass so quickly that we seem to take their "always there when we need them" presence for granted. This holiday called Mother's Day makes us stop, pause and give a great big hug to our maternal angels. After all, without them, we would not be here.

My mother always told me to give her flowers while she was alive and could enjoy their fragrance and beauty. She said she would not need them after she died. She did not want us to place them at her grave because she said she would not be there. When I asked her where she would be, she lovingly smiled, placed her hand on my chest and replied, "In your heart!"

Unfortunately, I can't thank my mother anymore for all she did for me. I certainly wish I could, but by urging you to thank and praise your mother on her special day, I am, in some magical way, doing the same for mine. Treasure every moment you have with your mother. Hug her and tell her what she means to you. After all, we never know when they, just like the most fragrant flowers, will fade away.

FRESH STRAWBERRY MUFFINS

Mark Ballard

2½ c. all-purpose flour
⅔ c. sugar
1 tsp. baking soda
¾ tsp. ground cinnamon
½ tsp. salt
1½ c. sliced fresh strawberries
1 c. nonfat buttermilk
⅓ c. margarine, melted
1¼ tsp. vanilla extract
1 egg, lightly beaten
1 egg white, lightly beaten
vegetable cooking spray
1½ T. sugar

Combine flour and next 4 ingredients in a large bowl, and stir well. Add fresh strawberries; stir well, and make a well in center of mixture. Combine buttermilk and next 4 ingredients; stir well. Add to dry ingredients, stirring just until moistened. Divide batter evenly among 18 muffin cups coated with cooking spray; sprinkle 1½ tablespoons sugar evenly over muffins. Bake at 350° for 25 minutes or until a wooden pick inserted in center comes out clean. Remove from pans immediately; let cool on a wire rack. Yield: 1½ dozen.

STRAWBERRY BREAD

Barbara Rouse

3 c. all-purpose flour
1 tsp. salt
1 tsp. soda
1 tsp. cinnamon
2 c. sugar
3 eggs, well beaten
1¼ c. oil
2 (10-oz.) pkg. frozen strawberries, thawed and drained
1¼ c. pecans, chopped

Combine flour, salt, soda, cinnamon, and sugar. Make a well in the center. Add eggs and oil stirring only until dry ingredients are moist. Stir in berries and pecans. Spoon into 2 greased 8-inch loaf pans. Bake for 1 hour or until done. Let cool before cutting.

LAZY CORNBREAD

Judy Harris

1 c. yellow or white plain meal
water
crazy salt (found in seasoning section at grocers)
black pepper
oil

Put frying pan over medium high heat and add oil to cover bottom. Put meal in bowl or measuring type pitcher with a spout. for ease in pouring. Sprinkle salt and pepper over this. Add enough water to make meal thin and very watery. When oil is very hot, pour enough of meal mixture to cover pan. If mixture has settled, stir enough to make it almost liquid when you pour it out. Add more water as needed if thickens. Add more oil as needed to keep it from sticking. This creates a wafer-thin bread that you can cook very crisply. Do not attempt to turn over until it hardens on bottom. After cooking both sides, put on paper towels to drain.

MAMA'S HOMEMADE BREAD

Jo Ballard

4 c. instant milk
3 pkg. dry yeast
½ c. plus 1 T. lukewarm water
½ c. vegetable oil
½ c. sugar
2 pinches salt
12 c. plain flour (preferably Martha White), divided

Scald milk and set aside until it reaches a lukewarm temperature. Dissolve yeast in water. Pour yeast mixture into the milk. Add oil, sugar and salt. Stir thoroughly. Pour the liquid mixture into a very large mixing bowl. Gradually add 6 cups of flour. When mixed well, beat the mixture. Then gradually add the rest of the flour. Roll the flour mixture out onto a floured surface. Knead thoroughly and beat air bubbles out with a rolling pin. Shape into a smooth ball. Put the dough ball into a clean bowl. Pour a little oil on hands and grease the whole ball of dough. Cover the dough inside the bowl with a towel and allow to rise once in the bowl. Pour the dough back out onto a floured surface and work it down. Divide the ball into smaller portions for each of your pans. This will make 4 regular sized loaves or 8 small loaves. Place the portions into the pans. Cover and allow to rise in pans until dough doubles in size. Bake in a moderate oven (350 degrees) until golden brown.

When I was growing up, our across-the-street neighbor's mother made this bread. Being a carbohydrate addict, even at that age, I asked Mother to get the recipe. She, my sister and I saved a day and a lot of elbow grease to make this fabulous bread. The smell alone is worth the effort!

ONION POPOVERS

Mark Ballard

3 T. margarine
1 c. flour, all-purpose, sifted two times
2 eggs
1 med. Vidalia Onion, chopped
¾ tsp. salt
1 T. shortening
1 c. evaporated milk

Saute onion in margarine. Grease custard cups (12 medium) and place on baking sheet. Preheat oven to 375°. Sift dry ingredients and cut in shortening. Beat eggs and milk with beater. Add flour mixture and heat until smooth. Fill cups ⅓ full. Bake 50 minutes. Remove from oven, cut slits in sides of popovers to release steam. Return to oven for 10 minutes. Quickly remove popovers so not to become soft. Serve promptly. Serves 12.

10 PANCAKES

Mark Ballard

1½ c. baking mix
1 egg
1 T. sugar
¾ c. water

Mix together. Cook on hot griddle.

BREAKFAST LASAGNA

Mark Ballard

16 slices white bread
1½ lb. ham, sliced
16 slices Swiss cheese
16 slices American cheese
8 eggs
2 c. milk
¾ tsp. dry mustard
½ tsp. onion salt
1½ sticks butter
corn flakes

Remove crust from bread. Layer bread, ham, Swiss cheese, American cheese in a 13x9x2-inch baking dish; . Repeat. In a blender, blend eggs, milk, mustard and onion salt.. Pour egg mixture over ham and cheese layers and refrigerate overnight. This is a must! About ½ hour before baking, remove from refrigerator. Heat oven to 350°. Melt butter and mix with enough corn flakes to cover top cheese layer. Bake for about 30 minutes. Serves 12.

STRAWBERRY SYRUP

Betty Leverett

Extra ripe strawberries
1½ c. sugar
¼ c. white Karo syrup
1 T. fresh lemon juice

Wash and stem strawberries. Crush berries in a food processor. Put on stove and boil 2 minutes. Measure 1¼ cups of liquid in a gal. pot. Add 1½ cups sugar, ¼ cup Karo and 1 tablespoon of fresh lemon juice. Boil for 2 minutes. Let cool slightly, skim off foam and pour in jar. Makes 1 pt..

VIDALIA ONION MARMALADE

Mark Ballard

3 T. extra-virgin olive oil
4 lb. Vidalia onions, thinly sliced (about 10 c.)
1 T. brown sugar
salt and pepper, to taste
¾ c. red wine vinegar
1¼ c. red wine

Heat olive oil in a large heavy-bottomed saucepan and add the onions. Cook over medium heat until they begin to soften, about 10 minutes, then add the brown sugar and stir to coat. Season with salt and pepper. Continue cooking over medium heat, stirring frequently, until the onions are golden brown, another 10-15 minutes. Add the vinegar and cook until it has completely evaporated, then add the red wine and repeat the process, stirring the onions frequently to prevent sticking and burning. When the red wine has evaporated, taste and correct the seasoning. Remove from the heat and serve warm (marmalade may be made up to 2 days ahead).

WAFFLES

Mark Ballard

1½ c. baking mix (do not pack)
2 T. sugar
1 egg
1 c. water

Blend baking mix and sugar. Add egg and water slowly, folding in. Cook on waffle iron. Makes about 5 waffles. Add seasonal fruit and serve to Mom on her special day.

ICEBOX VEGETABLE SALAD

Mrs. J. B. Franklin

1 can (16-oz.) cut green beans, drained
1 can (17-oz.) tiny peas, drained
1 can (16-oz.) shoe peg corn, drained
1 jar (4-oz.) chopped pimento, drained
1 c. finely chopped celery
1 med. onion, finely chopped
1 med. green pepper, finely chopped
1 c. sugar **½ c. vinegar**
½ c. vegetable oil **1 tsp. salt**
½ tsp. coarse-grind pepper

Combine all vegetables in a large bowl. In a saucepan, combine sugar, vinegar, oil, salt and pepper. Bring to a boil for 1 minute. Cool slightly and pour over vegetables. Cover and refrigerate overnight. 6 to 8 servings.

ONION SOUP

Mark Ballard

4 Vidalia onions, thinly sliced
3 T. butter
1 T. all-purpose flour
½ tsp. salt
2 c. chicken broth
1 c. milk
½ c. heavy whipping cream
3 egg yolks, beaten
1½ tsp. paprika
ground black pepper to taste
⅛ T. hot pepper sauce
2 T. chopped fresh parsley

In a saucepan, melt butter or margarine over medium heat. Add onions, and saute until golden brown, about 10 minutes. Stir in flour and salt, and mix thoroughly. Gradually add chicken broth, stirring constantly. Cover and simmer over low heat for about 10 minutes. When onions are very tender, stir in milk and cream. Heat thoroughly. Remove ½ cup soup and mix in egg yolks. Slowly stir egg-yolk mixture into soup in pan. Heat thoroughly, but do not allow soup to boil. Stir in paprika, black pepper, and hot pepper sauce. Serve hot and garnish with chopped parsley.

PINK CLOUD

Edith Sullivan

1 can crushed pineapple (20-oz.), drained
1 can condensed milk
1 can cherry pie filling
1 Cool Whip (8-oz.)
½ c. chopped pecans (optional)

Mix well all ingredients. Refrigerate.

SOUTHERN POTATO SALAD

Mark Ballard

6-8 med. white potatoes, peeled, cut into bite size pieces
5 eggs, boiled, peeled, chopped
2 c. mayonnaise
2 T. yellow table mustard
1 c. sour cream
3 T. sweet salad cube pickles
1 T. diced pimento
2 T. lemon juice
3 T. Vidalia sweet onion relish or finely chopped fresh onion
salt and pepper to taste
paprika

Boil diced potatoes and 2 tsp. salt until fork tender. Drain well. In a large bowl, fold mayonnaise, sour cream, mustard with potatoes, being careful not to mash potatoes. Add pimento, pickles, onion relish or onions, lemon juice, chopped eggs, black pepper and mix well. Sprinkle paprika on top. Serve warm.

STRAWBERRY PRETZEL SALAD

Janice Ballard

1⅓ c. pretzels, broken
¾ c. margarine
2 T. sugar
1 8-oz. pkg. cream cheese, softened
1 c. 4x confectioners sugar
8-oz. Cool Whip
1 lg. strawberry Jell-O
2 c. boiling water
2 pt. fresh or frozen strawberries

Cream margarine and sugar. Add pretzels and press into a 13 x 9-inch dish. Bake at 350° for 10 minutes. Let cool. Mix cream cheese and 4x sugar, fold in cool whip. Spread over pretzel mixture that has cooled. Dissolve Jell-O in boiling water; refrigerate until partially jelled, then add strawberries. Pour over cream cheese mixture and chill until firm.

STRAWBERRY SALAD

Jo Ann Stephens

¼ c. sliced almonds
1 T. and 1 tsp. sugar
⅓ head of lettuce
2 med. stalks celery
2 green onions with tops, thinly sliced
2½ c. fresh strawberries, sliced
1 (11-oz.) can mandarin oranges, drained

Toast almonds and sugar together in skillet on low heat, stirring constantly until sugar is dissolved and almonds are coated. Cool and break apart. Mix remaining ingredients with coated almonds. Toss with dressing

Dressing:
¼ c. vegetable oil
2 T. sugar
dash of pepper
½ tsp. salt
2 T. vinegar

Combine all ingredients in a tightly covered jar and shake to combine.

VIDALIA ONION, APPLE & CHICKEN SALAD

Mark Ballard

3 c. (1 lb.) diced, unpeeled sweet red apples
2 c. diced cooked diced chicken breast
1 c. coarsely chopped Vidalia onion
1 c. sliced celery
¼ c. dark raisins
¼ c. chopped toasted pecans
Creamy Apple Dressing (recipe follows)

In a large serving bowl, combine apples, chicken, Vidalia onion, celery, raisin and pecans. Top with Creamy Apple dressing; toss to coat. Serve immediately or cover and refrigerate until ready to serve.

Creamy Apple Dressing:
½ c. plain yogurt
¼ c. reduced-calorie mayonnaise
¼ c. apple juice concentrate
1 T. lemon juice
1¼ tsp. salt
⅛ tsp. ground black pepper

In a small bowl, combine yogurt, mayonnaise, apple juice concentrate, lemon juice, salt and black pepper. Yields about 1 cup.

ONION-SOUP RICE

Mrs. J. B. Franklin

1½ tsp. butter
1 c. med. or long-grain rice
1 c. water
1 can French Onion soup

In saucepan over low heat, melt 1½ teaspoon butter. Add 1 cup rice. Heat approximately 5 minutes, stirring occasionally. Then add 1 cup water and 1 can French Onion soup. Bring to boil over medium heat. Then cover and cook over very low heat until rice is tender - about 17 to 20 minutes.

RICE & ONIONS

Carolyn Pompei

2 c. rice
3½ c. water
1 pkg. onion soup
1 stick of oleo or margarine
1 can mushrooms, juice included
soy sauce

Mix ingredients together and bake for 1 hour. You may also cook it on top the stove.

SAUTEED NEW POTATOES

Mark Ballard

12 to 15 sm., select new potatoes
¼ c. olive oil
¼ butter, melted
2 T. minced garlic
3 T. brown sugar
1 tsp. salt

Clean potatoes leaving skin in place. Boil until done but firm. Drain. Add olive oil, butter, garlic, sugar and salt to pot. On low to medium heat saute potatoes until coated in mixture. Serves 4.

VIDALIA ONION PIE

Mark Ballard

2 9-inch pastry shells
2 lb. Vidalia onions, thinly sliced
¾ stick butter
3 eggs, well beaten
1 c. sour cream
dash of salt
dash of Tabasco sauce
dash of pepper
Parmesan cheese, grated

Preheat oven to 350°. Bake pastry shells for 8 minutes. Saute onions in butter. Combine eggs, sour cream, salt, Tabasco and pepper. Add to onions. Pour mixture into shells. Top with cheese. Bake for 20 minutes, then reduce oven to 325° and bake an additional 15 minutes, or until slightly brown.

CROCKPOT MACARONI & CHEESE

Janice Ballard

1 lb. elbow noodles **1 lb. shredded velveeta cheese**
1 stick margarine **1 can evaporated milk**
1 can cheddar cheese soup
2 eggs **¾ c. milk**

Cook noodles and drain. Add margarine and Velveeta cheese. Add other ingredients. Put in crock pot. You can add some shredded cheese on top. Cook on low for about 2½ hours.

"COMPANY'S COMING" ROAST

Mark Ballard

1 3 to 4 lb. chuck roast, boneless
2 cans cream of mushroom soup
1 pkg. Lipton Onion Soup Mix
Potatoes
Carrots
Onions

Place roast in a glass roasting pan (like Corning Ware) that has a cover. Layer vegetables around roast. Press dry soup mix onto top of raw roast. Spoon mushroom soup over meat and vegetables. Cover and place in oven preheated at 200 to 250 degrees. Cook for 8 to 10 hours for roast that will fall apart it's so tender.

I can still remember waking up on Sunday mornings to the smell of this roast that had cooked all night long. It was hard to focus during church knowing that roast was waiting on you at home!

BEEF VIDALIA

Debra Ballard

2 lbs. deli-style roast beef or sirloin steak, thinly sliced
1 lg. Vidalia onion, thinly sliced
1 lg. or 4 sm. loaves french bread
½ c. butter, softened
shredded lettuce and Provolone or Monterey Jack cheese

Marinade

¼ c. wine vinegar
1 cup salad oil
1 clove garlic, minced
1 tsp. salt
½ tsp. pepper
⅓ c. dill pickles, chopped

Mix ingredients for marinade and pour over beef and onions. Marinate overnight in a glass dish. Next day, slice bread and completely butter the cut surfaces. Drain beef and onions well and arrange over the bottom half of bread. Wrap in foil and bake in 350° oven until heated through. Remove and place cheese slice on bottom half. Wrap again until cheese melts. When ready to serve, remove to cutting, cutting board. Put shredded lettuce on top of beef mixture. Cover with top half of bread. Cut in 4 slices, toothpick together and place on serving platter. Serves 4.

CANNOLI FILLING

Carolyn Pompei

2 lb. ricotta, drained well (at least overnight)
2 T. vanilla
1 c. sugar

Gradually add sugar and vanilla to the ricotta, beat with electric mixer 10 minutes. You can add chocolate chips if you want. This will fill about 30 cannoli shells (small ones). Do not double recipe.

CHEESECAKE

Lucille Wientzen

24-oz. cream cheese
1½ c. sugar
4 eggs
2 c. sour cream
1 c. whipping cream
2 T. lemon juice
1 tsp. grated lemon peel
½ tsp. vanilla

Use your favorite graham cracker crust in a ten inch springform pan baked for ten minutes so it will be "set." Soften cream cheese and beat in the sugar until fluffy. Add eggs one at a time beating well between. Beat in the remaining ingredients. Pour into crust. Bake one hour in a 350° oven. Turn oven off and leave cake in the oven for an additional hour to set. Keep refrigerated. You can put fruit on top of this cake after baking but there is something about the simplicity of this cheesecake that makes it stand alone very well.

CHERRY CHEWBILEES

Blake Ballard

Crust:
1¼ c. all-purpose flour **½ c. packed brown sugar**
½ c. butter-flavored shortening
1 c. chopped pecans **½ c. flaked coconut**

Filling:
2 packages (8-oz. each) cream cheese, softened
⅔ c. sugar
2 eggs
2 tsp. vanilla extract
2 cans (21-oz. each) cherry pie filling

In a bowl, combine flour and brown sugar; cut in shortening until fine crumbs form. Stir in ½ cup nuts and coconut. Reserve ½ cup crumb mixture for topping. Press remaining mixture into the bottom of a greased 13 x 9 x 2-inch baking pan. Bake at 350° for 12-15 minutes or until lightly browned. Meanwhile, for filling, beat cream cheese, sugar, eggs, and vanilla in a mixing bowl until smooth. Spread over the hot crust. Bake 15 minutes longer. Spread pie filling on top. Combine remaining nuts and reserved crumbs; sprinkle over cheeries. Bake 15 minutes longer. Cool. Refrigerate until serving. Yield: 20 servings.

During our annual Cherry Blossom Festival, there used to be a cooking contest featuring all things cherry. One year, my mother assisted Blake and Courtney in finding, preparing and entering recipes in the kid's contest. Blake won with this recipe much to Courtney's dismay. Her recipe follows. Even if it didn't win, it's still pretty good!

CHERRY SQUARES

Courtney Ballard

1¾ c. flaked coconut
½ c. butter or margarine, softened
½ c. sugar
1 ½ c. all-purpose flour
1 can (21-oz.) cherry pie filling

In a mixing bowl, combine first four ingredients. Press half the mixture into the bottom of a greased 9x9 baking pan. Top with the pie filling and sprinkle with remaining crumbs. Bake 375° for about 40 minutes or until golden brown. Yield: 9 servings.

CREAM CHEESE PECAN PIE

William C. Kitchens

1 8-oz. pkg. cream cheese, softened
1 egg, beaten
1 tsp. vanilla
1¼ c. chopped pecans
½ c. sugar
½ tsp. salt
1 10-inch unbaked pie shell

Topping:
3 eggs
½ tsp. vanilla
1 c. light corn syrup

Cream together softened cheese, sugar, beaten egg, salt and vanilla. Spread over bottom of unbaked pie shell. Sprinkle pecans evenly over cream cheese layer. Combine all topping ingredients and beat until smooth. Pour over pecan layer. Bake for 35 to 45 minutes at 375° until pecan layer is golden brown. Serve slightly warm with Cool Whip, if desired. Yields 12 servings.

ENGLISH TRIFLE

Vicki Brantley

1 lg. pkg. strawberry Jell-O
2 (10-oz.) packages of frozen strawberries, partially thawed
1 angel food cake, cubed
2 pkg. instant vanilla pudding
3 c. milk
sliced bananas (dip banana slices in lemon juice to prevent discoloration)
1 sm. can crushed pineapple, drained
9-oz. Cool Whip
chopped pecans

Mix together and put in the glass container 1 large strawberry Jell-O and 2 (10-ounce) packages of frozen strawberries, partially thawed. Next, layer angel food cake, cubed. Mix packages of instant vanilla pudding and milk and pour over cake cubes. Layer bananas dipped in lemon juice next. Add crushed pineapple, cool whip and sprinkle with chopped pecans. Refrigerate.

FROZEN 3-LAYER LEMON DESSERT

Iris Ann Chambliss

Layer One
1½ c. vanilla wafer crumbs
4 T. sugar
1 stick butter, melted
1 c. chopped pecans

Grease a 9 x 13-inch pyrex dish with butter and set aside. Mix all ingredients and press into the dish and freeze until firm.

Layer Two
½ gallon vanilla ice cream
1 12-oz. can frozen lemonade

Soften the ice cream and stir in the can of thawed lemonade (do not dilute the lemonade). Mix together well and add to frozen crust. Return to the freezer until firm before adding the last layer.

Layer Three
4 T. lemon juice
1 c. sugar
6 T. butter
2 eggs, slightly beaten

Cook ingredients in a heavy boiler until butter melts and the sauce thickens and will coat a metal spoon. (Two 10-oz. jars of lemon curd may be used instead of the cooked mixture.) Pour into the pie shell on top of other layer. Return to freezer and freeze until firm enough to cut into squares.

STRAWBERRY SHORTCAKE

Mark Ballard

1¾ c. all-purpose flour
2 T. granulated sugar
1 T. baking powder
½ tsp. grated orange peel
3 T. unsalted butter or margarine, cut into pieces
¾ c. skim milk

Filling:
2 pt. fresh strawberries, sliced
1 T. orange juice
1 T. granulated sugar
Vanilla nonfat yogurt and mint leaves for garnish

Preheat oven to 450°. Spray a baking sheet with vegetable cooking spray. Set aside. In a large bowl, sift together flour, sugar, and baking powder. Stir in the orange peel. Using a pastry blender or 2 knives, cut the butter into the flour mixture until coarse crumbs form. Quickly stir in the milk until a soft dough forms. On a lightly floured surface, roll out dough to ½ inch thickness. Using a 2½-inch biscuit cutter, cut out biscuits. Gather trimmings, re-roll, and cut out more biscuits. Place on prepared baking sheet. Bake until golden, about 12 to 15 minutes. Place biscuits on a wire rack and cool slightly. To prepare filling, in a large bowl, combine strawberries, orange juice, and sugar. Mix well. Split warm biscuits in half horizontally. Place bottom halves on serving plates. Top each with some filling. Cover with biscuits tops. Serve with remaining filling, garnish with yogurt and mint. Serves 8.

POUND CAKE

Janice Ballard

1 c. real butter (2 sticks)
½ c. Crisco
3 c. sugar
6 eggs
3 c. cake flour
1 tsp. baking powder
½ tsp. salt
1 c. milk
2 tsp. of the combo Vanilla and Butter & Nut flavoring OR
1 tsp. *each*: Vanilla and Coconut flavorings
Glaze (recipe follows)

Cream well the butter, Crisco and sugar. Add eggs one at a time, beating one minute after each egg. Sift cake flour, measure and sift again. Add baking powder and salt to flour. Add flour mixture to shortening and eggs, alternately with milk and flavorings. Bake in a well-greased, floured tube or Bundt pan at 325° for 1 hour and 15 minutes or until done. Remove from oven and let stand 10 minutes. Remove from pan and flip cake right side up onto plate. While cake is hot, spoon on glaze. You can poke holes in top with a toothpick and the glaze will seep down into the cake.

Glaze:
½ c. sugar **¼ c. water**
1 tsp. butter flavoring

Boil together ½ cup sugar; ¼ cup water and 1 tsp. butter flavoring. Put on hot cake while hot.

VANILLA WAFER SPONGE CAKE

Beverly Futch

1 c. butter
2 c. sugar
6 eggs
1 tsp. vanilla
½ c. milk
1 c. chopped pecans
7-oz. flaked coconut
12-oz. vanilla wafers (crushed)
Vanilla Glaze (recipe follows)

Preheat oven to 350°. Grease and flour angel food pan. Cream butter with sugar in large bowl. Add eggs one at a time beating well after each addition. Add vanilla wafer crumbs in 4 batches alternately with milk. Add vanilla. Stir in pecans and coconut. Pour into prepared pan. Bake 60 minutes. Cool in pan. Top with vanilla glaze.

Vanilla Glaze:
⅓ c. butter
2 c. powdered sugar
1½ tsp. vanilla
2-4 T. water

Melt butter. Add powdered sugar and vanilla. Stir in water, 1 tablespoon at a time until smooth and of desired consistency. Spoon over cake.

BUTTERY CAKE MIX COOKIES

Janice Ballard

1 box Duncan Hines Butter Recipe Cake Mix
1 egg
1 stick margarine
1 c. chopped nuts

Mix together, will be stiff. Spoon onto a pan sprayed with Pam or you can roll into small balls. Bake at 325° for 6-8 minutes. You don't want these to brown. They should not look done when you remove.

EASY COOKIES

Mark Ballard

5 c. cornflakes
1 c. salted peanuts
1 c. light corn syrup
½ c. butter or margarine
4 c. crisp rice cereal
1 c. flaked coconut
1 c. sugar
½ c. light cream

In a large bowl, combine cereal, peanuts and coconut; set aside. In a saucepan combine corn syrup, sugar, butter and cream; cook and stir over medium heat until the mixture reaches soft-ball stage (240°), about 25-30 minutes. Pour over cereal mixture and toss to coat evenly. Pat into a greased 15 x 10 x 1-inch baking pan. Cool before cutting. Yield: 2½ to 3 dozen.

ICEBOX COOKIES

Connie Howard

1 pkg. graham crackers
2 sticks butter
1 c. sugar
1 egg
½ c. milk
1 c. finely chopped nuts
1 c. coconut
1 c. graham cracker crumbs

Line bottom of a 9 x 13-inch pan with whole graham crackers. Melt butter over low flame. Beat egg, sugar and milk together. Mix with butter and bring to a boil. Remove from heat; add nuts, coconut and graham cracker crumbs. Pour over layer of graham crackers. Top with whole graham crackers. Frost with icing.

Icing:
4 T. melted butter
2 tsp. vanilla
3 c. powdered sugar
4 T. milk

Mix all ingredients together and beat until smooth. Spread on top of crackers. Refrigerate overnight. When ready to eat, cut into small bars.

PEANUT BUTTER COOKIES

Gloria Sikes

2 c. self-rising flour
2 sticks oleo
1 c. brown sugar
1 c. sugar
2 eggs
1 c. peanut butter
2 T. water
1 tsp. vanilla

Combine oleo, brown sugar, sugar, eggs, peanut butter, water and vanilla. Add flour slowly into dough. Mix well. Drop by teaspoonful onto ungreased cookie sheet. Bake at 325° for 15-25 minutes. Makes 6 dozen.

POTATO CHIP COOKIES

Mark Ballard

1 lb. butter
3 c. flour
1 c. sugar
1½ c. crushed potato chips
2 tsp. vanilla

Preheat the oven to 325 degrees. Mix butter, flour and sugar until smooth. Add crushed potato chips and vanilla. Mix again. Drop by teaspoons onto greased cookie sheet. Bake at 325 until very light brown (about 20 minutes). Cool and sprinkle with powdered sugar. Yields about 100 cookies.

POUND CAKE COOKIES

Gail Harrison

2 sticks butter (no substitute)
1 tsp. vanilla
1 egg yolk
1 stick margarine
1 c. sugar
3 c. plain flour

Cream butter and sugar until mixture is fluffy. Add the egg yolk and vanilla and mix well. Add flour one cup at a time. Mix well after each addition. With fingers, roll dough into balls about 1 inch and place on greased cookie sheet and decorate with a pecan halve. Bake at 325° until cookie edges are lightly brown, 10-12 minutes. Do not overbake.

Summer

We seem to become best friends with the bright yellow, glowing sun during the season called Summer. Although hot and humid, there is something very restful and serene about this time of year. Our thoughts go to entertaining outdoors with various parties and cookouts. To stay cool and refreshed, we look to water in the form of oceans, lakes, swimming pools and backyard water hoses. We ride bicycles and drink lemonade, sit on porches and visit with friends, prepare cool and refreshing meals and confections and try, if only for a few months, to relax and have some fun! This season that is nestled between the holidays of Memorial Day and Labor Day is packed with celebrations honoring those who have fought so hard for our freedom and independence, our actual fathers who help us to know what to do when we gain the freedom of adulthood and those who labor to make our country great. Feel the warmth of the sun as it shines on your face as you think of Summer!

53231E-sg-2

Summer Celebrations

We Southerners sure know how to throw a party. Any old reason will suffice just fine. It doesn't even have to be special occasion. We have been known to invent a reason to celebrate. Bobby made an A on his report card, so let's call up a few friends. The guy Mary wants to date asked for her phone number. Let's immediately gather those closest to her. John got a great promotion, so let's bake a cake. Squeeze the lemons and brew up the sweet tea, because you and I both know one fact - Southerners like a PARTY! The more people that come, the merrier! What better time is there than summer to throw a casual party?

At least that's what my son thinks when he gathers ALL of his friends, and some people he doesn't even know, for the outdoor parties he gives just as soon as we go out of town. He keeps it quite simple though. You will never find him being bothered with all the hoopla that I often demonstrate. It just takes one call to order a pizza for him to have a party. In thirty minutes or less, his main course is delivered. He doesn't even worry with the hassle of invitations. He simply tells one of his friends, they tell two of their friends, their friends each tell two of their friends, and before you know it, you have a PARTY! And keep in mind, this all takes place in a matter of minutes. That's the reason we don't let him know when we will be leaving until the day we leave. I can only imagine what would happen if he had time to really plan.

He learned a lot from his older sister. My thoughts go back to one time when we were out of town and our daughter decided she would have a party. I guess being around me has made both of my children party-givers. I told you that it really doesn't require an occasion. Or, I guess that really IS an occasion

- the parents are out of town! So out of the blue, she gathered her group. Everything would have been just fine, except she had a guest attend that she had not invited. I wish I could have seen her face when her PaPa rang the doorbell. He was greeted by one of her friends, and after the color left her face, she yelled for our daughter to handle the situation. It was certainly handled, but not by our daughter. Daddy later told me that he CLEANED house that night with one clap of his hands. He said kids scattered like ants when their ant hill is disturbed. Why, I ask you, do we always miss the good parties?

I gave my first party when I was in the third grade. As you can imagine, it was well planned and attended. Being at school does make for a captive audience. With the help of another teacher, I secretly planned a going-away party for a teacher. I cut the invitations out of construction paper and used thick white paste to glue on the decorations. My adrenalin kicked in and excitement surrounded me. It was my first attempt at being creative with a party and I enjoyed it.

I have had tons of parties since then and have improved on my ability to entertain. One thing is for sure, parties and how we give them have changed over the years. Everyone seems to opt for my son's approach to entertaining these days. Less worry and hassle and more food and casual fun. We tend to set up what I like to refer to as a "grazing station" around which the guests can gather and partake. Since most guests enjoy this more casual form of entertaining, we need to put what Emily Post has told us was right in the past and surge forward into the 21st century.

The first thing you need to do is decide on a theme. Theme parties are great because they act as ice breakers for your guests. People will remember a theme party long after they have forgotten your formal sit-down dinner. I can still remember most of the fabulous theme parties I have attended over the years. An African Safari, a Circus Carnival, an Egyptian Soiree, a dark and gloomy "Over the Hill" celebration and even several Tacky parties! What fun we've had!

After you establish your theme, you must carry it out throughout the entire party starting with the invitations. Choose or create one that will let your guest know what to expect. If you wish for them to dress a certain way to carry out the theme, then your invitation is the place for you to address that. Most people are receptive to dressing in "costume" for a party as long as it is not too expensive or time consuming. You may want to give away prizes for the "best dressed" to encourage more people to participate. At some parties I have attended, the guests were provided "props" to put on once they arrived. Funny glasses, colorful masks, horrible teeth, to name a few.

Next, you must let your food reflect your theme. Please, don't drop the ball here. It is critical. I mean if you are having a Mexican Fiesta party, you do not want to serve hamburgers. Unless, that is, you decide to slice some avocados and bring on the sombreros, salsa and chips. Let your food be in harmony with your theme.

Finally, let your creative juices run wild with your decorations. Especially with your table presentations. Let your "grazing station" be both creative and whimsical. Since it's summer, instead of a regular centerpiece, why not do something different and use some"props" to help you decorate? Remember to think in terms of establishing some different heights on your table. I call this "multi-dimensional" dining. Look at some of the tricks that wonderful restaurants have always used at their salad bars and buffets to make them more appealing. Use seasonal fruits and garnishes to present your food and decorate your table at the same time. Go to your local fabric store and purchase some remnants of wonderful fabrics. Use these fabrics to disguise the boxes and crates that allowed you the multi-level look. Don't forget to invite some very special "guests" to attend your party and I don't mean the real ones. Look through your house and "borrow" some whimsical things to brighten your table.

This summer, create a fun party and a beautiful tablescape for your food. I know it's a different way of thinking, but I promise you will have fun both in planning and decorating. Take my word, people will love your extra effort and probably try to copy it at their next party. You know what we Southerners say, "Imitation is the sincerest form of flattery."

Memorial Day
Father's Day
Fourth of July
Labor Day

CRISPY ZUCCHINI CHIPS

Mark Ballard

¼ c. unbleached flour
½ tsp. dried oregano
¼ tsp. garlic powder
⅛ tsp. ground red pepper
2 egg whites
2 T. water
⅔ c. cornflake crumbs
¼ c. grated Parmesan cheese
2 zucchini, cut into ¼ -inch slices

Preheat oven to 350°. Coat a baking sheet with nonstick spray. Combine flour, oregano, garlic powder, and red pepper in a self-sealing plastic food-storage bag. Whisk egg whites and water in a pie plate. Combine crumbs and Parmesan in another plastic bag. Shake zucchini in flour mixture until slices are coated. Dip slices into egg-white mixture. Then shake in the crumb mixture. Place slices in single layer on the baking sheet. Bake for 10 minutes. Turn slices. Bake an additional 8 minutes until golden brown. Serves 8.

WHITE TRASH CAVIAR

Cele Minshew

1 15-oz. can black eyed peas, drained
1 15-oz. can shoepeg corn, drained
1 jar of Mrs. Braswell's pepper relish
1 8-oz. bottle of Wishbone Italian dressing
1 chopped onion
1 chopped bell pepper
1 chopped tomato

Mix all the ingredients together and serve with Frito Scoops.

FIRECRACKER DEVILED EGGS

Mark Ballard

6 hard-cooked eggs
⅓ c. mild salsa
3 T. reduced-fat sour cream
3 T. minced green onions
1 T. chopped black olives
1 tsp. lemon juice
green onions, red pepper strips or parsley, optional

Cut eggs in half. Remove yolks and set whites aside. Mash yolks with fork. Stir in remaining ingredients. Refill whites, using one heaping tablespoon yolk mixture for each egg half. Chill to blend flavors. Garnish with green onions, red pepper strips or parsley, if desired.

OYSTER & CRABMEAT MELT

Betty Jones

1 c. oysters
½ c. crushed Ritz crackers
salt and pepper to taste
¼ c. chopped onions
¼ c. parsley
1 c. crabmeat
½ c. melted butter
1 tsp. celery seeds
½ c. cream
½ c. bread crumbs

Mix undrained oysters, crabmeat, crackers. Add salt, pepper, celery seeds, parsley, chopped onions and cream. Top with bread crumbs. Top with melted butter; bake at 400° for 30 to 40 minutes.

SHRIMP ROLLS

Betty Jones

1 c. shrimp
¼ c. salad dressing
2 T. green olives
2 T. chili sauce
1 T. celery, chopped fine
1 pkg. crescent rolls

Mix first 5 ingredients. Place ¼ cup mixture on each of the triangles. Roll up. Cup each roll into bite-sized slices. Place cut side down on greased baking sheet. Bake at preheated over 375° for 10 to 12 minutes.

BANANA SMOOTHIE

Cindy Pate

1 lg. very ripe banana, peeled and cut into chunks
1 (8-oz.) container plain vanilla, or strawberry/banana yogurt
1 c. cold milk
2 or 3 T. honey
ground cinnamon

In a blender or food processor, combine banana, yogurt, milk and honey until smooth and creamy. To serve, pour into 2 tall glasses and sprinkle cinnamon. For a variety, add a few fresh or frozen strawberries with the other ingredients.

BLUEBERRY - PEACH SHAKE

Mark Ballard

½ c. orange juice
8-oz. fat-free vanilla or peach frozen yogurt
2½ c. sliced peaches
¾ c. fresh or frozen blueberries

Puree orange, yogurt, peaches and ½ blueberries in a blender. Pour into 4 glasses and garnish with remaining ¼ cup blueberries. Serves 4.

CAPPUCCINO FREEZE

Mark Ballard

2 T. instant decaffeinated coffee granules
⅔ c. boiling water
1 qt. low-fat vanilla frozen yogurt
ground cinnamon

In a large bowl, dissolve coffee in boiling water. Then slowly beat into frozen yogurt. If mixture is too soft, beat in additional frozen yogurt. Spoon into 4 coffee mugs and sprinkle with ground cinnamon. Freeze until ready to serve. Let soften for 15 minutes before serving. Serves 4.

FROSTY ORANGE

Mark Ballard

1 6-oz. can orange juice concentrate
1 c. milk
1 c. water
½ c. sugar
1 tsp. vanilla
12 ice cubes

Put the above ingredients in a blender and blend until smooth, about 45 seconds. Serve immediately. Yield: 6 cups.

LIME DROP

Debra Ballard

1½ c. plus 2 T. fresh lime juice
¼ c. superfine sugar
2 T. chopped fresh ginger
crushed ice
1½ c. gin
4 thinly slice lime rounds

In a large shaker, muddle ¼ cup of the lime juice with 2 tablespoons of the superfine sugar and the ginger. Fill the shaker with crushed ice, then add 1¼ cups of the lime juice and the gin; shake the drink vigorously. Pour the remaining 2 tablespoons of lime juice and 2 tablespoons of sugar into 2 bowls. Dip the rims of 4 cocktail glasses first in the lime juice and then in the sugar. Strain the cocktail into the glasses; garnish with the lime rounds. Makes 4 drinks.

PASSION-FRUIT COOLER

Debra Ballard

7½-oz. 100 percent blue-agave tequila
6-oz. passion-fruit purée
18-oz ginger beer
4½-oz. Cointreau
3-oz. lime juice
1 lime thinly sliced, for garnish

Mix together the tequila, passion-fruit puree, ginger beer, Cointreau, and lime juice in a pitcher. Pour into highball glasses filled with ice. Garnish with lime slices. Serves 6.

PEACH-AND-BERRY JULEP

Debra Ballard

1 slice peach
1 sprig of mint
1 sm. strawberry
2 raspberries
2 blueberries
¾-oz. simple syrup (recipe follows)
½ -oz. peach liqueur
1½-oz. bourbon

Muddle the peach slice, mint sprig, the berries, the lemon juice, and the syrup in a shaker until the fruit is crushed. Add peach liqueur, bourbon, and ice, and shake well. Strain into a highball glass filled with crushed ice. Garnish with peach slice and mint.

Simple syrup:
1 c. granulated sugar
1 c. water

Combine 1 cup granulated sugar and 1 cup water in a saucepan. Bring the mixture to a boil for a few seconds. Set aside to cool.

SUNNY CITRUS SMASH

Debra Ballard

6 c. freshly squeezed orange juice
1 12-oz. can mango nectar
1 6-oz. can frozen lemonade concentrate, thawed
1 6-oz. can frozen limeade concentrate, thawed
½ c. tequila
½ c. triple sec
2 L. bottle lemon-lime carbonated soda, chilled

Blend together first 6 ingredients. Chill thoroughly. . Blend "punch" with equal parts chilled soda. Serve by the glass or the pitcher. Serve over ice.

WATERMELON COOLER

Debra Ballard

5 lbs. seedless watermelon (about ½ med. melon)
10-oz. lemonade, homemade or high-quality prepared
12-oz. tequila (vodka or rum can be substituted)
watermelon wedges, for garnish

Cut the watermelon flesh into chunks, and, working in batches, puree in a blender until liquefied. Strain through a fine sieve to remove the pulp; you should have 4 cups of juice. Combine the watermelon juice, lemonade, and tequila in a 2-quart pitcher. Pour into tall glasses filled with ice, and garnish with a melon wedge. (Without the alcohol, this makes a great children's drink.)

PEACH QUICK BREAD

Mark Ballard

3 eggs
⅔ c. oil
1 c. sugar (if using fresh fruit, adjust to fruit's sweetness)
2 c. chopped peaches, fresh or canned
2 tsp. vanilla
3 c. flour
1 tsp. salt
1 tsp. soda
2 tsp. cinnamon
½ tsp. baking powder
1 c. chopped nuts of your choice

Beat eggs, add oil and sugar and cream well. Add peaches and vanilla. Stir in dry ingredients and nuts until blended; do not over beat. Pour batter into two greased bread pans. Bake at 325 degrees for 1 hour. (Makes 2 moist loaves. This batter can also be baked as muffins; adjust oven temperature to 375 degrees and time to 15 to 20 minutes.)

BLUEBERRY MUFFINS

Mark Ballard

3 T. light margarine, melted
¼ c. granulated sugar
¼ c. fat-free egg substitute
1 c. fat-free milk
2 c. unbleached flour
1 T. baking powder
1 c. blueberries

Preheat oven to 350°. Coat 12 muffin cups with nonstick spray. In a large bowl, combine margarine, sugar, egg substitute, and milk. In a small bowl, whisk together flour and baking powder. Add to milk mixture, and mix until just combined. Gently stir in blueberries. Divide batter among muffin cups. Bake until a toothpick inserted in center of a muffin comes out clean, about 30 minutes. Remove muffins from pan, and place on a wire rack to cool. Makes 12 muffins.

SUMMER TOMATO BREAD

Mark Ballard

4 fresh, very ripe tomatoes, cut in half
4 cloves garlic, cut in half
8 slices country-style bread, cut ½-inch thick
extra-virgin olive oil
sm. bowl of coarse (kosher or sea) salt
freshly ground black pepper

Preheat the grill to medium-high and prepare it for direct grilling. Place a half tomato and half garlic clove on each serving plate. Arrange the bread slices on the hot grate and grill until nicely browned, 2 to 4 minutes per side. Place a piece of grilled bread on each plate. To eat, rub a bread slice with cut garlic, then with cut tomato. Drizzle each slice with oil and sprinkle with salt and pepper, if desired. Serve immediately. Serves 8.

COCONUT BREAD

Mrs. J. B. Franklin

3 c. all-purpose flour
2 tsp. baking powder
½ tsp. baking soda
½ tsp. salt
2 c. sugar (less 2 T.)
1 c. vegetable oil
4 eggs, lightly beaten
2 tsp. coconut extract
1 c. buttermilk
1 c. shredded coconut
1 c. chopped walnuts (or pecans)

Combine flour, baking powder, baking soda and salt. Set aside. In a large bowl, combine sugar, oil, eggs, and coconut extract. Add dry ingredients alternately with buttermilk; stir just until moistened. Fold in coconut and nuts (which have been lightly sprinkled with about 2 tablespoons of flour mixture). Pour into 2 greased and floured 8½ x 4½-inch loaf pans. Bake at 325° for 1 hour, or until bread tests done. Cool 10 minute in pans before removing to a wire rack to cool completely. Yield: 2 loaves.

CORN CAKES WITH SUN-DRIED TOMATOES & GOAT CHEESE

Mark Ballard

¾-oz. sun-dried tomatoes (packed without oil)
¾ c. boiling water
2 ears fresh corn
1 clove garlic, minced
½ c. yellow cornmeal
½ c. whole wheat flour
½ tsp. baking powder
¼ tsp. salt
¼ tsp. freshly ground black pepper
¼ tsp. crushed red pepper
1 c. skim milk
¼ c. (1-oz.) chévre (mild goat cheese)
1 T. olive oil
2 egg whites

Combine tomatoes and ¾ c. boiling water in a bowl, and let stand 30 minutes; drain. Mince tomatoes. Cut whole kernels from corn to measure 1 c. Arrange cut corn in a vegetable steamer over boiling water; cover and steam 5 minutes or until tender. Combine tomatoes, cut corn, and garlic. Combine cornmeal and next 5 ingredients in a large bowl; stir well. Add corn mixture, stirring just until combined. Combine milk and last 3 ingredients in an electric blender and process until smooth. Add to cornmeal mixture, stirring just until dry ingredients are moistened. Let stand 15 minutes. Spoon 2 T. batter per cake onto a hot nonstick griddle. Cook for 2½ minutes or until the tops are covered with bubbles and edges look cooked. Turn corn cakes, and cook an additional 2½ minutes or until browned. Yield: 18 cakes.

DOUBLE BRAN-BRAN MUFFINS

Mark Ballard

½ c. low-fat sour cream
½ c. mashed ripe bananas
½ c. skim milk
⅓ c. sugar
2 T. vegetable oil
1 tsp. vanilla extract
1 egg, lightly beaten
1½ c. high-fiber morsels of bran cereal
½ c. unprocessed oat bran flour
1 tsp. baking powder
¾ tsp. baking soda
vegetable cooking spray

Combine first 7 ingredients in a bowl; stir well with a wire whisk. Add cereal; stir well. Let stand 10 minutes. Combine flour and baking powder and soda in a large bowl; make a well in center of mixture. Add cereal mixture to dry ingredients, stirring just until moistened. Divide batter among 12 muffin cups coated with cooking spray. Bake at 400° for 16 minutes or until a wooded pick inserted in center comes out clean. Remove from pans immediately; let cool on a wire rack. Yield: 1 dozen.

FRIED SQUASH FRITTERS

Edith Sullivan

1½ c. flour
½ tsp. salt and pepper, or to own taste
⅓ c. milk
1 or 2 T. grated Vidalia onion
3 or 4 c. grated yellow or green squash, do not peel

Mix well and drop by spoonful into hot oil, when brown turn over and cook other side till brown. Drain on paper towels. Serve.

GRILLED GARLIC BREAD

Mark Ballard

1 loaf (12-oz.) Italian bread, halved lengthwise
¼ c. fat-free Italian dressing
2 garlic cloves, minced

Brush cut sides of bread with dressing. Sprinkle with garlic. Coat a grill rack with nonstick spray. Place bread over medium-hot coals. Grill until crisp on both sides about 5 minutes. Serves 12.

HUSH PUPPIES

Mark Ballard

2¼ c. corn meal
3 T. self-rising flour
1 T. onion, finely chopped
1 egg
1 c. milk or water

Mix and drop by spoonfuls into hot grease. Cook until golden brown.

I don't eat fish but I sure do love the taste of these puppies!

RASPBERRY-BLUEBERRY KUCHEN

Mark Ballard

1¾ c. all-purpose flour
¼ c. plus 2 T. sugar
2¼ c. tsp. baking powder
¼ tsp. salt
¼ tsp. ground cinnamon
⅛ tsp. ground nutmeg
¼ c. plus 3 T. skim milk
3 T. vegetable oil
1 T. vanilla extract
1 egg, lightly beaten
vegetable cooking spray
2 c. fresh raspberries
1 c. fresh blueberries
3 T. sugar
½ c. red currant jell, melted

Combine first 6 ingredients in a large bowl; make a well in center of mixture. Combine milk and next 3 ingredients; stir well. Add to dry ingredients, stirring just until moistened. Spread batter evenly in a thin layer over bottom of a 13 x 9 x 2-inch baking pan coated with cooking spray. Scatter fresh raspberries and blueberries over batter; sprinkle with 3 tablespoons sugar. Cover and bake for 350° for 25 minutes. Uncover and bake an additional 15 minutes or until a wooden pick inserted in center comes out clean. Spoon melted jelly over kuchen. Serve warm or at room temperature. Yield: 15 servings.

FRENCH TOAST WITH PEACHES

Mark Ballard

1 loaf unsliced bread
1 pkg. vanilla pudding mix (not instant)
3 eggs
1 ¼ c. milk
½ tsp. vanilla
1 can peach pie filling

Slice bread one inch thick. Beat eggs until thick and add milk, pudding mix and vanilla. Dip bread into batter, turning to coat on both sides. Fry on buttered griddle until golden. Serve with butter and warmed peach pie filling.

COUNTRY SAUSAGE AND EGG PIE

Mark Ballard

2 sheets puff pastry, thawed
1 lb. sausage, maple flavored
1½ c. red potatoes, sliced thin
½ c. chopped onions
⅛ tsp. red pepper
¼ tsp. garlic powder
¼ tsp. salt
dash of pepper
1 c. apples, sliced thin
2 c. grated cheddar cheese
1 c. half and half
4 eggs
2 tablespoons apple juice
½ tsp. salt
dash of pepper

Preheat oven to 350°. Place one pastry sheet in pie plate and trim to fit. In a large skillet, cook sausage. Drain sausage, pat dry, then add next six ingredients. Cook on medium heat approximately 15 minutes until potatoes are tender. Add apples. Layer potato mixture, sausage and cheese in pie pan. Using whisk, mix together half and half, eggs, apple juice, salt and pepper. Pour over cheese. Place remaining puff pastry on top, cutting to fit. Crimp edges. Cook for approximately 30 to 45 minutes. May use excess pastry to decorate top of pie. Brush top with one egg and tablespoon of water if desired. Serves 8.

OVERNIGHT REFRIGERATOR PANCAKES

Rita and Bobby Miscinco

1 ¼-oz. env. active dry yeast
¼ c. warm water (100-110 degrees)
4 c. all-purpose flour
2 T. baking powder
2 tsp. baking soda
1 tsp. salt
2 tsp. sugar
6 lg. eggs
1 qt. buttermilk
¼ c. vegetable oil
chopped pecans, fresh or frozen fruit (optional)

Combine yeast and warm water in a 1-cup liquid measuring cup, let stand 5 minutes. Combine flour and next 4 ingredients in a large bowl; make a well in center. Combine eggs, buttermilk, and oil; add to flour mixture, stirring just until dry ingredients are moistened. Stir in yeast mixture. Cover. Refrigerate 8 hours or up 1 week. Remove batter from refrigerator, stir well. Pour ¼ cup for each pancake onto a hot, lightly greased griddle. Cook pancakes until tops are covered with bubbles and edges look cooked, turn and cook other side. Serve with pecans or fresh or frozen fruit, if desired.

PLANTATION CREOLE EGGS

Mark Ballard

6 eggs, hard cooked
salt and pepper, to taste
1 can whole tomatoes, crushed
1 sm. can tomato paste
1 med. onion
4 T. pepper flakes
4 T. celery flakes
1 T. curry powder
1 T. olive oil
2 cloves garlic, roasted
6 Ritz crackers, crushed

White Sauce:
¼ c. butter
3 T. flour
1 c. milk

Preheat oven to 350°. Slice eggs in half. Place in a greased 3 quart rectangular baking dish. Sprinkle with salt and pepper. In a medium pot, combine crushed tomatoes with tomato paste, set aside. Saute onion, pepper flakes, celery flakes, curry powder, olive oil and roasted garlic. Add to tomato mixture and simmer slowly for 3 to 4 minutes. In medium pan, melt butter and stir in flour; cook about a minute while stirring constantly. Add milk gradually and stir until thickened. Alternately layer white sauce and tomato mixture over eggs. Sprinkle with crushed crackers. Bake at 350° for 30 minutes.

BLUE CHEESE DRESSING

Gloria Sikes

2 containers crumbled blue cheese
½ c. mayonnaise
½ c. sour cream
2 T. mustard
1 clove garlic (crushed)
milk

Mix all ingredients together. Add milk for desired thickness. Refrigerate.

CREAMY APRICOT & BANANA SALAD

Betty Jones

1 16-oz. can apricots, sliced
2 bananas, sliced
1 6-oz. pkg. apricot gelatin
2 c. buttermilk
1 8-oz. ctn. whipped topping

Put apricots into saucepan and turn heat to medium. Add gelatin and stir until dissolved. Remove from heat and cool. Add sliced bananas, buttermilk and fold in whipped topping. Mix well. Pour into 9 x 13-inch pan and chill 4 to 6 hours. Cut into squares.

CHICKPEA SALAD

Mark Ballard

1 c. dried chickpeas, soaked according to pkg. directions, drained
1 (14½-oz.) can chicken broth
1 whole head garlic, with skin, halved horizontally
4 sprigs fresh thyme
3 tsp. coarse (kosher) salt
¾ tsp. pepper
¼ c. *each*: extra-virgin olive oil and fresh lemon juice
1 pt. cherry tomatoes, halved
¼ c. chopped fresh flat-leaf parsley

In Dutch oven, bring chickpeas, broth, garlic, thyme and cold water to cover chickpeas (by 2 inches) to a boil. Reduce heat to low; simmer 20 minutes. Stir in 2 teaspoon salt and ½ teaspoon pepper. Cook 20 to 30 minutes more, until very tender but still holding shape. Drain chickpeas. Reserve garlic halves; discard thyme. With tip of small knife, remove and mash enough garlic from skins to make 2 tablespoon paste. Discard any remaining garlic. Transfer chickpeas to bowl. Add garlic paste, remaining 1 teaspoon salt, remaining ¼ teaspoon pepper, the oil, lemon juice, tomatoes and parsley; toss to mix. Serve warm or at room temperature.

CRUNCHY SLAW

Mark Ballard

Dressing:
¼ c. rice-wine vinegar
2 T. dark Asian sesame oil
1 T. honey
½ tsp. salt
¼ tsp. freshly ground black pepper

Mix ingredients. Set aside.

Salad:
5 c. shredded green cabbage
3 c. shredded red cabbage
½ c. thin red-onion strips
¼ c. chopped scallions (white and green parts)
¼ c. loosely packed cilantro leaves
½ tsp. salt
¼ tsp. freshly ground black pepper
⅛ tsp. cayenne pepper
½ c. unsalted roasted peanuts

In large bowl, combine cabbages, onion strips, scallions, cilantro, salt, black pepper and cayenne. Add dressing; toss. Cover; refrigerate at least 4 hours or until cabbage wilts slightly. Stir in peanuts just before serving.

FROZEN SALAD

Mildred Gossett

1 (8-oz.) cream cheese
¾ c. sugar
1 lg. can crushed pineapple, drained
1 (10-oz.) pkg. frozen strawberries, do not drain
2 or 3 ripe bananas, mashed
12-oz. Cool Whip, thawed
1 c. chopped pecans

Cream together cream cheese and sugar. Stir together all ingredients real well. Freeze. Cut in squares to serve.

SUMMER TOMATO SALAD

Mark Ballard

1 T. coarse (kosher) salt
¼ lb. haricots verts (thin green beans), trimmed
¼ c. extra-virgin olive oil
2 T. *each*: red-wine vinegar, balsamic vinegar, minced chives
2 tsp. minced fresh thyme
1 tsp. minced garlic
¾ tsp. black pepper
3 lb. assorted tomatoes, cut into 2-inch chunks
1 sm. head fennel, trimmed and cut into ⅛-inch thick slices
2 c. loosely packed baby or regular arugula
½ c. finely chopped red onion
5½-oz. Gorgonzola, crumbled

In a small saucepan, bring water to a boil. Add ½ teaspoon salt and the haricots verts; cook just until tender, 2 minutes. Drain beans under cold running water. In large bowl, whisk oil, vinegars, chives, thyme, remaining salt, the garlic and pepper. Add tomatoes, fennel, arugula, onion and beans; toss. Divide among 8 plates. Top with Gorgonzola.

FRUIT SALAD

Mark Ballard

1 can pineapple chunks
1 can mandarin oranges
1 can sliced peaches
1 bottle maraschino cherries
1 lb. seedless grapes, cut in half
4 medium bananas, sliced
1 box vanilla pudding (non-instant)

Thoroughly drain all fruit reserving ⅔ cup pineapple juice and ⅓ cup juice from oranges. Mix these reserved juices and dry pudding in a sauce pan. (Mix pudding a little at a time to avoid lumps.) Cook, stirring constantly, until mixture begins to "gel" and look clear. Mix pineapple chunks, peaches, and oranges together with cooled, cooked pudding. Refrigerate overnight or at least for a few hours. Add sliced bananas, grapes, cherries shortly before serving.

HAWAIIAN SLAW

Mark Ballard

1 medium head cabbage
½ lb. small marshmallows
1 c. pineapple pieces, drained
¾ c. mayonnaise
celery seed to taste

Shred cabbage. Mix mayonnaise, pineapple juice and celery seed. Add cabbage and pineapple. Mix well. Refrigerate for at least 4 hours before serving.

HOT CHICKEN SALAD

Mary McPeters

4 c. chicken, cold, cut up and cooked
2 T. lemon juice
1 tsp. salt
2 c. chopped celery
1 can cream of chicken soup
1 tsp. finely minced onion
¾ c. mayonnaise
½ tsp. MSG
4 hard cooked eggs, sliced
1 can sliced water chestnuts
2 pimentos, cut fine

Topping:
⅔ c. toasted, finely chopped almonds
1½ c. crushed potato chips

Combine all ingredients and place in large rectangular casserole. Refrigerate overnight. Add topping. Bake at 400° for 25 minutes. Serves 8.

LEMON JELL-O FRUIT SALAD

Jo Ann Stephens

2 6-oz. lemon Jell-O
1 lg. can pears
1 lg. can peaches
1 lg. bottle Maraschino cherries
1 lg. can pineapple chunks
1 lg. can Mandarin oranges
3 bananas, sliced
2 apples, diced
2 c. grapes
1 c. peach juice

Drain all fruit well, reserving 1 cup peach juice. Dissolve Jell-O in 2 cups of hot water. Add 1 cup of cold water and the cup of peach juice. Stir well. Fill a large bowl with fruit and pour Jell-O mixture over it.

The can be done with any type Jell-o. For a more tropical flavor, try half lemon and half pineapple Jell-O.

POTATO SALAD

Mark Ballard

4½ lb. potatoes, peeled, cut into ¾-to-1-inch pieces
2 c. mayonnaise
1 c. chopped sweet onion
1½ c. finely diced celery
1 tsp. sugar
¼ c. red-wine vinegar
¼ c. yellow mustard
1 T. salt
¾ tsp. freshly ground black pepper
9 hard-boiled eggs, shelled and coarsely chopped
1 T. snipped chives

Place the potatoes in a large pot, and cover with cold salted water. Bring to a boil, and cook until tender, 10 to 15 minutes. Remove the pot from the heat, and allow the potatoes to cool in the cooking liquid. Drain the potatoes while they are still warm. Combine the mayonnaise, onions, celery, sugar, vinegar, mustard, and salt and pepper in a large bowl. Add the potatoes to the dressing while they are still warm. Gently fold in the chopped eggs, and garnish with chives.

MISS NELL'S
ROMAINE LETTUCE SALAD

Nell Pipkins

1 head Romaine Lettuce
1 pkg. Ramen Noodles, crushed
1 c. chopped walnuts (or other nuts of your choice)
4 T. butter
Dressing (recipe follows)

Wash, tear and set aside lettuce. Mix noodles, nuts and butter and toast in oven until brown. Arrange lettuce, sprinkle toasted mixture over it and finish off with dressing.

Dressing:
1 c. sugar
1 c. olive oil
3 T. soy sauce
½ c. red wine vinegar

Blend all ingredients together and always shake well before using.

SANFORD HOUSE DRESSING

Mary Ballard

1 tsp. salt
1 tsp. paprika
1 tsp. dry mustard
1 tsp. celery seed
½ c. sugar
1 c. salad oil
¼ c. Tarragon vinegar
½ tsp. grated onion

Combine dry ingredients in bowl of electric mixer. Add oil and vinegar, alternately, beating well after each addition. Add onion last. This dressing keeps well in refrigerator. If it separates, stir it together again. Makes about 2 cups.

SUMMERTIME BREAD SALAD

Mark Ballard

½ lb. 3-4 day old, good quality bread (preferably Italian), torn, or cut into cubes
1 cucumber, peeled, seeded and cubed
⅓ c. Balsamic vinegar
3 cloves garlic, minced
1 red onion, chopped
5 tomatoes, seeded and cut into pieces
½ c. basil leaves torn into small pieces
½ c. extra virgin olive oil
12 calamata olives, pitted and halved (optional)

Combine all veggies and basil in a large bowl; mix oil and vinegar together with garlic. Pour over salad. Toss gently. Let salad sit up to 30 minutes for bread to absorb dressing.

SUNNY FRUIT FIESTA

Mark Ballard

1 cantaloupe melon, halved and seeded
½ honeydew melon, seeded
¼ c. superfine or granulated sugar
¼ c. fresh lime juice
2 T. fresh lemon juice
1 T. orange-flavored liqueur (optional)
1½ tsp. grated lime peel
1 c. sliced fresh strawberries
1 c. black or red seedless grapes

Using a melon baller, scoop flesh from cantaloupe and honeydew into balls; set aside. In a large glass or ceramic bowl, combine the sugar, lime juice, lemon juice, orange liqueur, and lime peel. Stir well to dissolve sugar. Add the cantaloupe and honeydew balls, strawberries, and grapes. Toss gently to combine. Cover the bowl with plastic wrap and refrigerate for at least 1 hour to blend flavors, stirring once or twice. Spoon the fruit mixture into serving bowls or hollowed-out melon halves, dividing evenly. Serve immediately.

GREEN JACKET SALAD

The Green Jacket Restaurant

1 head of lettuce, shredded to your liking
Toasted Pita Bread, broken into crouton-sized pieces
2 T. red wine vinegar
2 T. olive oil
1 bunch green onions, chopped
1 tsp. Lawry's seasoning salt
1 tsp. Accent
Parmesan Cheese
Salt and Pepper to taste
1 to 2 chopped tomatoes

Combine lettuce, onions, tomatoes. Combine vinegar, oil, seasoning salt, Accent , cheese and salt and pepper, and pour over salad ingredients. Mix in croutons. Toss gently and serve immediately.

This salad was served table-side at one of our favorite "special-occasion" restaurants. The waiter would chop and mix the salad for you at your table in a big wooden bowl and serve it to you on ice-cold plates. It was wonderful. Regrettably, the restaurant closed a number of years ago but it's still one of our favorites.

BLUEBERRY SALAD

Beverly Futch

2 sm. pkg. grape Jell-O
1 can. blueberry pie filling
1 lg. can crushed pineapple

Topping:
1 8-oz. pkg. cream cheese
1 sm. sour cream
½ c. sugar
1 tsp. vanilla

Dissolve Jell-O in 2 cups of hot water. Add pineapple and pie filling and stir well. Chill in 9 x 13-inch dish until firm. Mix topping ingredients and spread on firm Jell-O. Sprinkle with chopped pecans if desired.

BETTY JOE'S BAKED BEANS

Betty Joe Greene

4 strips bacon, fried and drained
1 lb. ground beef, browned and drained
2 sm. onions, chopped
1 bell pepper, chopped
garlic salt to taste
½ c. brown sugar
1 tsp. yellow mustard
1 3-oz. can tomato sauce
2 med. cans pork and beans

Fry bacon. Brown ground beef, onions and pepper in bacon grease. Combine remaining ingredients, except beans, in separate bowl. Stir in beans. Finally, stir in ground beef mixture. Pour into a large Dutch oven or baking dish. Top with crumbled bacon. Bake at 325 degrees fo 20 to 25 minutes until simmering hot.

I grew up eating and then making these at every cookout we ever had. They are, to this day, the best baked beans I've ever tasted.

BARBECUED GREEN BEANS

Diane Nickels

4 slices bacon, cooked crisply and crumbled
or ½ c. bacon bits
¼ c. chopped onion **½ c. catsup**
¼ c. light brown sugar **1 T. Worcestershire sauce**
2 16-oz. cans green beans, drained

Saute onion lightly in about a tablespoon of olive oil. Drain any remaining fat and add rest of ingredients except for green beans. Bring to a boil and stir to dissolve sugar. Stir in beans and return to a boil. Reduce heat and simmer uncovered over low heat 5 minutes, stirring twice during the 5 minutes.
Alternative: Place in a 1-quart casserole and bake covered at 350° for 30-35 minutes until heated through.

(Diane says she prefers to fix this dish up to the point of returning to the boil after adding the green beans. At that point, she refrigerates them overnight, if possible. This way, the flavors blend and all you need to do heat thoroughly and serve.)

COLD SPICED FRUIT

Betty Sewell Ragland

1 20-oz. can pineapple chunks
1 16-oz. can peach slices
1 16-oz. can apricots
1 16-oz. pear slices
Drain all and reserve all except ½ c. liquid
3 sticks cinnamon
10 whole cloves
2 sliced oranges, seeded, sliced into 8ths (Leave peel on)
1 c. sugar
⅔ c. vinegar
1 3-oz. cherry gelatin

Bring spices, oranges, sugar, vinegar, gelatin and juices to a boil. Simmer for 30 minutes. Pour liquid over fruits and refrigerate. Serves 12.

MARY-MAC'S HONEY BAKED ONION

Mary Mac's Tearoom, Atlanta

6 medium Vidalia onions
1½ c. tomato juice **1½ c. water**
6 tsp. melted butter **6 tsp. honey**

Peel onions. Cut in half. Place in a buttered baking dish. Mix other ingredients, pour over onions. Bake 1 hour at 325 degrees or until soft.

CRISPY ONION RINGS

Mark Ballard

1 lg. sweet onion
2½ c. crushed cornflakes cereal
1 tsp. seasoned salt
2 tsp. sugar
1 tsp. paprika
½ c. nonfat buttermilk
vegetable cooking spray

Cut onion into 4 thick slices; separate into rings, reserving smallest rings for another use. Set aside. Stir together crushed cornflakes cereal and next 3 ingredients; divide mixture in half. Dip half onion rings in buttermilk, and dredge in half of cornflakes crumb mixture. Place in a single layer on baking sheets with vegetable cooking spray. Repeat procedure with remaining onion rings and remaining crumb mixture. Bake at 375° for 15 minutes or until crisp; serve warm.

EASY FRIES

Mark Ballard

1 lb. Idaho potatoes
2 c. peanut oil, at room temperature
2½ -inch onion slices
salt

Wash and peel the potatoes. Cut them into long strips with a square cross-section about ⅜-inch on each side. Wash them briefly under cold water and dry with a cloth. Put them in a large pot and just cover with the peanut oil. Add the onion. Place the pot over high heat (attach a candy thermometer, if you have one). When the oil exceeds 200°, it will begin to bubble, first softly and then furiously, and by the time it reaches 350°, the potatoes will be a deep golden brown and ready to eat. This should take 20 to 25 minutes. (The oil temperature should not exceed 370°.) When the fries are to your liking (taste one or two to check), remove them from the oil and blot them with paper towels. Salt the fries just before serving. Serves two.

GRILLED ONION

Mark Ballard

1 very lg. Vidalia onion
5 strips of bacon
butter
garlic salt
Dale's Seasoning
black pepper

Cut one end off of the onion and core it. Pour two caps of Dale's Seasoning in the hole. Add black pepper to taste, and fill the hole the rest of the way with butter. Cross 5 strips of bacon like a star, put the onion on top and wrap the bacon around it. Add garlic salt to taste. Wrap in aluminum foil and grill over indirect heat for the about one hour.

GRILLED POTATOES AND CORN

Mark Ballard

24 sm. red potatoes (about 3 lb.) with skins
2 T. extra-virgin olive oil
1 tsp. coarse (kosher) salt
½ tsp. black pepper
8 ears fresh corn, unhusked
softened unsalted butter (optional)

In 6-quart pot, bring potatoes and enough cold water to cover potatoes (by 1 inch) to a boil; boil 8 minutes, until just barely tender. Drain, rinse under cold water. Transfer to bowl; toss potatoes with oil, salt and pepper. Place on skewers or in grilling basket. Peel off enough of tough outer corn husks to leave an even layer around cobs. Peel back remaining husks to reveal silks; discard silks. Re-cover cobs with husks to enclose. Soak in cold water to cover, 10 minutes. Prepare outdoor grill with medium-hot coals. Grill potatoes and corn, turning frequently, until potatoes are lightly charred and browned, and corn husks are lightly charred, with some kernels beginning to brown, 15 to 20 minutes. Serve with butter, if desired

SAVORY SUMMER PIE

Mark Ballard

½ (15-oz.) pkg. refrigerated piecrusts
1 sm. red bell pepper, chopped
½ purple onion, chopped
2 garlic cloves, minced
2 T. olive oil
2 T. chopped fresh basil
4 lg. eggs
1 c. half-and-half
1 tsp. salt
½ tsp. pepper
2 c. (8-oz.) shredded Monterey Jack cheese
⅓ c. shredded Parmesan cheese
3 plum tomatoes, cut into ¼-inch-thick slices

Fit pie crust into a 9-inch deep-dish tart pan; prick bottom and sides of pie crust with a fork. Bake at 425° for 10 minutes. Remove from oven; set aside. Saute bell pepper, onion, and garlic in hot oil in a large skillet 5 minutes or until tender; stir in basil. Whisk together eggs and next 3 ingredients in a large bowl; stir in sauteed vegetables and cheeses. Pour into crust; top with tomato. Bake at 375° for 45 to 50 minutes or until set, shielding edges with strips of aluminum foil after 30 minutes to prevent excessive browning. Let stand 5 minutes before serving. Yield: 8 servings.

SCALLOPED TOMATOES

Mark Ballard

6 Ripe tomatoes
4 c. fresh bread crumbs
¼ c. melted butter or extra-virgin olive oil
2 T. chopped fresh chives
2 T. chopped fresh parsley
1 T. fresh thyme leaves
salt and freshly ground pepper to taste

Preheat oven to 375°. Combine 4 cups fresh bread crumbs, ¼ cup melted butter or extra-virgin olive oil, 2 tablespoons chopped fresh chives, 2 tablespoons chopped fresh parsley, 1 tablespoon fresh thyme leaves, and salt and freshly ground black pepper to taste. Press half the bread crumb mixture into a large baking dish to form a "crust". Bake until lightly golden, about 10 minutes. Thickly slice 6 ripe tomatoes. Remove dish from oven, arrange a layer of tomatoes over bread crumbs, and sprinkle with more crumbs. Repeat process until tomatoes are used up, ending with a layer of bread crumbs. Bake until crumbs are golden and tomatoes are warm about 10 minutes. Serves 8.

SPICED CORN ON THE COB

Mark Ballard

2 T. canola oil
1 T. coriander seeds
½ cinnamon stick
½ T. allspice berries
½ tsp. turmeric
½ tsp. cracked black pepper
½ dried red chile
1 med. shallot, coarsely chopped
2 tsp. finely chopped fresh ginger
1 gal. water
4 ears of corn, shucked
1 tsp. ground cumin
1 tsp. kosher or coarse sea salt
½ tsp. cayenne pepper
3 T. melted unsalted butter
2 T. fresh lime juice

In a large saucepan, heat the canola oil. Add the coriander seeds, cinnamon stick, allspice berries, turmeric, cracked black pepper and dried chile and cook over moderate heat until fragrant, about 1 minute. Add the shallot and ginger and cook, stirring, until softened, about 2 minutes. Add the water and bring to a boil over moderate heat. Cover and simmer for 20 minutes. Add the corn and simmer, uncovered, until tender, about 5 minutes. Meanwhile, in a small skillet, toast the ground cumin over moderate heat until fragrant, about 10 seconds. Scrape the cumin into a small bowl and let cool. Stir in salt and cayenne. Brush the corn with melted butter and drizzle with the lime juice. Sprinkle the spiced salt over the corn and serve at once.

SPICY CORN CHUTNEY

Mark Ballard

4 ears fresh corn
2 c. diced, unpeeled tomato (about ¾ lb.)
1½ c. diced onion
1 c. currants
½ c. chopped fresh cilantro
3 T. diced jalapeño pepper
1 tsp. cumin
1½ c. frozen apple juice concentrate, thawed and undiluted
1½ c. rice vinegar
1 4-oz. can diced green chiles, undrained

Cut whole kernels from ears of corn to measure 2 cups. Combine corn and remaining ingredients in a saucepan; stir well. Bring to a boil; cook, uncovered, over medium-low heat 3 hours or until liquid is nearly absorbed, stirring occasionally. Serve with poultry. Yield: 1 quart. Note: Store chutney in an airtight container in refrigerator for up to 2 weeks.

SQUASH CASSEROLE

Mildred Gossett

2 cans squash, drained
1 stick margarine
2 eggs
2 c. crushed Ritz Crackers
½ c. milk
1 c. grated cheese
1 sm. onion, chopped
salt and pepper to taste

Melt margarine in large baking dish, then pour into mixture. Stir, then pour into dish, cover with a little cheese and crackers. Bake at 350° for 30 to 40 minutes.

TOMATO PIE

Betty Ragland

2 c. Bisquick
1½ c. grated cheese
¾ c. half-and-half
4 lg. tomatoes
1 c. mayonnaise
¼ c. finely chopped green onions

Mix together Bisquick, 1 c. cheese, half and half. Form into a ball and press into a 14x9-inch Pyrex sprayed with Pam. Bake 15 minutes at 400°. Peel and slice tomatoes and spread over the crust. Sprinkle salt and pepper. Mix mayonnaise, onion and ½ c. cheese over tomatoes. Bake at 350° for 15 minutes.

ZUCCHINI CASSEROLE

Edith Sullivan

2 lb. zucchini squash, cut into cubes - do not peel
1 Vidalia onion, chopped
½ tsp. oregano
1 pkg. saltine crackers, crumbled
1 can (15-oz.) crushed tomatoes
1½ c. grated Medium Cheddar cheese
2 T. butter, melted
½ c. Parmesan cheese

Cover zucchini, onion, and oregano with water and cook 10 to 15 minutes (do not overcook). Drain. Add crumbled saltine crackers, cheddar cheese, tomatoes and butter. Mix well, grease 9 x 12-inch pan. Top with Parmesan cheese and bake at 350° for 1 hour.

CRABBY CAROLINA RICE

Debra Ballard

1½ c. Carolina or other long-grain white rice
1 T. Old Bay Seasoning
2½ T. unsalted butter
14-oz. crabmeat, preferably Main crab claw meat
1 T. vegetable oil
1 med. onion, finely chopped
2 garlic cloves, minced
½ c. chopped canned tomatoes, drained
1 tsp. fresh lemon juice
salt
2 scallions, thinly sliced

In a large saucepan of boiling water, cook the rice over moderately high heat, stirring occasionally, until tender, about 12 minutes. Drain and spread on a baking sheet to cool. In a large skillet, toast the Old Bay Seasoning over low heat until fragrant, about 40 seconds. Scrape the spice mixture into a small bowl and let cool. Melt the butter in the skillet. Add the crabmeat and 1 teaspoon of the Old Bay Seasoning and cook over moderately high heat for 1½ minutes, tossing gently with spatula. Transfer to a plate. Heat the oil in the skillet. Add the onion and cook over moderately low heat until softened, about 4 minutes. Add the garlic and the remaining 2 teaspoons of Old Bay and cook, stirring, until fragrant, about 2 minutes. Add the tomatoes and cook until dry, about 4 minutes. Add the rice and cook over moderate heat, stirring, until heated through, about 3 minutes. Add the crabmeat and lemon juice and cook, stirring, until hot. Season with salt and transfer to warmed bowls. Sprinkle the scallions over the rice and serve.

PASTA PRIMAVERA

Mark Ballard

1 lb. fresh asparagus
2 c. fresh broccoli florets
1 med. onion, chopped
1 lg. clove garlic, chopped
1 T. olive oil
1 lg. carrot, scraped and diagonally sliced
1 med.-size sweet red pepper, coarsely chopped
1 med.-size sweet yellow pepper, coarsely chopped
1 c. whipping cream
½ c. chicken broth
3 green onions, chopped
2 T. chopped fresh basil OR 2 tsp. dried whole basil
½ tsp. salt
8-oz. uncooked linguine, broken
½ lb. fresh mushrooms, sliced
1 c. freshly grated Parmesan cheese
¼ tsp. freshly ground pepper

Snap off tough ends of asparagus. Remove scales with a vegetable peeler or knife. Cut asparagus diagonally in 1½-inch pieces. Place asparagus pieces and broccoli florets in a vegetable steamer over boiling water; cover, steam 6 to 8 minutes or until vegetables are crisp-tender. Remove from heat. Saute onion and garlic in oil in a large skillet until tender. Add carrot and chopped peppers to onion mixture; saute until crisp-tender. Remove from heat; drain. Combine whipping cream, broth, green onions, basil, and salt in a medium skillet. Cook over medium-high heat for 5 minutes, stirring occasionally. Cook linguine according to package directions. Drain well; place in a large serving bowl. Add reserved vegetables, whipping cream mixture, and sliced mushrooms; toss gently. Sprinkle with Parmesan cheese and pepper; toss gently. Serve immediately. Yield: 8 servings.

PORTOBELO BENEDICT

Edwina Barnes

2 T. margarine
4 Portobelo mushrooms
4 (⅜-inch) slices of large tomato
¾ c. chopped onion
1 tsp. savory salt
½ tsp. salt
½ tsp. pepper
4 (1-oz.) pitettes (small pita bread)
4-oz. Monterey Jack cheese, sliced into 8 slices
4-oz. Cheddar cheese, sliced into 8 slices
4 eggs, poached (free range eggs, if possible)

In a medium skillet, melt the margarine over medium heat. Wash the mushrooms, remove the stems from the mushrooms, and place in the skillet. Saute for 3 minutes on one side and turn. Add tomatoes, onion, salts and pepper to the skillet and saute for 4 minutes. Remove from heat. Toast the pitettes in a toaster. Place a mushroom on each. Top with one slice of the Monterey Jack cheese and sprinkle with onions. Top with one slice of tomato and another slice of Monterey Jack cheese. Top with a poached egg and criss-cross 2 slices of cheddar on the top of each. Place on a toast pan and place under a broiler approximately 10 inches from heat. Broil for approximately 4 minutes or until the cheddar is bubbly. Serve immediately.

THREE CHEESE CHICKEN BREASTS IN TOMATO SAUCE

Denise Chambers

¼ . olive oil
6 skinless boneless chicken breast halves
½ lg. onion, chopped
2 lg. cloves garlic, chopped
1 T. dried oregano
1 (15 oz.) can tomato sauce
1 (14 oz.) can Italian-style stewed tomatoes
⅓ c. dry white wine
2 bay leaves
8 oz. Penne pasta, freshly cooked
1 c. grated mozzarella
⅓ c. grated Asiago or Romano cheese
⅓ c. grated Parmesan cheese

Preheat oven to 375 degrees. Butter a 13x 9 x 2-inch glass baking dish. Heat oil in heavy skillet over high heat. Season chicken with salt and pepper. Add chicken to skillet; saute until outside is white, about 1 minute per side. Transfer to plate. Add onion, garlic and oregano to skillet and saute until onion begins to soften, about 4 minutes. Add tomato sauce, stewed tomatoes with their juices, wine and bay leaves and cook until sauce thickens (about 8 minutes). Break up tomatoes with a spoon. Discard bay leaves. Line prepared dish with penne. Arrange chicken over this pasta layer. Spoon sauce over this, covering chicken and pasta completely. Mix cheeses in small bowl. Sprinkle cheese over sauce. Bake until chicken is just cooked through and sauce bubbles; about 20 minutes.

CHEESEBURGER PIE

Mark Ballard

1 deep dish pie crust
1 lb. ground beef
1 tsp. salt
¼ tsp. pepper
¼ c. onion
½ c. oatmeal or bread crumbs
½ c. catsup

Brown meat and add rest of ingredients. Press into pie crust.

Topping:
½ lb. cheddar cheese
1 egg
¼ c. milk
½ tsp. salt
½ tsp. dry mustard
½ tsp. worcestershire sauce

Mix all these ingredients well. Spread onto top of ground beef mixture. Bake 30 minutes at 375 degrees.

MARY'S CHICKEN CASSEROLE

Mary Ballard

2 lbs. chicken breasts
1 onion
Salt and pepper to taste
1 8-oz. carton sour cream
1 can cream of chicken soup

Boil chicken with the onion, salt and pepper until done. Allow cooked chicken to cool and pull off bone. Place deboned chicken in a baking dish. Mix sour cream and soup and pour over the chicken.

Topping:
1½ pkg. Ritz Crackers, crushed
1 stick butter
1 tsp. poppy seeds

Combine and place on top of sour cream and soup mixture. Bake at 450 degrees until bubbly and crackers are golden brown.

HOT DOGS DELICIOUS

Judy Harris

½ c. chopped onion
1 T. butter or margarine
1¼ c. catsup (14-oz. bottle)
2 T. sweet pickle relish
1 T. vinegar
1 T. sugar
¼ tsp. salt
dash of black pepper
1 lb. hotdogs
toasted buns

Saute onion in butter. Stir in catsup, relish, vinegar, sugar, salt and pepper. Score hotdogs, add to sauce, and simmer 10 minutes. Serve on toasted buns. Note: If buns are not toasted, they will get soggy. They also taste better if toasted.

LOW-CAL CRABMEAT FRITTATA

Debra Ballard

4 T. butter
2 cloves garlic, mashed
1 c. chopped onion
2 c. chopped zucchini
1 c. sliced mushrooms
salt and pepper, to taste
6 eggs
1 c. powdered milk
1 c. Parmesan cheese
1 lb. crab meat

Preheat oven to 350°. In large skillet, melt butter and add garlic, onion, zucchini and mushrooms. Saute until tender. Add salt and pepper and cook 5 to 7 minutes. In a large bowl, beat together eggs, milk and Parmesan cheese. Combine egg mixture with crabmeat and pour on top of vegetable mixture and bake 25 minutes or until firm.

LOW COUNTRY BOIL

Martha Armstrong

Water
¾ c. salt
1 bag dry crab boil
1 T. liquid shrimp and crab boil
2 head garlic, unpeeled and cut in half horizontally
2 lemons, cut in half
1 yellow onion, peeled and quartered
10 small red potatoes, washed and halved
1 lb. andouille or Polish sausage, cut into 2-inch pieces
4 ears corn, cleaned and cut in half
1½ lbs. shrimp, unpeeled

Fill a 6 to 8 quart stock pot three-quarters full with water. Add the salt, crab boils, garlic, lemons and onion. Cover and bring to a boil. Remove the lid and add the potatoes and cook for 5 minutes. Add the sausage and corn, cover and bring to a boil and cook for 5 minutes more. Add the shrimp and turn the flame off. Let sit 15 minutes. Drain and serve. Makes 6 servings.

POLYNESIAN CHICKEN

Betty Jones

6 whole chicken breasts, split
6 chicken legs and thighs
3 cans of mixed fruit for salads
1 sm. bottle soy sauce
1 clove garlic, crushed
3 jars of sweet and sour sauce

Preheat oven to 350°. Place clean chicken pieces on towels to dry. Arrange in shallow pan. Drain fruit, reserving syrup. Pour syrup and soy sauce over chicken and add garlic. Bake uncovered, basting often and rearranging chicken so all pieces will brown, about 1 hour. Chicken should be golden brown. Pour liquid from chicken into large saucer. Cover pan of chicken with foil. Add sweet and sour sauce to liquid. Bring to boil over medium heat; boil until sauce thickens and is reduced to about 3½ cups - about 40 minutes. Pour over chicken. Refrigerate over night covered. Also refrigerate the fruit in separate container. Next day, about 1½ hours before serving, preheat oven to 350 degrees. Bake chicken uncovered and basting often about 30 minutes. Add fruit and bake about 15 minutes longer or until piping hot.

SPAGHETTI PIE

Betty Jones

1 c. cooked spaghetti
1 T. butter
2 T. Parmesan cheese
1 egg
½ lb. ground beef
¼ c. onion
2 T. green pepper
½ c. tomatoes
sugar
salt
pinch of oregano
chopped garlic

Combine 1 cup of cooked spaghetti with 1 tablespoon soft butter, 2 tablespoons Parmesan cheese and 1 well beaten egg. Press mixture into a baking dish. In a skillet, cook ½ pound ground beef, ¼ cup onion and 2 tablespoons chopped green pepper. Cook until meat is browned. Add ½ cup tomatoes, a pinch of sugar, oregano and one chopped garlic clove. When mixture is heated, spread over spaghetti and bake uncovered at 350° for 15 minutes. Sprinkle with more cheese and serve.

STUFFED GREEN PEPPERS

Mildred Gossett

6 lg. green peppers
1 lb. hamburger
1 chopped onion
1 tsp. salt
½ tsp. garlic salt
1 c. cooked rice
1 can (15-oz.) tomato sauce
¾ c. shredded mozzarella cheese

Cut thin slices off top of peppers. Remove seeds and membranes. Rinse. Cook peppers in enough boiling water to cover for 5 minutes. Drain. Cook hamburger and onion in skillet until light brown. Drain. Stir in salt, garlic salt, rice and 1 cup tomato sauce. Heat. Stuff each pepper. Put in ungreased baking dish. Pour remaining sauce over peppers. Cover and cook in 350° oven for 45 minutes. Uncover and cook 15 minutes longer. Sprinkle with cheese.

SWEET AND SOUR PASTA

Loutrell Edenfield

1 lb. bag of Mueller's Salad Twist pasta
1 pkg. of Italian dressing
1 env. Good Seasons Italian dressing
1 c. Italian dressing
½ c. sugar, more or less
½ c. vinegar
2 T. of parsley flakes
4-oz. bottle sliced pimentos
1 T. green pepper, diced

Cook pasta according to package directions and drain. Bring all other ingredients almost to a boil (do not boil) and pour over pasta. When cool, place in refrigerator overnight.

APRICOT CHICKEN

Gladys Aaron

6 each any chicken parts
1 pkg. Lipton onion soup mix
1 c. Russian dressing
½ apricot preserves
¼ c. honey

Preheat oven to 350°. Mix together, Russian dressing, onion soup mix, apricot preserves and honey. Place chicken in oven baking dish that has cover. Cover chicken with mix. Place in oven uncovered for 15 minutes. Cover and cook for another 45 minutes, basting chicken periodically.

VIDALIA ONION SUMMER TACOS

Mark Ballard

1½ lb. lean ground beef
1 env. taco spice
¼ c. water
1 pkg. corn tortilla taco shells (1 doz.)
2 c. lettuce, torn into bite-sized pieces
1 c. cheddar cheese, shredded
1 lg. Sweet Vidalia Onion, chopped
1 lg. tomato, chopped

Brown ground beef and drain. Add taco spice and water. Simmer on low heat, uncovered, for ten minutes. To serve, fill each shell with two tablespoons of meat and sprinkle with lettuce, cheese, chopped Vidalia Onions, and tomatoes. Serve with Vidalia Onion salsa. Makes 4 servings.

Vidalia Onion Salsa:
1 lg. Vidalia Onion
1 lg. tomato
2 jalapeño peppers
1 can (16-oz.) chopped tomatoes
salt and pepper to taste

Chop one large Vidalia onion, 1 large tomato and two fresh jalapeño peppers. Stir together with one 16 ounces can of chopped tomatoes, undrained. Add salt and pepper to taste. Refrigerate one hour before serving. Makes 3 cups salsa.

VEGETARIAN LASAGNA

Edwina Barnes

½ lb. lasagna noodles, cooked
2 med. onions, chopped
4 cloves garlic, minced
3 T. oil
2 c. tomato sauce, canned tomatoes, or thinned tomato paste
2 tsp. dried oregano
1 tsp. basil
¼ c. chopped fresh parsley (optional)
2-3 tsp. salt
½ - ¾ lb. sliced fresh mushrooms, sauteed
1 can (1 lb.) kidney beans
¾ lb. thinly sliced Mozzarella cheese
2 c. ricotta or cottage cheese
½ c. grated Parmesan cheese

Rinse noodles in cold water so they won't stick together; set aside. Saute onions and garlic in oil until soft. Stir in tomato, seasonings and salt. Cook and stir about 30 minutes until sauce has thickened. Stir in mushrooms and beans. To assemble lasagna: place a layer of noodles in shallow baking dish 9 x 9-inch, cover with ⅓ of the tomato sauce, then ⅓ of each of the cheeses. Repeat layers twice more, ending with Parmesan cheese. Bake in 375° oven about 20 minutes. Cut in squares to serve. Makes about 8 servings.

BASIL GRILLED CHICKEN

Mark Ballard

¾ tsp. coarsely ground pepper
4 chicken breast halves, skinned
⅓ c. butter or margarine, melted
¼ c. chopped fresh basil
½ c. butter or margarine, softened
2 T. minced fresh basil
1 T. grated Parmesan cheese
¼ tsp. garlic powder
⅛ tsp. salt
⅛ tsp. pepper
fresh basil sprigs (optional)

Press ¾ teaspoon pepper into meaty sides of chicken breast halves. Combine ⅓ cup melted butter and ¼ cup chopped basil; stir well. Brush chicken lightly with melted butter mixture. Combine ½ cup softened butter, 2 tablespoons basil, Parmesan cheese, garlic powder, salt, and pepper in a small bowl. Beat at low speed of an electric mixer until mixture is well blended and smooth. Transfer to a small serving bowl; set aside. Grill chicken over medium coals 8 to 10 minutes on each side, basting frequently with remaining melted butter mixture. Serve grilled chicken with basil-butter mixture. Garnish with fresh basil sprigs, if desired. Yield: 4 servings.

BUFFALO BILL BURGERS

Blake Ballard

1 lb. extra-lean ground round or sirloin
½ tsp. crushed black peppercorns **¼ tsp. ground red pepper**
1 c. vegetarian baked beans **4 Kaiser rolls, split**

Gently shape beef into 4 burgers. Sprinkle peppercorns and red pepper on both sides of burgers. Coat a large nonstick skillet with nonstick spray and heat over high heat. Add burgers and cook over medium heat until browned on both sides and no longer pink in the center, about 10 minutes, or until internal temperature is 155° to 160°. Add beans to skillet with burgers. Cook until hot, about 4 minutes. Place burgers in rolls. Top with beans.

GRILLED PORTERHOUSE STEAKS

Blake Ballard

4 (1-inch-thick) porterhouse steaks (about 1¼ to 1½ lb. each)
3 T. cracked black pepper **1 T. coarse (kosher) salt**
2 T. olive oil

Prepare grill with medium heat. Let steaks stand at room temperature 20 minutes. Season with pepper and salt, pressing pepper into steaks. With brush, dab meat with oil. Grill steaks 5 minutes per side for medium-rare, 7 minutes for medium. Let rest 5 minutes. Slice and serve.

Blake has taken the grilling "reins" from his PaPa who was a master griller after working in the propane gas industry for years. Blake's steaks and burgers are always wonderful!

CRISPY SHRIMP BURGERS

Debra Ballard

1½ tsp. unsalted butter **⅓ c. chopped onion**
2 T. *each*: chopped celery and green bell pepper
¾ tsp. salt **¼ tsp. cayenne pepper**
1 lb. medium shrimp, peeled, deveined and chopped
1 tsp. finely chopped garlic
2 T. chopped scallion (green part)
2 lg. eggs **1 c. fine plain bread crumbs**
¼ c. all-purpose flour **1 tsp. creole seasoning**
1 T. water **2 T. vegetable oil**
4 hamburger buns, toasted
shredded lettuce and tomato slices

In large skillet, melt butter over medium heat. Add onion, celery, bell pepper, salt, and cayenne; cook until softened, 6 minutes. Add shrimp; cook 3 minutes, until opaque. Transfer mixture to large bowl; let cool slightly. Add garlic, scallion, 1 egg and ½ cup crumbs; mix. Divide into 4 equal portions; shape into 4 patties. In shallow bowl, combine flour with ½ teaspoon creole seasoning. In another shallow bowl, beat remaining egg with 1 tablespoon water. In third small bowl, combine remaining ½ cup crumbs and ½ teaspoon creole seasoning. Dredge each party in flour mixture, then egg, then crumbs. In nonstick skillet, heat oil over medium. Add patties; cook 3 minutes a side, to brown. Drain on paper towels. Spread buns with tarter sauce. Fill with patty, lettuce and tomato.

ARTICHOKE & RED PEPPER LASAGNA

Courtney Ballard

2 26-oz. jars roasted red pepper pasta sauce
1 15-oz. ricotta cheese
2 c. shredded mozzarella cheese
1 egg, slightly beaten
6 lasagna noodles (cooked and drained)
1 12-oz. jar roasted red bell peppers (drained/chopped)
¼ c. oregano
1 14-oz. can artichoke hearts
Parmesan cheese

Cook noodles, drain and lay flat on a platter. You will need to stuff and roll these up later. Spread one jar of the pasta sauce in a 13 x 9 pan. Mix cheeses together with egg. Spread this mixture evenly onto each noodle. Sprinkles red pepper, oregano and artichoke hearts on top of cheese mixture. Roll the noodles up and place them into pan on top of pasta sauce. Pour rest of pasta sauce onto top of rolled noodles and sprinkle with Parmesan cheese. Cover and bake at 350 degrees for 30 minutes. Then uncover and bake another 15 minutes. You can also add more cheese on top if desired.

Our daughter Courtney has turned into quite the cook. She enjoys preparing this special vegetarian dish for her friends and entertaining in creative and innovative ways. I wonder where she gets that from?

GRILLED CHICKEN
Marinated in Cumin, Lemon, and Garlic

Mark Ballard

1½ T. white peppercorns
2 tsp. cumin seeds
1 tsp. coriander seeds
½ tsp. ground cinnamon
12 cloves garlic
1 T. coarse (kosher) salt
1 c. finely chopped onion
2 T. grated lemon zest
¼ c. *each*: lemon juice and canola oil
¼ c. chopped parsley
2 (3-lb.) chickens, quartered

In skillet, toast peppercorns, cumin, coriander and cinnamon over medium heat, stirring, until fragrant, 1 minute. Finely grind in small food processor. Add garlic and 2 teaspoons salt; pulse until paste forms. Transfer to large bowl. Add the onion, zest, juice, oil and parsley. Add chicken quarters; turn to coat. Cover; refrigerate 8 hours or overnight. Prepare outdoor grill with medium-hot coals. Remove chicken from bowl; scrape off excess marinade. Sprinkle chicken with remaining salt. Grill, turning, 20 to 25 minutes, until cooked.

PORK AND PEACHES

Danny Bullington

1 c. peach sauce (recipe follows)
1 fresh orange, sliced into wedges and seeded
½ c. French Brandy
18 to 24 ea. fresh asparagus tips
2 c. bread dressing
2 c. self-rising flour
2 fresh peaches, peeled and sliced into wedges
2 T. vegetable oil
3 tsp. lemon pepper
6 boneless center-cut pork chops
6 whole long stem cherries

Split chops and stuff with the bread dressing. Sprinkle chops with lemon pepper. Heat oil in large skillet over medium high heat. Add chops to oil and brown about 7 minutes on each side or until done. Transfer chops to a serving platter and set aside. Remove excess oil and flour bits from the skillet. Leave the skillet bottom coated with oil and place chops back into the skillet. Bring up heat to a simmer, cover chops with peach sauce. Place asparagus in a separate pan with butter and a little water and steam until crisp. Turn heat under the chops up and pour brandy over the chops and ignite. The brandy will burn off the chops and leave a glaze on the sauce. Serve on a bed of rice or orzo. Garnish the sides with peach and orange wedges and asparagus tips. Top chop and peach sauce with long stem cherry. Serve immediately!

Peach Sauce
¼ c. almond extract
½ medium orange, quartered and seeded
½ tsp. salt

1 c. honey
3 lbs. peaches, peeled and quartered
4 c. sugar

Chop peaches in food processor, but don't make mushy. Combine peaches, sugar and honey in a large Dutch oven. Cover and let stand about 45 minutes. In a food processor, add orange and chop finely. Measure orange and add a like amount of water into a sauce pan. Cover and cook until the orange peel is soft. Bring peaches slowly to a boil, stirring frequently, until sugar dissolves. Cook about 15 minutes, stirring constantly. Add orange mixture, return to a boil and cook about 20 to 25 minutes. Remove from the heat. Stir in salt and almond extract. Skim off any foam with spoon and set aside until needed.

TACO BURGERS

Mark Ballard

½ lb. ground turkey breast
½ lb. extra-lean ground beef
¼ c. low-sodium salsa
4 pita breads
¼ c. fat-free sour cream
½ c. shredded lettuce
½ c. diced tomatoes

Preheat broiler. Coat broiler pan with nonstick spray. In a large bowl, gently mix turkey, beef, and salsa. Shape into 4 burgers. Broil burgers 4 inches from heat until browned on both sides and no longer pink in the center, about 10 to 12 minutes or until internal temperature is 155° to 160°. Slit top of each pita to form a pocket. Place burgers in pita pockets. Add sour cream, lettuce, and tomato. Serves 4.

STEAK KEBOBS

Debra Ballard

2 T. reduced-sodium soy sauce
2 T. honey
1 T. grated fresh ginger or 1 tsp. ground ginger
1 clove garlic, crushed
1 tsp. grated lemon peel
½ tsp. crushed red hot pepper flakes
12-oz. boneless sirloin steak, trimmed and cut into 1-inch cubes
8 cherry tomatoes
4 lg. mushrooms, cut in half
1 green bell pepper, cored, seeded, and cut into 8 squares

In a shallow glass dish, combine soy sauce, honey, ginger, garlic, lemon peel, and red pepper flakes. Mix well. Add beef; stir to coat. Cover with plastic wrap and refrigerate for 1 to 2 hours, stirring occasionally. Preheat broiler. Remove beef from the marinade. Discard marinade. Using four 10-inch metal skewers, alternately thread beef, tomatoes, mushrooms, and bell pepper. Place on broiler pan. Broil 2 inches from heat, turning 2 or 3 times, until meat is medium-rare and vegetables are lightly browned, about 10 minutes. Place on serving plates and serve immediately.

A Taste of Summer

Each and every one of us loves a present. You know, something that is created especially for us. Something we will definitely treasure. This season brings us a gift that is absolutely fit for a king. We must be the most special people on Earth because here, in our neck of the woods, the conditions are perfect for growing an incredible fruit we fondly call the peach!

You don't have to travel very far in central Georgia to see the rows of green trees standing in perfect lines like royal guardsmen holding court. They are in many ways. In the early spring they give us a profusion of blossoms that create the illusion of petal pink clouds. This should be enough of a gift to herald Spring, but the best is certainly yet to come.

The May sun seems to blister the newly formed fruit as though it was suntanning on the Riviera. Right before our eyes we see its golden skin turn luscious shades of pink and red as if its cheeks have been painted by a magical make-up brush. We try to patiently wait. At the precise moment when their flavor becomes more than their fuzzy little jackets can hold, the peaches are plucked quickly from the trees. Oh, how privileged we are to be able to watch them grow! Some less fortunate people have to wait for their arrival by mail or purchase them in supermarkets. They should thank God we share, but we gloat because we can enjoy their oozing ripeness only minutes after harvesting.

Take a second to conjure up the smell of a tree-ripened peach. Close your eyes and let it engulf you. Peel back the delicate skin that has protected it these past months from the harsh elements. The sweet juice runs down your arms as you carefully try to slice the fruit. Finally, impatience wins the battle and you take a big bite of one of the best pleasures Summer has to offer.

Don't you want one right now? We should never take them for granted because there is nothing quite like a 'Georgia Peach!'

Years ago when I needed some realistic peaches for a demonstration, I was out of luck. So I developed this paper maché version that will suffice in a pinch. You can create these clever look-a-likes with a little patience and skill. Unlike their real counterparts, these beauties last forever!

Painted, Paper Mache' Peaches

Materials:

3" styrofoam balls
orange tissue paper
Elmer's Glue
Water
Bowl for glue/water mixture
Plate for paint
Sea Sponge
Wax Paper
Acrylic Paint: Apricot Bright Yellow Dusty Mauve
Leaf Green Tapestry Wine
Satin Cream Cranberry Bright Red
Dried stems
Dried peach pits

Instructions:

Shape styrofoam balls into peach shape, cut in half for halves and then again for quarters. Tear tissue paper into 2 to 3 inch ragged pieces. Prepare the glue mixture using a ratio of half water, half glue. Dredge the styrofoam ball in the glue mixture, completely coating it. Be careful not to over-saturate with glue. Apply the tissue paper to the balls, overlapping the pieces slightly so that the entire area is covered. Keep fingers moist with water or glue mixture so that the tissue paper doesn't adhere to the fingers when working with the tissue.

Place the covered balls on a flat wax papered surface. Turn frequently to avoid sticking. Allow to completely dry. This may take from one to three days depending on temperature and humidity.

When completely dry, paint using sponge in a dabbing motion. Begin with apricot for the base and then use yellow, mauve and wine for highlights. Mix satin cream with paint to lighten and add depth. Use leaf green to highlight around the area where stem will be attached.

For the halves and quarters, use a peach pit to make an impression and then use cranberry and bright red paint in addition to other colors to paint the concave "inside" area.

Affix stem and peach pit using hot glue, if desired.

PEACH CUSTARD PIE

Mark Ballard

1 un-baked 9" pie shell
2 large or 4 small, ripe peaches
1 c. sugar
⅓ c. plain flour
2 eggs, well beaten
½ stick butter, melted
¼ teaspoon almond flavoring, or flavoring of your choice

Preheat oven to 350 degrees. Peel and slice peaches and arrange them to cover the bottom of the pie crust with one layer. Mix the sugar and flour. Add the well beaten eggs, melted butter and flavoring, mixing well. Pour over the peaches. Bake until crust browns and custard thickens and sets. Time will range from 25 to 35 minutes depending on the oven.

This is absolutely the BEST peach pie I've ever tasted. And, it's proven to be quite popular with my viewers and readers who've requested and prepared the recipe.

BANANA BROWNIES

Mary McPeters

¾ c. flour
¾ c. sugar
½ tsp. baking powder
¼ tsp. salt
½ c. soft margarine
2 eggs
½ c. mashed fully ripe banana (1 med.)

Blend dry ingredients together. Add margarine, eggs, and banana. Beat until well mixed. Add ½ chopped nuts. Pour into greased 8 x 8 x 1-inch pan. Bake 350° for 30 minutes. Cool and sprinkle with powdered sugar and cut into squares.

BLUEBERRY CRUNCH

Marie Shepard

1 lg. can of pineapple undrained
3 c. fresh blueberries
4 T. dark brown sugar
1 box yellow cake mix
1 c. chopped pecans
5 T. dark brown sugar
1 stick melted butter or margarine

Preheat oven to 350° and place rack in middle of oven. Spray oblong Pyrex dish with vegetable oil, layer pineapple; then blueberries, sprinkle on 4 tablespoons brown sugar. Top those with the dry cake mix, then chopped pecans and rest of brown sugar. Drizzle top with melted butter. Bake for 15 minutes. Using a long handle spoon, make holes every 4 inches to let the juices rise through the cake mixture. Continue cooking for 30 minutes. Make a foil tent if browns too quickly. Serve warm with a scoop of vanilla ice cream. Yield: 8 to 10 servings.

CHOCOLATE PUDDING

Mark Ballard

2 egg whites
⅔ c. unsweetened cocoa powder
2 T. cornstarch
2¼ c. skim milk, divided
½ c. granulated sugar
⅛ tsp. salt
1 tsp. vanilla extract
Fresh strawberries, mint leaves, and unsweetened cocoa powder for garnish

In a small bowl, lightly beat egg whites and set aside. In a large bowl, combine ⅔ cup of cocoa and cornstarch. Whisk ¾ cup of milk into cocoa mixture until completely smooth. In a large heavy saucepan, combine remaining milk, sugar, and salt. Mix well. Bring to a boil over high heat, whisking constantly. Remove pan from heat. Whisk cocoa mixture into hot milk mixture. Bring to a boil over medium-high heat; cook for 2 minutes, whisking constantly. Remove pan from heat. Add vanilla; blend well. Pour pudding into serving dishes. Cool to room temperature. Cover and chill for 1 hour. Garnish with berries, mint leaves, and cocoa. Serves 4.

DANG GOOD PIE

Melanie Wheeler

¾ stick butter
3 eggs
3 T. flour
1 ½ c. sugar
1 c. crushed pineapple, drained
1 c. coconut flakes
9-inch unbaked pie shell

Melt butter and mix with remaining ingredients. Pour filling into unbaked pie shell. Bake at 350° for 45 minutes or until set and brown.

FAT FREE BANANA PUDDING

Barbara Rouse

5-7 med. bananas
1 box fat free vanilla wafers
1 sm. box sugar free instant vanilla pudding
1½ c. water
1 fat free eagle brand milk
1 (8-oz.) fat free cool whip

Place layer of vanilla wafers in bottom of deep dish. Cut bananas into pieces and place over cookies. Combine water with eagle brand milk. Mix in vanilla pudding until soft set. Place in refrigerate for 10-15 minutes. Fold in cool whip. Pour ½ mixture over bananas. Layer cookies, bananas, and pudding mixture again. Top can be trimmed with cool whip and chopped pecans.

FRIED BANANAS

Betty Jones

3 bananas
¼ c. confectioners' sugar
½ tsp. cinnamon
¼ c. flour
1 egg, beaten
¾ c. dry bread crumbs

Peel bananas and cut into halves crosswise. Dust with sugar mixed with cinnamon and roll in flour. Dip into beaten egg, then roll in bread crumbs. Fry in deep, hot oil until golden brown. Makes 6 servings.

FROZEN PEANUT BUTTER PIE

Mark Ballard

8-oz. cream cheese
1 c. powdered sugar
½ c. crunchy peanut butter
½ c. milk
9-oz. Cool Whip
1 graham cracker crust

Combine cream cheese, powdered sugar, peanut butter and milk. Fold in Cool Whip. Pour into crust and freeze.

HENRIETTA'S HAWAIIAN PIE

Betty S. Ragland

1 c. granulated sugar
¼ c. buttermilk
3 eggs
1 tsp. vanilla
2 c. sweetened flaked coconut
6 T. margarine, melted
1 (20-oz.) can crushed pineapple, drained
½ c. chopped walnuts
½ c. maraschino cherries, chopped
2 regular 9-inch pie shells, unbaked

Preheat oven to 350 degrees. In a medium bowl, combine sugar, buttermilk, eggs, vanilla, coconut, margarine, pineapple, walnuts and cherries. Stir to mix well. Pour into pie shells. Bake 45 to 50 minutes or until done and golden brown.

IMPOSSIBLE PIE

Gloria Sikes

1 lg. Cool Whip
1 can Eagle Brand milk
½ c. lemon juice
1 lg. can crushed pineapple, drained
½ c. chopped nuts
2 graham cracker crusts

Mix first five ingredients together and pour into graham cracker crusts. Chill thoroughly before serving.

ROLL THE CAN ICE CREAM

Martha Armstrong

1 c. heavy cream
1 c. milk
⅓ to ½ c. sugar
1 beaten egg
1½ tsp. vanilla
½ c. diced peaches
1 1 lb. coffee can (or 12 oz.)
1 3- lb. coffee can
20 c. crushed ice
1½ c. rock salt

Combine all ingredients except ice and salt in the smaller coffee can with a tight-fitting plastic lid, filling only two-thirds full and tape the lid. In the larger can, layer some ice and salt in the bottom. Place smaller, filled can on top of ice in larger can and pack ice and salt in the space between cans and on top. Cover large can. Roll can back and forth with your foot for 10 minutes. Open large can and drain off melted ice. Repack with ice and salt and roll for another 5 to 10 minutes. Remove small can and serve. Makes 2½ cups of ice cream.

PEACH ICE CREAM

Mark Ballard

5 eggs
1¼ c. sugar
1 tsp. vanilla
1 13-oz. can evaporated milk
2½ c. chopped peaches (may be pureed)
milk to fill 2 quart freezer ¾ of the way full

Beat eggs; add sugar and enough milk to mix thoroughly. Cook over low heat stirring constantly until eggs are cooked. Remove from heat and add evaporated milk. Stir in fruit and flavoring. Pour into ice cream freezer container and add milk. Remember to allow for expansion as mixture freezes. Freeze according to freezer directions. Makes one-half gallon.

MOMMA'S NO CRUST COCONUT PIE

Diane Nickels

¾ stick butter, melted
1½ c. sugar
3 eggs, beaten
2 T. self-rising flour
1 tsp. vanilla
1 lg. can evaporated milk
1 c. coconut

Flour and grease one large glass baking dish (deep dish). Mix together above ingredients and pour in baking dish. Bake 375° for 35 minutes.

PEACH DELIGHT

Imogene J. Scarborough

2½ c. self rising flour
2 stick butter, softened
1 c. chopped nuts
8-oz. cream cheese, room temperature
2½ c. powdered sugar, sifted
8-oz. Cool Whip
4 c. sliced peaches
1 c. sugar
1 c. water
4 T. plain flour
4 T. peach Jell-O

Mix 2½ cups of flour, butter and nuts well with spoon and spread in 9 x 13-inch pan. Bake at 350° for 20-25 minutes. Set aside to cool. Beat together cream cheese, powdered sugar, and Cool Whip with electric mixer and spread on crust. Add peaches. Mix sugar, water, plain flour and peach Jell-O and cook over med. heat until thick. Stir constantly. Cool slightly and pour over peaches, evenly coating all. Refrigerate.

PEACH DESSERT

Gladys Aaron

2 sticks butter, melted
1½ c. plain flour
1 c. chopped nuts
½ c. brown sugar
8-oz. cream cheese
8-oz. Cool Whip
2 c. powdered sugar
4 c. sliced peaches

Topping:
3-oz. peach Jell-O
¾ c. sugar
1 c. boiling water
2 T. cornstarch (mix in little bit of cold water to prevent lumping)

Combine butter, flour, nuts, and brown sugar. Put in dish sprayed with vegetable spray. Bake at 350° for 25 minutes. Let cool. Combine cream cheese, Cool Whip and powdered sugar and spread on top of first layer. Mix Jell-O, sugar, cornstarch, and boiling water and cook until thick. Remove from heat and cool. Add four cups peaches, spread on top.

BLUEBERRY CAKE

Betty S. Ragland

1 box Duncan Hines Butter Cake mix
1 lg. (8-oz.) cream cheese
½ c. granulated sugar
1 med. Cool Whip (12-oz.)
1 c. powdered sugar
1 can blueberry pie filling

Bake a 3-layered cake according to box directions. Combine cream cheese, sugar, Cool Whip and powdered sugar. Place cake layer on bottom, spread with ⅓ creamed mixture; spread with ⅓ can of blueberry pie filling. Repeat for other layers, topping with pie filling and drizzle down the sides a little.

DREAMCICLE CAKE

Mary McPeters

1 box Duncan Hines orange cake mix
1 (3-oz.) box orange Jell-O
1 tsp. orange flavoring **3 eggs**
⅓ c. oil **1¼ c. water**

Preheat oven 350°. Grease and flour two or three cake pans and set aside. Mix Jell-O and cake mix, then add eggs, oil, water and flavoring. Mix well. Bake 20 to 25 minutes at 350°. Let cakes cook 20 minutes. After each cake cools, slice each layer to make 4 (or 6) layers.

Icing:
8-oz. sour cream
1 7-oz. can of shredded coconut
1 c. white sugar
¼ c. orange juice
12-oz. Cool Whip

Mix sour cream and coconut in bowl. In a separate bowl add sugar to the orange juice until sugar is dissolved. Combine the 2 bowls and fold in the Cool Whip. Ice cake. Garnish with mandarin oranges and or nuts on top. Keep refrigerated until ready to serve.

FRUIT COCKTAIL CAKE

Barbara Rouse

2 eggs
2 c. self-rising flour
2 c. sugar
1 lg. can fruit cocktail, with juice

Mix all ingredients together. Bake in a 9 x 13-inch pan at 325° for 30 to 40 minutes.

Topping:
1 stick butter
1 c. sugar
1 c. coconut
1 c. chopped pecans
1 sm. can Pet milk

Mix all together in sauce pan. Cook on medium heat on stove until mixture boils for 8 minutes. Pour over cake while mixture is still warm. Let cake and topping cool.

HIBISCUS NECTAR CAKE

Mark Ballard

½ c. butter, softened
½ c. shortening
2 c. sugar
5 lg. eggs, separated
1¼ tsp. vanilla extract
1 teaspoon coconut extract
1 c. buttermilk
¼ c. sour cream
2 c. all-purpose flour
1 tsp. baking soda
½ tsp. salt
1 c. chopped pecans
½ c. chopped maraschino cherries, drained

Beat butter and shortening at medium speed with an electric mixer until fluffy; gradually add sugar, beating well. Add egg yolks, 1 at time, beating until blended after each addition. Add extracts; beat until blended. Combine buttermilk and sour cream, stirring until blended. Combine flour, baking soda and salt, and add to butter and buttermilk mixture alternately beginning and ending with flour mixture. Beat at low speed with an electric mixer until blended after addition. Beat egg whites until stiff peaks form; fold into batter. Fold in pecans and cherries. Pour batter into 3 greased, floured 9-inch round cake pans. Bake at 350° for 20 minutes or until wooden pick inserted in center comes out clean. Cool in pans 10 minutes, remove from pans, and cool completely.

Cherry-Nut Cream Cheese Frosting:
½ c. butter, softened
1 (8-oz.) cream cheese
1 tsp. vanilla extract
½ tsp. coconut extract
1 (16-oz.) pkg. powdered sugar, sifted
1 c. chopped pecans
½ c. maraschino cherries

Beat butter, cream cheese at medium speed until creamy; mix in extracts. Gradually add powdered sugar, beating well. Fold in pecans and drained, chopped cherries. Yield: 4½ cups.

KEY LIME CAKE

Barbara Rouse

1⅓ c. sugar
2 c. all-purpose flour
½ tsp. salt
½ tsp. baking soda
1 tsp. baking powder
1 (6-oz.) pkg. lime gelatin
5 eggs
1½ c. vegetable oil
¾ c. orange juice
½ tsp. vanilla extract
1 tsp. lemon extract
⅓ c. lime juice
⅓ c. 4x powdered sugar

Icing:
6-oz. cream cheese (room temperature)
½ stick butter or margarine (room temperature)
2 tsp. vanilla
¼ tsp. salt
1 box powdered sugar plus ½ c. powdered sugar

Blend sugar, flour, salt, baking soda, baking powder, gelatin, eggs, oil, orange juice and extract at low speed until moist. Beat 2-4 minutes at medium speed. Pour batter into three 8 or 9-inch greased and floured baking pans. Bake at 350° for 30 to 40 minutes. Pour lime juice mixture (⅓ cup lime juice, ⅓ cup powdered sugar) over warm cake while the cake is in the pan, prick cake with fork to allow mixture to soak into the cake. In medium bowl, mix icing ingredients together and frost cake.

PEACH UPSIDE-DOWN CAKE

Mark Ballard

Caramel:
6 T. butter plus additional for the pan
1 c. sugar
4 to 6 fresh peaches, halved and pitted

Butter a 10-inch cake pan, line the bottom with parchment paper, and butter the paper. Place 2 T. water and sugar in a saucepan, and stir together. Cook over high heat, swirling the pan (do not stir), until the mixture turns a golden caramel color. Immediately remove the pan from the heat, and whisk in the butter (be careful; the mixture will foam). Pour the caramel into the bottom of the prepared cake pan and cover with peach halves, cut-side-down.

Cake:

1 c. granulated sugar	**½ c. melted butter**
2 eggs	**1½ c. all-purpose flour**
2 tsp. baking powder	**1 tsp. salt**
½ c. buttermilk	**2 tsp. vanilla extract**

Preheat oven to 350 degrees. Add sugar and melted butter to the bowl of mixer fitted with a whisk attachment and beat until combined. Add eggs. Whisk until the mixture is light and fluffy. Sift together flour, baking powder, and salt. Stir the buttermilk and vanilla extract together. With mixer set on low speed, add the dry ingredients by thirds, alternating with the liquid ingredients, to the butter mixture. When all is fully blended, pour the batter into the pan over the peaches and bake, rotating it front-to-back after the first 15 minutes, for about 50 minutes or until the cake is golden brown and springy to the touch. Allow to sit for about 10 minutes before inverting onto a platter.

CANDY CLAY

Mark Ballard

⅓ c. butter
½ tsp. salt
⅓ c. light corn syrup
1 tsp. flavoring oil or extract
1 lb. box Dixie Crystals confectioners' sugar, sifted
food coloring

Cream butter until light and fluffy. Add corn syrup, salt and flavoring. Gradually beat in confectioners' sugar. Knead until smooth. Recipe yields about 1 pound of edible clay.

Kids love making all sorts of creations from this edible Play Dough-like concoction.

PICKLES

Mildred Gossett

1 lg. jar of Vlasic Dill Whole pickles
2¾ c. sugar
½ c. tarragon vinegar
¼ tsp. alum
1 T. allspice

Cut pickles into slices and drain in colander. Mix sugar and vinegar in bowl. Stir and add pickles. Add alum and stir until sugar is melted. Tie allspice in a bag. Put one-third of pickles in jar. Drop the allspice in and add rest of pickles and juice in jar. Keep refrigerated.

Showers
Weddings
Ladies Luncheons
Teas

APRICOT-PECAN BRIE TARTS

Mark Ballard

25 pecan halves
1 (8-oz.) pkg. Brie, chilled
1½ (17¼-oz.) pkg. frozen puff pastry sheets, thawed
⅓ apricot preserves

Bake pecans at 350° degrees in a shallow pan for 10 to 15 minutes or until toasted; cool. Remove rind from cheese; cut cheese into 24 cubes, and set aside. Roll pastry into a 15 x 10-inch rectangle on a lightly floured surface; cut into 24 squares. Fit squares into miniature muffin pans, extending corners slightly above cup rims. Bake pastry at 425° for 10 to 12 minutes or until it begins to brown. Remove from oven, and gently press handle of wooden spoon into center of each pastry, forming tart shells. Spoon ½ teaspoon preserves into each shell; top with a cheese cube and pecan half. Bake 5 more minutes or until cheese melts; serve immediately. Yield: 2 dozen

These pesto recipes can be used in a variety of ways - as a dips, spreads, with pastas or other dishes. Delicious!

BASIL PESTO

Mark Ballard

½ c. packed fresh basil
½ c. shredded Parmesan sauce
¼ c. pine nuts, toasted
⅔ c. olive oil
3 garlic cloves
1 T. lemon juice
½ tsp. salt
½ tsp. pepper

Process all ingredients in a blender or food processor until smooth, stopping once to scrape down sides.

CILANTRO PESTO

Mark Ballard

½ c. loosely packed fresh cilantro leaves
½ c. shredded Parmesan cheese
¼ c. pecan pieces, toasted
¼ c. olive oil
3 garlic cloves
1 T. lime juice
½ tsp. salt
½ tsp. ground cumin

Process all ingredients in a blender or food processor until smooth, stopping once to scrape down sides.

DRIED TOMATO PESTO

Mark Ballard

1 (8-oz.) jar minced dried tomatoes in oil, undrained
½ c. shredded Parmesan cheese
½ c. loosely packed fresh Italian parsley
¼ c. pine nuts, toasted
3 green onions, cut into pieces
3 garlic cloves
1 T. lemon juices

Process all ingredients in a blender or food processor until smooth, stopping once to scrape down sides.

OLIVE PESTO

Mark Ballard

1 (16-oz.) bottle pitted kalamata olives, drained
1 (7-oz.) bottle pimento-stuffed olives, drained
¼ c. shredded Parmesan cheese
3 T. olive oil
3 garlic cloves
1 T. pepper

Process all ingredients in a blender or food processor until smooth, stopping once to scrape down sides.

MINT PESTO

Mark Ballard

2 c. loosely packed fresh mint leaves
½ c. shredded Parmesan cheese
¼ c. olive oil
¼ c. pine nuts, toasted
2 garlic cloves
1 T. lemon juice

Process all ingredients in a blender or food processor until smooth, stopping once to scrape down sides.

HIDDEN VALLEY RANCH CHEESE BALL

Barbara Rouse

½ c. Hidden Valley Ranch Milk Recipe Original Salad Dressing, prepared double strength
½ c. mayonnaise
½ c. milk
6-oz. cream cheese, room temperature for 1 hour
8-oz. shredded cheddar cheese, room temperature for 1 hour
5-oz. sliced almonds, toasted

Prepare the salad dressing double strength by combining 1 pkg. dry ranch dressing mix, ½ c. mayonnaise and ½ c. milk. Mix the double strength salad dressing and cream cheese. Beat well with electric mixer. Add cheddar and blend. Cover and freeze for 30 minutes. Shape mixture into a ball. Roll cheese ball in toasted almonds.

HOME MADE BOURSIN

Betty Jones

1 (8-oz.) cream cheese
1 clove garlic, crushed
1 tsp. basil
1 tsp. caraway seeds
1 tsp. dill weed
1 tsp. chives, chopped
cracked black or lemon pepper

Blend cream cheese with garlic, basil, caraway, dill and chives. Pat into a round flat shape. Roll all sides (lightly) in lemon pepper or cracked black pepper. May be made a few days ahead or serve at once with crackers.

PARMESAN-RICE CRISPS

Mark Ballard

1 c. brown rice
¼ c. wild rice
¾ c. freshly grated Parmesan cheese
salt and freshly ground pepper

Bring a large saucepan of water to a boil. Add both the brown rice and the wild rice to the boiling water, cover and cook over low heat until the rice mixture is very soft, about 55 minutes. Drain the rice mixture and spread it on a platter, then let it cool completely. In a food processor, pulse the cooled rice mixture until it is coarsely chopped and sticky. Scrape the chopped rice mixture into a large bowl and stir in the grated Parmesan cheese until well blended. Season the rice mixture with salt and pepper. Preheat the oven to 450°. Line a large cookie sheet with parchment paper. Scoop ½ cup of the rice mixture onto one half of the prepared cookie sheet and pat it into a disk. Cover the rice disk with plastic wrap, then press or roll it out to a very thin 7 x 10-inch rectangle. Repeat on the other half of the cookie sheet. Bake the rice crisps in the lower third of the oven for about 12 minutes, or until they are crisp and golden brown. Using a spatula, carefully transfer the parchment paper with the crisps to a wire rack and let the crisps cool completely. Repeat with the remaining rice.

SWEDISH NUTS

Nita Kunkel

4 c. nuts
¾ c. sugar
2 egg whites
1 stick of butter or margarine
1 tsp. vanilla

Heat nuts (approximately 10 minutes at 325°). Beat egg whites until stiff. Add sugar and vanilla; add pecans to egg whites. Melt butter on cookie sheet. Add pecans to butter. Bake at 350°, about 25 minutes or until all butter is gone. Stir four times.

CLAM CANAPES

Betty Jones

1 can 10½-oz. minced clams, reserve liquid
¾ c. blue cheese (about 4-oz. crumbled)
1 3-oz. pkg. cream cheese

Drain minced clams and reserve liquid. Combine clams with blue cheese, cream cheese and enough clam juice to make cheese mixture easy to spread. Blend the ingredients well and serve with crackers.

MRS. BRYANT'S SANDWICHES

Jo Ballard

1 pound carrots, ground and drained
½ cup ground celery
1 cup ground pecans
garlic salt to taste
Juice of 1 lemon
1 cup mayonnise
salt and pepper to taste

Mix all ingredients together and refrigerate overnight. Spread on bread with crust removed. Cut into desired shapes and serve.

MAE'S TOMATO SANDWICHES

Jo Ballard

1 loaf Roman Meal Bread
1 8-ounce package cream cheese, softened
Mayonnaise **½ teaspoon seasoning salt**
Juice of 1 lemon **1 cup coarsely chopped pecans**
6 small tomatoes, thinly sliced
Dried Parsley

Mix cream cheese with mayonnaise to make cream cheese of spreading consistency. Add seasoning salt, lemon juice and pecans. Cut bread into 2-inch rounds using a cookie cutter and a corresponding number of crescent shapes using the same cookie cutter. Spread cream cheese mixture on bread circles. Add a tomato slice. Sprinkle with more seasoning salt and dry parsley. Top with crescent shapes. Refrigerate prior to serving.

HAM & PINEAPPLE ROLLS

Jeannie Cox

1 can (8¼-oz.) crushed pineapple
1 pkg. (6-oz.) Stove Top chicken flavor stuffing mix
12 thin slices boiled ham **1 or 2 T. butter or margarine**

Drain pineapple, measuring syrup; add water to make 1½ cups. Prepare stuffing mix as directed on package, substituting measured liquid for the water, and adding the pineapple with the Stuffing Crumbs. Spoon about ¼ cup stuffing on each ham slice; roll up, and place, seam side down in melted butter in a skillet. Heat, uncovered, turning occasionally. Makes 12 rolls or 6 servings.

Mustard Sauce for Ham & Pineapple Rolls:
1 T. butter or margarine
1 T. flour
2 T. dry mustard
⅓ c. hot water
⅓ c. vinegar
¼ c. sugar
¼ tsp. salt

Melt 1 tablespoon butter or margarine in a saucepan. Blend in 1 tablespoon flour and 2 tablespoons dry mustard. Stir in ⅓ cup hot water and ⅓ cup vinegar; add ¼ cup sugar and ¼ teaspoon salt. Cook and stir until thickened; stir in ⅓ cup mayonnaise. Makes 1¼ cups.

HERBED TOMATO CHEESE

Mary Ballard

1 c. fat-free cream cheese
2 cloves garlic, minced
1 T. freshly snipped or frozen chives
1 T. freshly snipped dill, or ½ tsp. dried
4 tomatoes, peeled, seeded, and diced

In a medium bowl, combine cheese, garlic, chives, and dill. Add tomatoes and mix well. Yield: 1½ cup.

CHEESE STRAWS

Diane Nickels

½ lb. grated extra sharp cheddar cheese
2 sticks margarine, softened
2 c. plain flour
¼ tsp. red pepper
¼ tsp. salt

Grate cheese. Add margarine. Mix together. Sift flour, red pepper, and salt. Add to cheese/butter mixture by hand. Use a cookie press with star shape. Bake at 350° for 10 minutes.

COCKTAIL CUCUMBERS

Mary McPeters

½ c. sugar
½ c. white vinegar
¼ c. water
1 tsp. salt
1 tsp. dill weed
2 med. unpeeled cucumbers, sliced thin

Make one day in advance.
Bring to a boil in a saucepan the sugar, vinegar, water, salt and dill weed. Mix to dissolve and blend. Place cucumbers in a glass bowl, and pour the hot marinade over them. Cover and refrigerate overnight. Drain before serving.

FRUIT DIP

Betty S. Ragland

1 12-oz. jar marshmallow cream
1 8-oz. cream cheese, softened

Mix well and serve with fruit.

MARINATED SHRIMP

Carolyn Pompei

2½ lb. of shrimp
2½ tsp. capers with juice
2 lg. onions, sliced
1½ tsp. salt
1¼ c. oil
¾ c. dark cider vinegar
1 tsp. sugar
1 T. Lea & Perrin Sauce
½ tsp. paprika
1 dash Tabasco sauce

Layer shrimp and onions. Top with juice, cover tightly and refrigerate for 24 hours. Every now and then shake bowl with shrimp. Serve with large corn chips. Yield: 6 cups.

CARROT RIBBON SANDWICHES

Vicki Brantley

2 c. finely grated carrot (1 lb. pkg.)
1 tsp. garlic salt or ½ clove of finely chopped garlic
½ c. finely chopped pecans
2 T. sweet pickle relish
mayonnaise (enough for good spreading consistency)
loaf of white bread
loaf of whole wheat bread

To get the carrots finely chopped, it's best to use a food processor. First use the food processor to grate the carrots. Then place the grated carrots in food processor with the chopping blade and finely chop. Place the finely chopped carrots in layers of cheesecloth. Squeeze as much liquid as you can from the carrots. Mix carrots with garlic salt, pecans, and sweet pickle relish. Add just enough mayonnaise until the mixture is thick but can be easily spread. Then layer the following to make one sandwich; slice of wheat bread, carrot mixture, slice of white bread, carrot mixture, slice of wheat bread. Using a sharp knife, trim the edges off of the bread and slice the stack into 4 long pieces. These little sandwiches can be frozen ahead of time. Just wrap well to prevent freezer burn and thaw before serving. Hint: The sandwiches cut better and the edges look neater if the bread is frozen when making and cutting the sandwiches.

ALMOND FLAVORED PUNCH

Dell Taylor

1 (12-oz.) can orange juice
1 (12-oz.) can lemonade
2 qt. water
½ c. pineapple juice
1¾ c. sugar
1 T. almond flavoring
1 T. vanilla
1 qt. ginger ale

Mix all together, except ginger ale, the day before serving. Add chilled ginger ale just before serving.

AMARETTO-COFFEE FREEZE

Caroline Kennedy

½ c. almond liqueur
¼ c. coffee liqueur
1 qt. frozen vanilla yogurt, softened

Process half of each of all ingredients in a blender until smooth, stopping to scrape down sides. Repeat procedure with remaining ingredients. Serve immediately. Yield: 5½ cups.

BANANA PUNCH

Georgia Bell

6 c. water **3 c. sugar**
3 (32-oz.) cans unsweetened pineapple juice
1 (6-oz.) can frozen orange juice concentrate, undiluted
½ c. lemon juice
3 c. mashed rip bananas (about 9)
3 (l L.) bottles ginger ale, chilled

Bring 6 cups water and sugar to a boil in a Dutch oven, stirring until sugar dissolves. Remove from heat; stir in pineapple juice and next 3 ingredients. Pour into a 2-gallon container. Freeze 2 hours or until firm. Let stand at room temperature 45 minutes before serving. Pour ginger ale over banana mixture, stirring until slushy. Serve immediately. Yield: 7 quarts.

CALIFORNIA PUNCH

Barbara Rouse

2 cans (46-oz.) Dole Pineapple Orange Juice
1 can (12-oz.) frozen lemonade concentrate
1 qt. ginger ale **2 c. fresh or frozen berries**
ice cubes **1 orange, lemon or lime, thinly sliced**

In large punch bowl, combine pineapple orange juice with reconstituted lemonade. Add ginger ale, berries and ice cubes. Garnish with orange, lemon or lime slices. Makes about 6 quarts.

CHILLED STRAWBERRY COCKTAIL

Mark Ballard

4 lemons **3½ c. orange-pineapple juice**
½ c. low-calorie cranberry juice cocktail
1 T. honey
½ c. fresh or thawed frozen strawberries, sliced

Thinly slice 1 lemon. Squeeze juice from remaining lemons. In a large pitcher, combine lemon juice, orange-pineapple juice, cranberry juice, and honey. In a small bowl, use a fork to crush strawberries until they resemble a coarse puree. Stir strawberries into juice mixture and add lemon slices. Refrigerate until ready to serve. Yields 6 servings.

SPARKLING FRUIT SPRITZER

Debra Ballard

1 white peach **5 strawberries**
1 slice watermelon **½ apple**
¼ c. sugar **3-oz. Grand Marnier**
5-oz. vodka
8-oz. fruity white wine (Sauvignon Blanc or Pinot Grigio)
10-oz. champagne

Cut fruit into small cubes or slices. Place in a large pitcher. Add sugar, Grand Marnier, vodka, and white wine. Allow mixture to steep in the fridge for up to a day (it can also be served immediately). Pour into a pitcher half filled with ice. Top off with champagne.

GINGER-BERRY LEMONADE

Mark Ballard

½ lb. fresh ginger, in chunks
3½ c. sugar
10 c. + 1 c. water
1 pt. raspberries
4 c. fresh lemon juice (about 16 lemons)
Garnishes:
raspberries, lemon slices and mint sprigs

In food processor, pulse ginger until very coarsely chopped. In Dutch oven, bring 10 cups water, sugar and ginger to a boil. Boil 15 minutes, stirring occasionally, until sugar dissolves. Let cool 15 minutes. Strain syrup through sieve into bowl; discard solids. Refrigerate syrup until cold, about 2 hours or overnight. In processor or blender, puree raspberries. Scrape through fine sieve; discard seeds. In a large bowl, combine syrup, raspberry puree, lemon juice and remaining 1 cup water. Pour into large pitchers filled with ice. Garnish. Makes 16 cups.

JELL-O PUNCH

Jerry Cochran

1 lg. box Jell-O (flavor depends on color preference)
2 c. boiling water
3 sm. cans frozen lemonade (add water as directed on can)
1 lg. can pineapple juice
2 qt. ginger ale
sliced oranges or limes for garnish

Dissolve Jell-O in boiling water. Add other ingredients in order given. If made in advance, add ginger ale just before serving.

KOOL-AID PUNCH

Barbara Rouse

2 pkg. pre-sweetened Kool-Aid, any flavor
2 qt. water
46-oz. pineapple juice
2 L. ginger ale

Mix and enjoy.

LIME PUNCH

Mark Ballard

1 3-oz. pkg. lime gelatin
2 c. boiling water
2 6-oz. cans frozen limeade concentrate
½ c. sugar
1 tsp. almond extract
¼ c. fresh lemon juice
½ gallon lime sherbet
4 qt. lemon-lime carbonated beverage, chilled

Dissolve gelatin in boiling water. Prepare limeade according to package directions. Combine liquid gelatin, limeade, sugar, almond extract and lemon juice; chill. Shortly before serving place in punch bowl; add lime sherbet by scoops. Carefully pour carbonated beverage into punch bowl, stirring to mix, and letting sherbet partially melt. Makes 35 to 40 5-oz. servings.

JUST PEACHY PUNCH

Mark Ballard

½ c. sugar
1 c. water
4 c. peach nectar
1 c. orange juice
1 c. lemon juice
1 qt. ginger ale

Bring sugar and water to a boil, stirring until sugar is dissolved. Cool, add fruit juices and chill. At serving time, pour over ice ring in a punch bowl and add ginger ale.

PEACH TEA

Mark Ballard

3 c. strong tea
½ c. lemon juice
5 c. peach nectar
2 12-oz. cans ginger ale
sugar to taste
lemon slices

In a large pitcher, combine all ingredients except lemon slices. Pour into ice-filled glasses and garnish with lemon slices.

ORANGE FRUIT PUNCH

Diane Nickels

1 pkg. Orange Kool-Aid w/o sugar
1 sm. can frozen orange juice
1 sm. can frozen lemonade
1 lg. can pineapple juice
2 c. sugar

Combine dry Kool-Aid mix with remaining ingredients. Add enough water to make 1 gallon. (Can change flavor of Kool-Aid and add sherbet when serving.)

TANGY FRUIT PUNCH

Carol Streetman

1 can (46-oz.) pineapple juice
1 can (12-oz.) frozen orange juice concentrate
¾ c. frozen lemonade concentrate
1 c. water, divided into ½ cups
½ c. sugar
2 lg. ripe bananas
2 c. fresh strawberries
2 L. ginger ale

In a punch bowl, combine pineapple juice, orange juice concentrate, lemonade concentrate, ½ cup water and sugar. Place bananas, strawberries and ½ cup water in blender, cover and process until smooth. Stir into juice mixture. Cover and refrigerate. Just before serving, stir in ginger ale. Yield: 25-30 servings.

CHEESE SCONES

Mark Ballard

2 c. flour
1 tsp. *each*: cream of tartar, baking soda
3 T. unsalted butter, chilled and divided
¼ tsp. *each*: ground red pepper, ground mustard, salt
½ c. plus 3 T. milk, divided
½ c. shredded cheddar cheese

Sift together the flour, cream of tartar, baking soda, red pepper, mustard and salt into the bowl of a food processor with metal blade inserted; add 2 tablespoons of butter. Pulse until lumps resemble tiny peas, about 5 times. Add ½ cup milk; pulse. Add up to 3 tablespoons of additional milk until dough is soft but not sticky; add cheese. Pulse 4 times. Heat oven to 425°. Place dough on floured surface; knead lightly 2 or 3 times. Roll dough to ¾-inch thickness. Cut out scones with a 2-inch cutter. Leftover dough scraps can be re-rolled for cutting. Melt remaining tablespoon butter; brush over scone tops. Place scones on a greased baking sheet. Bake until golden, about 10 minutes.

GRAPE SALAD

Betty S. Ragland

5 lb. seedless grapes, red and green, mixed
1 8-oz. cream cheese
1 c. sour cream
1 c. sugar
brown sugar to lightly cover grapes
½ to 1 c. chopped toasted pecans

Thoroughly blend sugar, cream cheese and sour cream. Fold in grapes and place in pan in a single layer. (Use something like a Pyrex container.) Sprinkle with brown sugar and then pecans.

ONE CUP SALAD

Barbara Rouse

1 c. mini marshmallows
1 c. pineapple chunks
1 c. fruit cocktail
1 c. (8-oz.) sour cream
1 c. coconut

Drain fruit, mix all ingredients together and chill.

CRUSTLESS VEGETABLE QUICHE

Mark Ballard

1 zucchini, thinly sliced
1 c. thinly sliced carrots
½ c. chopped onions
½ c. chopped red bell peppers
6 tsp. butter
¾ c. cracker meal
1 tsp. baking powder
ground red pepper
1 c. fat-free egg substitute
1½ c. fat-free milk

Preheat oven to 400°. Coat a 9-inch pie plate with nonstick spray. Saute zucchini, carrots, onions, and peppers in 1 teaspoon butter over medium heat until tender, about 6 minutes. Spoon into pie plate. In a medium bowl, combine cracker meal and baking powder. Add red pepper to taste. Using a pastry blender or 2 knives, cut in remaining butter until mixture resembles crumbs. Whisk in egg substitute and milk until blended. Pour over vegetables. Bake until quiche is puffed and golden, about 30 minutes. Let stand for 5 minutes before serving. Serves 6.

CHOCOLATE ECLAIR DESSERT

Carolyn Pompei

1 12-oz. container Cool Whip
3 c. milk
2 pkg. instant French Vanilla pudding
1 box Honey Graham crackers
1 container chocolate frosting

Mix pudding with milk until almost set. Fold Cool Whip into pudding mixture. Alternate layers of Graham crackers and this mixture in 9x13-inch container. Start and end with Graham crackers. Microwave frosting 15-30 seconds. Spread on top of crackers. Refrigerate.

ORANGE BLOSSOMS

Gail Harrison

1 box yellow cake mix
1 sm. box instant lemon pudding
4 eggs
¾ c. oil
¾ c. water

Glaze:
⅔ c. orange juice
4 c. confectioners' sugar
6 T. oil
6 T. water
Add a little yellow food coloring

Mix cake mix, lemon pudding, eggs, oil and water and bake in small cupcake cups. Mix orange juice, confectioners' sugar, oil, water, and food coloring. Dip cupcake into glaze.

PETIS FOURS

Mark Ballard

1 box yellow or white cake mix
9 c. sifted confectioners' sugar
½ c. water
½ c. light corn syrup
1 tsp. vanilla
½ tsp. almond

Mix and bake cake mix according to box directions. Bake cake in sheet pans so it is thin enough to cut with cookie cutters. Cool, cut and arrange on wire racks. Mix confectioners' sugar, water, corn syrup, vanilla and almond together in top of double boiler. Heat over boiling water to lukewarm. Do not overheat or the icing will not shine. Pour over cake pieces sitting on wire rack. Use wax paper or pans under the racks for easy clean-up.

SMALL LEMON CUP CAKES

Jo Ann Stephens

1 box Duncan Hines Lemon Supreme Cake mix
grated rind of 1 lemon
grated rind of 1 orange
juice of 2 lemons
juice of 2 oranges
1½ box powdered sugar

Mix cake as directed on box. Bake cup cakes in small muffin tins for 20 minutes and while hot, drop in glaze, then drain on cake rack.. Makes 8 dozen.

STRAWBERRY BLOSSOMS

Judy Harris

12 lg. strawberries, rinsed and drained
3-oz. cream cheese, softened
2 T. powdered sugar **1 T. sour cream**

Remove stems from berries to form flat base. May take a very thin slice off bottom if needed to make it stand alone. Place each berry on cutting board with pointed end up. Use a sharp knife to slice each berry in half vertically cutting within ¼-inch of base. Cut each half into 3 wedges to form 6 petals, being careful not to slice through base. Pull petals slightly apart. Combine cream cheese, powdered sugar, and sour cream and beat until light and fluffy. Use pastry bag with star tip or small spoon to fill berries with cream mixture. Keep chilled until ready to serve.

ALMOND CRESCENTS

Martha Armstrong

2 c. all-purpose flour **¾ c. butter or margarine**
1 c. ground pecans **⅔ c. powdered sugar, divided**
1 T. ice water **1 T. milk**

Combine flour, butter, pecans, ⅓ cup powdered sugar, ice water and milk. Mix thoroughly. Shape dough into 2½ x ½-inch crescent-shaped logs and place on a greased cookie sheets. Bake at 350 degrees for 17 minutes or until lightly browned. Transfer to wire rack. Roll in remaining powdered sugar while still warm. Makes about 3 dozen.

ORANGE COFFEE CAKE

Jo Ann Stephens

¾ c. sugar
1 T. grated orange rind
2 11-oz. cans refrigerated buttermilk biscuits
½ c. butter, melted
2 T. orange juice
½ c. chopped pecans
1 c. sifted powdered sugar

Combine sugar, pecans, orange rind in small bowl. Dip each biscuit in melted butter and dredge in sugar mixture. Stand each biscuit on edge in a lightly greased Bundt pan. Drizzle with remaining butter and sugar mixture. Bake at 350° for about 45 minutes or until golden brown. In the meantime, mix powdered sugar and orange juice for glaze. Immediately invert pan onto a plate when removed from oven. Spoon glaze over warm bread. Best served warm.

JAM THUMBPRINTS

Mark Ballard

⅔ c. butter
⅓ c. sugar
2 egg yolks
1 tsp. vanilla
½ tsp. salt
1½ c. sifted all-purpose flour
2 slightly beaten egg whites
¾ c. finely chopped walnuts
⅓ c. cherry or strawberry preserves

Cream butter and sugar till fluffy. Add egg yolks, vanilla, and ½ teaspoon salt; beat well. Gradually add flour, mixing well. Shape in ¾-inch ball; dip in egg whites, then roll in nuts. Place 1 inch apart on greased cookie sheet. Press down centers with thumb. Bake 350° for 15 to 17 minutes. Cool slightly; remove from pan and cool on rack. Just before serving, fill centers with preserves. Makes 36.

LEMON PECAN SLICES

Mark Ballard

1 c. flour plus 2 T. flour, divided
½ c. melted butter
½ tsp. baking powder
2 eggs, beaten
½ tsp. salt
1½ c. brown sugar
1 tsp. vanilla extract
½ c. grated coconut
1 cup chopped pecans
1½ c. confectioners sugar
lemon juice

Combine 1 cup flour with the butter to make a smooth paste. Spread this in a 9 x 13 inch pan. Bake at 350 degrees for 12 minutes. Combine the 2 T. flour, baking powder, eggs, salt, brown sugar, vanilla extract, coconut and pecans. Spread this mixture on top of the baked paste. Bake at 350 degrees for 25 minutes. When cooked, cover with the confectioners sugar thinned to the desired consistency with the lemon juice. Cut into oblong slices.

BETTY SUE'S PIMENTO CHEESE

Vicki Brantley

1 lb. sharp cheddar, grated
1 lb. mild cheddar, grated
1 med. jar pimentos
1 sm. can evaporated milk
1 pt. mayonnaise
salt and pepper to taste

Mix all the above ingredients and chill.

GOOD PIMENTO CHEESE

Betty Jones

4 T. mayonnaise
1 3-oz. cream cheese
3 cloves garlic, chopped
fresh parsley, chopped to taste
4 shots of Tabasco
1 c. pecans
1 sm. jar diced pimento (do not drain)
12-oz. extra sharp cheddar cheese

Puree mayonnaise, cream cheese, garlic, parsley and Tabasco in blender or food processor until smooth. Turn into bowl. Process the pecans until coarsely chopped and add. Add pimento with juice to mayonnaise mixture. Grate cheese and combine with remaining ingredients, stirring well. Let stand in refrigerator at least one hour prior to serving.

PIMENTO CHEESE

Stephen T. Southerland

2 lb. Kraft Extra Sharp cheese, grated
1 qt. mayonnaise
1½ lg. jar of diced pimento
juice of 1 lemon, sometimes 2
seasoning salt
black pepper
About 6 T. sugar, depending on taste

Mix all of the above ingredients in order listed and chill prior to serving.

Fall

When all the heat and humidity has just about won the battle, a cooler wind blows in to offer relief. The greens of summer give way to the wonderful golds, yellows, oranges and russets of autumn. Shiny and orange, plump pumpkins and gourds take the place of peaches and other summer fruits. Sandals and shorts give way to warmer clothes and polished new shoes. With long lists of school supplies, brand new pencils and book bags, school is back in session. Not far behind, with the sharp sound of a whistle, football season begins to the loud cheers of the fans. We rake and bag leaves while taking time out to "Trick or Treat" ourselves to caramel apples, popcorn balls and candy. We look to the earth for the bounty we need to prepare for the cold months ahead. We set aside a special day to give thanks for all that we have to be grateful. This is truly a season of gathering. So, take a seat on your front porch swing and watch the leaves slowly fall.

53231E-sg-3

Tailgating

BAKE AHEAD APPETIZERS

Betty Jones

1 egg
1 (8-oz.) can tomato sauce with cheese, divided
1 lb. ground beef
½ c. bread crumbs
1 tsp. salt
½ tsp. chilli powder
½ tsp. Worcestershire sauce
60 to 70 cubes of cheddar cheese

Beat egg and ½ can tomato sauce in mixing bowl. Add beef, bread crumbs, salt, chilli powder and Worcestershire sauce. Mix well. Shape one teaspoonful meat around one cube of cheese. Place meatballs in baking pan and bake at 350° for 18 to 20 minutes. Turn once to brown. Remove and keep warm or store in refrigerator until ready to use. Drain fat from pan and scrape cheese drippings from pan and combine with remaining ½ can of tomato sauce with cheese. Add parsley. Heat sauce to melt cheese. Serve hot with meatballs that have been heated. Serve with toothpicks and dipping sauce. Makes 60 to 70 meatballs.

BETTY'S EASY DIP

Betty Jones

1 8-oz. cream cheese, room temperature
1 8-oz. bottle Catalina dressing

Mix the 2 ingredients together. Chill. Serve with raw vegetables.

CHICKEN WINGS WITH HONEY AND ORANGE SAUCE

Sharon Freeman

12 chicken wings (2 lb.)
1 1.3-oz. env. Lipton Golden Onion Recipe Secrets Soup Mix
⅓ c. honey
¼ c. water
¼ c. frozen concentrated orange juice, partially thawed and undiluted
¼ c. dry sherry
1 T. prepared Dijon-style mustard
2 tsp. soy sauce
¼ tsp. ground ginger
3 dashes of hot pepper sauce or to taste

Preheat oven to 350°. Cut tips off of the chicken wings. Halve trimmed wing pieces at joints. Place in a glass 13 x 9-inch baking pan. Stir together remaining ingredients and pour over chicken pieces. Turn each piece to coat with sauce. Bake uncovered, basting occasionally, 40 minutes or until chicken is well done and sauce has thickened. Makes 24 appetizer pieces.

HAM & CHEESE PARTY SANDWICHES

Traci Freeman

2 pkg. party rolls
deli-sliced ham **cheese slices, Swiss or Provolone**
2 sticks butter
2 T. Worcestershire sauce
2 T. mustard
4 T. light brown sugar
2 T. poppy seed

Combine butter, sauce, mustard and sugar and bring to a boil until sugar is dissolved. Cut rolls in half, lay ham and cheese (Provolone or Swiss) slices between rolls and spread a little of the sauce on top of ham and cheese. Place tops of bread back on and pour the rest of sauce on the top of the bread. Sprinkle with poppy seeds. Bake at 350° and 10 minutes until cheese is melted.

HOT FETA ARTICHOKE DIP

Barbara Rouse

1 can 14-oz. artichoke hearts, drained, chopped
2 pkg. 4-oz. Feta Cheese crumbles
1 c. mayonnaise
½ c. 2-oz. shredded Parmesan Cheese
1 jar 2-oz. diced pimentos, drained
1 clove garlic

Mix all ingredients. Spoon into 9-inch pie plate or 3-cup shallow baking dish. Bake at 350° for 20-25 minutes or until lightly brown. Garnish with chopped tomato and green onions. Serve with assorted crackers or chips.

MEATY CHEESE DIP

Mark Ballard

1 lb. ground chuck
½ lb. ground hot pork sausage
1 2 lb. loaf Velvetta, cubed
1 8-oz. jar med. salsa
Lg. bag corn chips

Brown ground chuck and sausage in a large skillet, stirring until meat crumbles; drain. Add cheese and salsa; cook over low heat, stirring constantly, until cheese melts. Serve warm with corn chips.

SCRABBLES

Mark Ballard

1 box Rice Chex
1 box Wheat Chex
1 box pretzel sticks
2 c. peanuts
1 c. pecan halves
2 sticks of butter
1 tsp. garlic salt
1 T. Worcestershire sauce

Preheat oven to 300 degrees. Melt 2 sticks of butter, 1 heaping teaspoon garlic salt, and 1 tablespoon Worcestershire sauce. Pour mixture over dry ingredients, stirring. Spread on cookie sheets and bake for 30 or so minutes. Stir often.

PECAN PRALINE CRUNCH

Bettye Cox

1 box toasted oat cereal
2 c. pecan halves
1 c. white Karo syrup
1 stick butter
1 c. brown sugar
1 tsp. baking powder
1 tsp. vanilla

Toss toasted oat cereal and pecan halves together in a large mixing bowl. Set aside. Cook the Karo syrup, butter and brown sugar on top of the stove until boiling, stirring constantly. Remove from heat immediately and add baking powder and vanilla.. Pour immediately into cereal and nut mix, stirring to coat. Spread mixture on a large baking sheet or jelly roll pan. Bake at 250° 1 hour. DO NOT STIR WHILE BAKING. Remove from oven and turn out quickly onto wax paper. When cool, break into chunks.

SPICY SHRIMP DIP IN A JIFFY

Betty Jones

1 chicken bouillon cube
⅓ c. hot water
2 tsp. minced onion
1 8-oz. pkg. cream cheese
½ tsp. Worcestershire sauce
¼ tsp. hot pepper sauce
2 T. lemon juice
2 4½-oz. cans of small shrimp, drained and chopped

Dissolve chicken bouillon cube in ⅓ cup of hot water. Add minced onion. Stir a little bouillon at a time into cream cheese. Add Worcestershire sauce, hot pepper sauce and lemon juice. Blend until smooth. Add shrimp. Refrigerate until serving time. Makes 2⅓ cups.

YUMMY SAUSAGE BUNDLES

Mark Ballard

½ lb. bulk sausage
½ c. finely chopped Vidalia onion
½ c. chopped fresh mushrooms
¾ c. grated sharp cheddar cheese
¾ tsp. prepared mustard
¾ tsp. Worcestershire sauce
¼ c. milk
nonstick cooking spray
1 (8-count) can big, flaky biscuits
1 egg white, beaten

Preheat oven to 375° degrees. Brown sausage and drain, leaving 1 tablespoon of the drippings in pan. Rinse sausage to remove fat. Saute onions and mushrooms in pan until softened. Mix with sausage. Mix together cheese, mustard, Worcestershire and milk; add to sausage mixture. Spray at 12-count muffin tin with cooking spray. Separate the biscuits into two layers of dough from each biscuit and set aside. Use fingers to flatten each biscuit and line muffin cups, forming 12 crusts. Fill crusts with 2 tablespoons sausage mix. Place remaining layers on top of filling, pressing into bottom crust around edges. Brush tops of bundles with egg white. Bake 12-15 minutes or until golden brown.

RED SNAPPER

Debra Ballard

¼ c. tomato juice
3 T. vodka
½ tsp. Worcestershire sauce
¼ tsp. *each*: salt, freshly ground black pepper, ground red pepper
1 dash lemon juice

Combine all ingredients with ice cubes in cocktail shaker. Shake just long enough to chill thoroughly ; strain into highball glass. Makes 1 drink.

PECAN PIE MUFFINS

Jeannie Cox

1 c. chopped pecans
1 c. firmly packed brown sugar
½ c. all-purpose flour
2 lg. eggs
½ c. butter or margarine, melted

Combine pecans, brown sugar, and flour in large bowl. Combine eggs and butter. Add to dry mix. Stir just until moistened. Place in muffin tin cups. Bake 350° for 20-25 minutes. Cool on rack.

BLACK-EYED PEA & CORN SALAD

Ida Powell

1 15-oz. can black-eyed peas
1 15-oz. can white shoe peg corn
1 1½-oz. sliced ripe black olives
2 lg. tomatoes, chopped
3 to 4 green onions, chopped
1 clove garlic, minced
½ lg. green bell pepper
1 jalapeño, chopped (optional)
¼ chopped sweet onion
¼ c. chopped fresh parsley
1 8-oz. Italian salad dressing

Mix well together. Serves 8.

BRUNSWICK STEW

I. J. Branch

1 Boston butt
1 chicken fryer
1 gal. stewed tomatoes
1 gal. ketchup (use ½ and then add more)
2 lemons - use juice (let rind stay in stew until cooked)
1 stick butter
5 lb. onions, chopped
1 lb. bacon, fried crisp and crumbled
1 gal. English peas, drained
½ bottle Worcestershire sauce
½ bottle Crystal Hot sauce
8 lb. Irish potatoes, cubed
1 gal. corn (½ kernel and ½ cream)

Cook pork and chicken until tender, then chip into small pieces. Add all above ingredients except corn and potatoes. Add salt and pepper to taste. Add ½ small bottle Worcestershire sauce and ½ bottle Crystal Hot sauce. Cook for several hours, simmering to be sure flavors merge. A while before done, add corn and potatoes. If not thick enough, add 3 cups of instant potatoes as needed. Use a wooden spoon to stir.

CORNBREAD SALAD

Barbara Rouse

1 c. mayonnaise
½ c. sweet pickle relish
1 box Jiffy Corn bread mix (prepare according to pkg.)
2 lg. tomatoes, chopped
1 lg. onion, chopped
1 lg. bell pepper, chopped
1 jar of Hormel bacon bits

Cook the cornbread and crumble. In a small bowl combine mayonnaise and pickle relish. In a separate bowl or triffle dish, layer ½ of each: cornbread, chopped tomatoes, chopped onions, chopped bell pepper, salt and pepper to taste and ½ jar bacon bits. Spread ½ mayonnaise mixture over this. Repeat layer with remaining ½ of ingredients. Top with a sprinkle of paprika. Best if made a day ahead or several hours before serving.

KAT'S CAPTAIN SOUP

Vicki Brantley

1 lb. extra-lean ground beef
46-oz. V-8 juice
10¾-oz. can cream of mushroom soup
1 tsp. chopped garlic
10-oz. pkg. frozen chopped okra
2 1 lb. pkg. frozen mixed vegetables
1 lg. onion, chopped
salt to taste

Brown ground beef with garlic until done. Drain well. Add the remaining ingredients. Simmer for 2 hours. This soup is not good unless it is cooked for 2 hours.

CUBAN BLACK BEANS AND RICE

Mark Ballard

1 T. olive oil
½ c. finely chopped onions
½ c. finely chopped green bell peppers
1 tsp. minced fresh garlic
1 tsp. chili powder
¼ tsp. dry mustard
⅛ tsp. ground red pepper
1 can 28-oz. crushed tomatoes
1 can 15-oz. black beans, rinsed and drained
2 c. cooked quick-cooking brown rice

In a large nonstick skillet, heat oil over medium-high heat. Add onions and green peppers, and cook, stirring often, until onions are translucent, about 3 minutes. Add garlic, chili powder, mustard, and red pepper to onion-pepper mixture. Cook and stir for 1 minute. Add tomatoes and beans to onion-pepper mixture. Bring to a boil. Cover and cook for 10 minutes. Serve over rice. Serves 4.

OLD-FASHIONED BEEF STEW

Mark Ballard

1 lb. lean beef chuck, trimmed and cut into 1-inch cubes
2 T. all-purpose flour
2 tsp. vegetable oil
2 lg. yellow onions, thinly sliced (about 3 c.)
2 c. sliced mushrooms
2 cloves garlic, minced
2 tsp. reduced-sodium tomato paste
2 c. reduced-sodium beef broth
4 c. sliced carrots
2 med. russet potatoes, thinly sliced (about 2 c.)
1 c. 1-inch green bean pieces
1 T. cornstarch
1 T. cold water
¼ c. chopped freshly parsley

Coat beef with flour, shaking off excess. In a large nonstick pot, heat oil over medium-high heat. Add beef; saute until browned, about 6 minutes. Place on a plate. Add onions and mushrooms to pot; saute for 6 minutes. Add garlic; saute, stirring for 1 minute. Pour off fat. Return beef to pot; stir in tomato paste, then broth. Add enough water to just cover; bring to boil. Reduce heat to low; simmer until beef is tender, about 1¼ hours. Skim off any foam. Add carrots, potatoes, and green beans. Cover partially; simmer for 15 minutes. In a small bowl, mix cornstarch and cold water; stir into stew. Increase heat and boil uncovered for 1 minute. Sprinkle with parsley and serve.
Serves 6.

BARBECUE CHICKEN

Mark Ballard

½ c. brewed coffee
⅓ c. ketchup
2 T. fresh lemon juice
2 T. red wine vinegar
1 T. olive oil
3 T. pure maple syrup or brown sugar
2 T. orange juice concentrate
1 garlic clove, minced
2 T. chopped onion
One 3½ lb. chicken, cut into 8 pieces or chicken breasts

In a small saucepan mix all of the ingredients except the chicken. Bring to a boil, reduce the heat and simmer the barbecue sauce until thickened, 5 to 10 minutes. Sprinkle the chicken with salt and freshly ground pepper. On an oiled rack set 4 to 6 inches over a medium-low fire, grill the chicken for 10 to 15 minutes on each side, or until it is cooked through. Brush the chicken liberally with the sauce 5 minutes before it is done. Bring the barbecue sauce back to a boil and boil for 3 minutes. Serve the chicken with the sauce. Serves 4.

BAR-B-QUE MEATBALLS

Barbara Rouse

1 lb. lean hamburger
1 c. canned milk
1 c. bread crumbs (any type)
1 egg
¼ c. vinegar
¾ tsp. salt
1 sm. green pepper, chopped
2 T. Worcestershire sauce
3 T. sugar
½ chopped onion
1 c. ketchup

Mix hamburger, canned milk, bread crumbs, and egg together in bowl and form into round balls. Place in baking dish. Mix remaining ingredients all together and pour over meat balls. Bake in 350° oven to 45 minutes to 1 hours.

CHICKEN FINGERS

Janice Ballard

6 boneless, skinless chicken breasts (cut in ½-inch strips) or 1 bag frozen boneless, skinless breast strips
1 egg, beaten
1 c. buttermilk
1 tsp. garlic powder
1 c. plain flour
1 c. seasoned bread crumbs
1 tsp. salt
1 tsp. baking powder

Mix egg, buttermilk, and garlic powder together in a bowl. Mix flour, bread crumbs, salt and baking powder in another bowl. Put chicken in the buttermilk mixture for 2 hours or overnight, covered in fridge. Drain. Place chicken fingers, a few at a time, into crumb mixture, coating all over. Fry in vegetable oil for about 4-5 minutes, until golden brown

PEANUT BUTTER OATMEAL FINGERS

Jerry Cochran

½ c. margarine
½ c. shortening
1 c. granulated sugar
1 c. brown sugar
2 eggs
¾ c. peanut butter
1 tsp. soda
½ tsp. salt
1 tsp. vanilla
2 c. plain flour
2 c. quick oats

Mix. Pat dough into a greased 13x9-inch pan and bake at 350° for 20 to 25 minutes. Frost with your favorite chocolate frosting. Cut into finger length cookies.

MICROWAVE PEANUT BRITTLE

William C. Kitchens

1 c. raw peanuts
1 c. sugar
½ c white corn syrup
⅛ tsp. salt
1 tsp. butter
1 tsp. vanilla
1 tsp. baking soda

Stir together peanuts, sugar, syrup and salt. Cook 4 minutes on high. Stir well and cook another 4 minutes. Add butter and vanilla to peanut mixture, stirring to blend. Return and cook 2 minutes. (Peanuts will be slightly brown and syrup hot). Add baking soda and gently stir till foamy. Pour onto aluminum foil. Let cool, break into pieces and store in air tight container.

CARAMEL STICKS

Mark Ballard

1 c. brown sugar
1 tsp. baking powder
1 c. nuts
1 egg
confectioners sugar
1 c. plain flour
1 tsp. vanilla
1 stick butter
¼ tsp. salt

Melt butter and stir in remainder of ingredients except confectioners sugar. Bake at 350° for 30 minutes in a 9x13-inch pan. Allow to cool and cut into squares. Place in bag with confectioners sugar and shake gently to coat.

TIGER BITES

Pauline Miles

1 lb. vanilla candy coating **1 c. extra crunchy peanut butter**
6-oz. semi-sweet chocolate chips

Melt candy coating in microwave. Stir in peanut butter and pour into a foil lined, greased jelly roll pan. Melt chocolate chips and drizzle over candy mixture. Swirl with a knife to create marbleized effect. Chill until firm. Break into pieces. Store in air tight container.

CHOCOLATE SHEET CAKE

June Ewing

1 stick margarine
1 c. water
2 c. self-rising flour
2 eggs, well beaten
1 tsp. vanilla
½ c. Crisco
4 T. Hershey's cocoa
2 c. sugar
½ c. buttermilk

Bring margarine, Crisco, water and cocoa to a boil. Add flour and sugar. Stir well and add eggs, buttermilk and vanilla. Bake at 350° for about 30 minutes.

Icing:
1½ c. sugar
½ c. Pet milk
1 teaspoon vanilla
⅓ c. cocoa
1 stick butter

Combine all but vanilla in saucepan and boil 2 minutes. Add 1 teaspoon vanilla and let cool before putting on cake.

APPLE POUND CAKE

Mark Ballard

3 c. flour
1 tsp. baking soda
1 tsp. salt
1 tsp. cinnamon
1½ c. corn oil
2 c. sugar
3 eggs
2 tsp. vanilla
½ c. butter
½ c. packed light brown sugar
2 tsp. milk
2 c. (3 med. size) pared and shredded apples
1 c. finely chopped pecans

Stir together flour, baking soda, salt, cinnamon. Beat together oil, sugar, eggs and vanilla. Gradually beat in dry ingredient mixture until smooth. Fold in apples and nuts. Turn into greased and floured 10-inch Bundt or tube pan. Bake at 325° for 1 hour and 20 minutes. Cool in pan on wire rack for 20 minutes. Heat butter, brown sugar and milk to boiling. Boil 2 minutes. Loosen cake in pan and turn out on rack. Spoon hot sugar mixture over warm cake, allowing it to run down sides. Cool completely before serving. (To store for more than a day or two, cover completely and refrigerate.) Makes 12 to 16 slices.

It's just not fall unless an apple cake is baked!

ONE BOWL FRESH APPLE CAKE

Lucille Wientzen

1 c. salad oil
2 c. sugar
3 egg, slightly beaten
1 tsp. vanilla
1½ tsp. baking soda 1 tsp. salt
3 c. flour
½ tsp. cinnamon
½ tsp. nutmeg
½ tsp. cloves
3 c. chopped, unpeeled apples
1 c. pecans or walnuts, chopped

In a large bowl mix everything but apples and nuts. Stir in chopped unpeeled apples and nuts. Bake in a greased 10-inch tube pan at 350° for one hour or until done. **NOW THE IMPORTANT PART!!!** Place in a brown grocery bag and close. Cool. Remove from pan. (Cooling in bag gives the top of the cake a wonderful finish.)

APPLESAUCE COOKIES

Mark Ballard

¾ c. soft shortening
1 egg
2¼ c. all-purpose flour
½ tsp. salt
¼ tsp. cloves
½ c. chopped nuts
1 c. brown sugar, packed
½ c. applesauce
½ tsp. soda
¾ tsp. cinnamon
1 c. seedless raisins

Heat oven to 350°. Mix shortening, sugar and egg thoroughly. Stir in applesauce. Measure flour and sift. Blend flour and other dry ingredients; mix well. Mix in cloves, raisins and nuts. Drop by teaspoonful onto greased baking sheet. Bake 10 to 12 minutes. Makes approximately 4 dozen cookies.

CORN-OAT COOKIES

Jeannie Cox

1 c. margarine
1 c. sugar
1 egg (well beaten)
1 tsp. vanilla
½ tsp. salt
1 c. quick oatmeal
1 c. crushed corn flakes
½ c. flaked coconut
½ c. chopped pecans
1 c. brown sugar
1 c. vegetable oil
3½ c. plain four
1 tsp. baking soda

Cream margarine and add sugars, beating well; add egg, oil and vanilla, mix well. Combine flour, soda, salt to creamed mixture, mix well; stir in oats and remaining ingredients. Shape dough into 1-inch balls; place on ungreased cookie sheet and flatten balls with fork. Bake at 325 degrees for 10 to 12 minutes. Cool slightly and remove from cookie sheet. Yields: 10 dozen.

CRISPY BRAN-RAISIN COOKIES

Diane Nickels

1¼ c. flour
½ tsp. baking soda
¼ tsp. salt
½ c. margarine, softened
1 c. sugar
1 egg
1 tsp. vanilla
2 c. bran cereal with raisins
½ c. chopped nuts

Stir together flour, baking soda, and salt; set aside. Cream margarine and sugar until light; beat in egg and vanilla until fluffy. Stir in flour mixture at low speed, then fold in cereal and nuts. Drop by teaspoonful on greased cooking sheet. Bake in preheated oven, 350°, 12 minutes or until golden brown. Remove to rack to cool.

DAPHNE'S OATMEAL COOKIES

Daphne Sides

1½ c. all-purpose
1 c. butter
¾ c. light brown sugar
1 tsp. vanilla
1 c. chocolate chips
1½ c. oatmeal
1 tsp. baking soda
¾ c. sugar
1 egg
1 c. dried cranberries
1 c. Heath Bars, cracked up

Sift flour and baking soda. Cream butter, sugar, and light brown sugar. Mix together and add egg and vanilla. Add cranberries, chocolate chips, Heath bar, and oatmeal and mix. Drop by tablespoonfuls on baking sheet. Bake 350° for 8-12 minutes.

PECAN CRISPIES

Mark Ballard

½ c. butter or margarine
6 T. granulated sugar
½ tsp. vanilla
1 tsp. baking powder
1 c. chopped pecans
6 T. brown sugar
1 egg
1¼ c. sifted all-purpose flour
¼ tsp. *each*: soda and salt

Cream butter and sugars until light. Beat in egg and vanilla. Sift together dry ingredients; blend into creamed mixture. Stir in nuts. Drop from teaspoon on ungreased cookie sheet. Bake at 375° about 10 minutes. Cool cookies slightly before removing from pan. Makes 2½ dozen.

RANGER COOKIES

Jo Ballard

1 c. white sugar
1 c. brown sugar
1 c. butter
2 eggs
2 c. all-purpose flour
1 tsp. baking powder
1 tsp. baking soda
1 tsp. salt
2 c. Rice Krispies
2 c. Oatmeal
1 c. nuts (pecans)
1 can coconut (small)
1 tsp. vanilla

Mix ingredients in order listed. Drop onto greased cookie sheet. Bake at 350 degrees until golden brown.

My mother made these every fall before we made our annual trip to the mountains. You can add butterscotch or chocolate chips for a little more decadence.

Halloween

Trick or Treat but....
Please don't eat the spiders!

On television I give neat ideas about how to decorate for a party and how to "doll up" food in really creative ways. It was Halloween and I wanted to do this for our party with my chocolate iced brownies. I had taken lime green icing and made little spider webs on top of each brownie. I wanted to add a little spider on top as if it was caught in the web. How CUTE! I didn't have time to draw the spiders so I found these plastic ones that were about the size of a dime. I piled the brownies on an orange plate and they looked fabulous! Our party guests began to arrive. I placed the plate of brownies on the dining room table surrounded by fake spider webs and a little sign that read, "BEWARE, Spider Brownies!"

My wife Debra said that she was concerned about the fake spiders because, besides our guests, our kids were having friends over. She was afraid that they might not see the sign and choke on the plastic spiders. I couldn't believe that anyone would do this, but the damage was done. With my obsessive-compulsive disorder, I decided to make another sign. This one read:

"BEWARE! THE SPIDER WEBS ARE EDIBLE. THE BROWNIES ARE FABULOUS. BUT, DON'T EAT THE PLASTIC SPIDERS!!!!!!

Soon the party was in full swing. Blake and Courtney's friends didn't seem to have any problems because their spiders and little bits of lime green icing were ending up on the dining room rug. I was still worried and pretty much stationed myself near the brownies all night. Our friend Marianne arrived a little late, as usual. She loves my brownies and when she saw them exclaimed that she hadn't eaten all afternoon and was dying for a brownie. I gave her one and issued the spider warning. She began to eat and we got to talking about something else. All of the sudden, she began pointing frantically at her throat. I had just told her about the spider so I said, "Yeah, right! Ha-Ha!" Marianne began to turn slightly blue and said she had the spider stuck in her throat. I didn't believe her because she's always playing tricks on me.

When she didn't get the right reaction from me, she went to the back of the house to try to get some water or something. Debra confronted her in the kitchen and asked what was going on. Marianne choked out that she had swallowed one of the spiders. Debra was horrified and, since Marianne was even bluer, decided to call Ask-A-Nurse - on Halloween night! The nurse that answered listened as Debra explained that her friend had swallowed a spider. The nurse, thinking that Debra was pulling her leg, said, "Yeah, right. Happy Halloween to you, too!" and hung up. Debra called back and explained, "You don't understand. My husband is Mark Ballard and he put these plastic spiders on the brownies we are serving and our friend has really eaten one!" The nurse believed her at this point and, after asking if Marianne was having problems breathing (which by this time she was not), suggested that Marianne eat a piece of bread to move the spider along. After Debra told me off about the plastic spiders, we both turned to Marianne and told her, "If you think we're looking for that spider, after it moves along, you can just think again!"

Here's the recipe for the fabulous and infamous brownies. Use plastic spiders at your own risk!

MARK'S CHEWY BROWNIES

6 eggs
3 c. sugar
1 c. corn oil
2 c. all-purpose flour
1 c. cocoa
1 tsp. salt
½ c. chopped nuts
2 tsp. vanilla

Preheat oven to 350 degrees. Beat eggs. Add sugar and oil and beat again. Sift flour with cocoa and salt; add to egg mixture. Add nuts and vanilla. Pour batter into a 13 x 9 x 2-inch pan and bake for 30 minutes. Leave in pan and frost. Cut into squares while still warm.

Frosting:
1 box confectioners sugar
4 heaping T. cocoa
⅓ c. evaporated milk
1 stick butter, melted
2 tsp. vanilla

Combine sugar and cocoa until well mixed. Stir in milk and butter until creamy. Add vanilla and mix well before frosting the brownies.

CIDER PUNCH

Mark Ballard

3 c. apple juice
2½ c. unsweetened pineapple juice
2 c. cranberry juice
¼ c. brown sugar
2 cinnamon sticks
2 tsp. whole cloves
2 tsp. allspice

Mix juices and sugar and pour into percolator coffee pot. In coffee basket, put spices. Perk and serve hot.

FROZEN FINGER PUNCH

Mark Ballard

12 surgical gloves (without powder)
15 c. colored water or fruit juice
1 64-oz. bottle white grape juice
1 2-L. bottle ginger ale

Fill each glove with 1¼ cups colored water; tie top into a knot. Freeze 8 hours. Place frozen gloves, fingers up, in a punch bowl. Add white grape juice and ginger ale.

INSTANT SPICED TEA MIX

Mary Jane Rensler

2 c. Tang
½ c. sugar
½ c. instant tea
1 tsp. cinnamon
½ tsp. powdered cloves
1 sm. pkg. lemonade mix

Blend together and store in airtight jars. To serve - use 1½ to 2 teaspoons and add to a cup of boiling water. This may be fixed and served from percolator.

MULLED APPLE-ORANGE DRINK

Mark Ballard

1 c. water
½ c. sugar
2 sticks cinnamon
4 whole allspice
6 whole cloves
½ teaspoon ground ginger
4 c. apple juice
2 c. orange juice
¼ c. lemon juice

In large saucepan combine water and sugar; bring to boil over medium heat; boil 3 minutes. Add spices, reduce heat and simmer 10 minutes; discard spices. Add juices and heat to boiling. Serve hot. Makes 8 servings.

PIRATE'S PAINKILLER

Debra Ballard

3 T. dark rum
2 T. pineapple juice
3 T. cream of coconut
2 T. orange juice
1 c. ice cubes
1 T. orange liqueur
ground nutmeg, ground cinnamon, maraschino cheeries, kiwi fruit slices, for garnish

Process first 4 ingredients in a blender until smooth. Serve over ice; top each serving with orange liqueur. Garnish, if desired. Yield: 1½ cup.

HARVEST PUMPKIN BREAD

Mark Ballard

½ c. butter or margarine, softened
1 c. firmly packed brown sugar
2 lg. eggs
2 c. all-purpose flour
2 tsp. baking powder
¼ tsp. baking soda
½ tsp. salt
2 tsp. pumpkin pie spice
1 c. mashed cooked pumpkin
½ c. chopped pecans, toasted
1 tsp. vanilla extract

Beat butter at medium speed with an electric mixer until creamy; gradually add brown sugar, beating well. Add eggs, 1 at a time, beating until blended after each addition. Combine flour and next 4 ingredients; add to butter mixture alternately with pumpkin, beginning and ending with flour mixture. Beat at low speed after each addition, just until dry ingredients are moistened. Stir pecans and vanilla into batter. Spoon batter into a greased 8 x 14-inch loaf pan. Bake at 350° for 1 hour or until a wooden pick inserted in center comes out clean. Cool in pan on a wire rack 10 minutes; remove from pan, and cool on wire rack.

Peachy Cream Cheese Spread:
1 8-oz. pkg. cream cheese, softened
⅓ c. peach preserves
¼ tsp. ground ginger

Beat all ingredients at low speed with an electric mixer until blended. Slice bread and serve with spread.

PUMPKIN CRANBERRY NUT BREAD

Mark Ballard

3½ c. flour
2 tsp. ground cinnamon
1 tsp. salt
1 tsp. baking soda
½ tsp. baking powder
2 tsp. grated orange rind
¾ c. butter or margarine, softened
2 c. sugar
3 eggs
1 can (16-oz.) solid pack pumpkin
1 c. chopped walnuts
1 c. chopped cranberries

Preheat oven to 350°. Combine dry ingredients; set aside. Cream butter and sugar. Add eggs one at one time, mixing after each addition. Alternate additions of pumpkin and dry ingredients. Stir in nuts and cranberries. Pour batter into 2 lightly greased 8½ x 4½ x 2½-inch loaf pans. Bake 60-65 minutes or until bread tests done. If desired, drizzle with icing (mix just enough cream or milk into confectioners' sugar to make a slightly runny consistency); garnish with walnut halves and a cranberry.
Yield: 2 loaves.

CURRIED PUMPKIN SOUP

Mark Ballard

2 T. butter or margarine
1 8-oz. pkg. sliced fresh mushrooms
1 sm. onion, chopped
2 T. all-purpose flour
1 T. curry powder
3 c. chicken broth
1 16-oz. can pumpkin
1 T. honey
½ tsp. salt
¼ tsp. ground nutmeg
¼ tsp. pepper
1 12-oz. can evaporated milk

Melt butter in a large saucepan over medium-high heat. Add mushrooms and onion, saute until tender. Stir in flour and curry powder; gradually add chicken broth, and cook over medium heat, stirring constantly, until thickened. Stir in pumpkin and next 4 ingredients; reduce heat, and simmer, stirring occasionally, 10 minutes. Stir in milk, and cook, stirring constantly, until thoroughly heated.

MOUNTAIN APPLE-ONION SOUP

Betty S. Ragland

1 qt. beef broth, undiluted
1½ c. (12-oz.) apple cider
1 bay leaf
½ tsp. dried thyme
1 tsp. coarsely ground black pepper
½ tsp. salt
2 T. unsalted butter
1 lb. Vidalia onions, thin sliced and separated into strips
½ tsp. sugar
½ c. cooking sherry or dry sherry
½ c. garlic croutons
½ c. freshly grated Parmesan cheese
½ c. (4-oz.) sliced Gruyere cheese
Red apples, finely diced and chilled, for garnish

Combine beef broth and apple cider in a large saucepan. Bring to a light boil. Add bay leaf, dried thyme, ground black pepper and salt. Simmer for 1 hour. Saute onions in unsalted butter in a medium skillet; add sugar and continue cooking onions until tender (about 3-5 minutes). Remove onions from skillet and add cooking sherry (or dry sherry) to the hot skillet. Allow to simmer for 1 minute. Add sauteed onions and cooking sherry to beef broth mixture and simmer for 1 hour, stirring occasionally. Remove from heat.

Ladle soup into oven safe soup bowls and top each bowl with 1½ teaspoons croutons, 1½ teaspoons grated Parmesan cheese and two slices of Gruyere cheese. Broil 1-2 minutes or until cheese melts and slightly browns. Carefully remove the bowls from the oven. Garnish with diced apples before serving.

PUMPKIN AND PEANUT BUTTER SOUP

Mark Ballard

1 sm. pumpkin
2 T. water
2 med. leeks, white part only, chopped
1 med. onion, chopped
6 c. chicken stock
7 T. unsalted butter, unsoftened
¾ c. all-purpose flour
1 c. heavy cream
1 c. unsalted roasted peanuts, chopped
1 T. peanut oil
4 stalks celery, chopped
salt and pepper to taste
4 T. creamy peanut butter

Peel and split pumpkin in half. Remove and discard seeds. Julienne ¼ of pumpkin meat. Cut remaining meat into 1-inch cubes. Heat the oil and water in a 5-quart saucepan over medium heat. When hot, add the chopped celery, leeks, and onion. Season with salt and pepper. Saute for 5 minutes. Add pumpkin cubes and continue to saute for an additional 5 minutes. Add chicken stock, bring to a simmer, then adjust heat to maintain stock at a low simmer for 20 minutes. Melt butter in 2½-quart saucepan over low heat. Add flour to make a roux. Whisk vigorously until smooth. Add this mixture to a 5-quart saucepan with remaining stock and vegetables. Whisk until smooth. Allow to simmer for 10 minutes. Adjust seasoning with salt and pepper. Remove soup from heat. Puree in food processor and then strain. Return soup to heat and bring to a simmer. Heat cream and pumpkin julienne together in a nonstick pan. When warm, add to soup. Adjust seasoning with salt and pepper. Portion soup into warm serving dishes and garnish with peanuts. Yield: 8 servings.

Any of these fall soups would taste even better served from small, hulled-out pumpkins. Get creative with your presentations!

WHITE CHICKEN CROCK-POT CHILI

Mark Ballard

1 c. chopped onion
1 can (or the equivalent) chicken broth
2 cloves of garlic, chopped finely
2 tsp. Cumin seed (the whole seed is important-the ground type will not withstand the long cooking time and will make your chili "muddy")
½ tsp dried oregano leaves (same as with the cumin, use the leaves, not ground)
3 15-oz cans white beans
1 or 2 chopped red, green or yellow bell peppers
jalapeno chili peppers, fresh, jarred or canned, (optional or 'to taste')

In a 4 or 6-quart crockery cooker combine the chicken, onions, chicken broth, garlic, cumin and oregano. Let cook a while on low (approx. 3-5 hours, depending on your schedule). Add drained beans. (Remember, you are just heating them up here. They have already been cooked.) Now, here is the important part if you don't want mushy chili. Add the bell peppers and jalapeno peppers (if using) no earlier than the last 60 to 90 minutes before serving. Top each serving with shredded Monterey jack cheese and or broken tortilla chips if desired.

ALL-AMERICAN APPLE PIE

Mark Ballard

¼ c. packed light brown sugar
¼ c. granulated sugar
1 T. all-purpose flour
1 tsp. grated lemon peel
¼ tsp. ground cinnamon
¼ tsp. ground nutmeg
6 med. baking apples, peeled, cored, and thinly sliced (about 2 lbs.)
1 c. dark raisins
1 un-baked, ready-made 9-inch pie crust

For The Glaze:
1 lg. egg, beaten (optional)
1 tsp. granulated sugar (optional)

Preheat oven to 425°. Spray a 9-inch deep-dish pie plate with vegetable cooking spray. In a large bowl, combine brown sugar, granulated sugar, flour, lemon peel, cinnamon, and nutmeg. Mix well. Add apples to sugar mixture; stir until coated. Stir in raisins. Spoon into prepared plate. Place pie crust on top of filling. Trim edges, pressing against edge of pan. Using a sharp knife, cut steam vents in pie crust. To glaze, lightly brush pie crust with beaten egg. Sprinkle with sugar. Bake until pie crust is golden brown, about 35 to 40 minutes. Place on a wire rack and cool for 30 minutes. Serve warm. Make 10 slices.

APPLE CARAMEL SQUARES

Judy Harris

2½ c. sugar
3 eggs
1½ c. oil
3 c. self-rising flour
1 tsp. baking powder
2½ c. apples, peeled and finely diced
1 c. chopped pecans
1 T. vanilla

Glaze:
½ c. butter
1 c. light brown sugar
¼ c. milk

Combine sugar, eggs, and oil. Add flour and powder and mix well. Fold in apples and nuts and add vanilla. Pour into 15 x 10 x 2-inch baking dish and bake at 300° for one hour. Combine glaze ingredients in small saucepan. Bring to a boil and let boil, stirring constantly, for 3 minutes. Pour over hot pastry. Cool and cut into squares. Store covered in refrigerator.

APPLE CRISP

Ellen NeSmith

¼ c. of peanut butter - smooth or crunchy
¼ c. butter
¼ c. rolled oats
¼ c. flour
¾ c. brown sugar
¼ tsp. salt
6 or 8 med. sized apples
1 T. lemon juice
3 T. water

With pastry blender or two knives, cut peanut butter and butter into combined oats, flour, sugar and salt. Peel, core and slice apples into buttered shallow baking dish. Sprinkle with lemon juice and water. Spoon peanut butter mixture over apples, bake in 375° degrees for 40 minutes until apples are tender. Serve hot or cold with cream, whipped cream, or softened ice cream. Makes 6 servings.

APPLE DUMPLINGS

Diane Nickels

1 Granny Smith apple, peeled and cut into 8 pieces
1 pkg. Crescent Rolls (8 rolls)
1 stick butter
½ c. water
1 c. granulated sugar
½ c. brown sugar
cinnamon and sugar to taste

Wrap each apple slice in a crescent roll triangle. Place in a baking dish. Sprinkle brown sugar between the individual dumplings in the bottom of the pan. Heat butter, water and granulated sugar and pour over dumplings. Sprinkle cinnamon and sugar over the dumplings. Bake at 350° for 30 minutes. Serve warm with vanilla ice cream.

APPLE GOODIE

Mildred Gossett

3 c. apples, diced
1 c. sugar and ¾ c. sugar, divided
¾ c. oatmeal
½ c. flour
½ c. butter
1 tsp. baking powder
¼ tsp. soda

Place apples in shallow pan and cover with 1 cup sugar. Sprinkle with nutmeg. In mixing bowl mix ¾ c. sugar, oatmeal, flour, butter, baking powder and soda together until grainy. Sprinkle mixture over apples and bake in a slow oven until apples are tender and top is brown (about 30 minutes). Serve with or without whipped cream or ice cream.

BAKED APPLE PUFF

Mark Ballard

2 lg. apples, peeled, cored and sliced
3 T. lemon juice
¼ tsp. cinnamon
5 T. 10x sugar
4 T. cream cheese softened
6 T. butter
4 eggs, beaten
½ c. milk
¼ tsp. salt
½ c. flour
10x sugar for topping

In a medium bowl, mix first four ingredients together. In a medium pan, melt cream cheese and butter and then add apple mixture. Cook five minutes. Put cooked apples in well greased round oven proof casserole dish. Mix eggs, milk, salt and flour and pore over apples. Bake at 425° 20 minutes or until golden and puffed. Sprinkle with additional 10x sugar. Yield: 4 servings

CARAMEL PIE

Becky Haltom

1 c. sugar
½ c. sugar
¼ tsp. salt
3 egg yolks
1 tsp. vanilla
1½ c. milk
½ c. flour
½ c. milk
½ stick margarine/butter
1 pie shell

Brown 1 cup sugar until syrupy. Add 1½ cups of milk and stir until mixed well and sugar is dissolved. Combine ½ c. sugar, flour, salt and ½ c. milk. Remove a couple of spoonfuls of the hot mixture from pot into a smaller bowl. Mix egg yolks with this small portion of the mixture and gradually add back to pot. (This prevents eggs from cooking rapidly and spoiling the pudding texture.) Cook until thickened. Add margarine/butter and vanilla. Pour into baked pie shell and top with meringue.

CHOCOLATE PEANUT BUTTER DIPPED APPLES

Mark Ballard

10 apples, stems removed
10 to 12 wooden ice cream sticks
1 c. Hershey's Bake Shoppe Semi-sweet Chocolate Chips
1 (10-oz.) pkg. Reese's Peanut Butter Chips, chopped
⅜ c. shortening, divided

Line tray with wax paper. Wash apples; dry thoroughly. Insert wooden stick into each apple; place on prepared tray. Place chocolate chips, ⅔ cup peanut butter chips and ¼ cup shortening in medium-size microwave-safe bowl. Microwave at HIGH (100%) 1 minute; stir. If necessary, microwave at HIGH an additional 30 seconds at a time, stirring after each heating, just until chips are melted when stirred. Dip bottom three-fourths of each apple into mixture. Twirl and gently shake to remove excess; return to prepared tray. Place remaining 1 cup peanut butter chips and remaining 2 tablespoons shortening in small microwave-safe bowl. Microwave at HIGH 30 seconds; stir. If necessary, microwave at HIGH an additional 15 seconds at a time, stirring after each heating, just until chips are melted when stirred. Spoon over top section of each apple, allowing to drip down sides. Refrigerate until ready to serve. Makes 10 dipped apples (10 servings).

FIVE-MINUTE CARAMEL SAUCE

Judy Harris

½ c. butter | **1 c. firmly packed, light brown sugar**
1 c. heavy cream | **1 c. pecan pieces (optional)**

Place butter and sugar in a 1-quart microwave proof container. (A jar or pitcher works best.) Microwave on high for 2-2½ minutes until butter and sugar are melted and mixture is bubbling, stirring once during cooking. Remove from microwave and stir in cream. Microwave on high 2-3 more minutes until mixture is bubbling rapidly. Remove from microwave and stir again. Stir in pecans if using them. Store covered in refrigerator. Serve over ice cream. This keeps well about 3 days. To reheat, place uncovered in microwave on high for 1-1½ minutes.

FLUFFY PUMPKIN DESSERT

Mark Ballard

1 c. graham cracker crumbs
¼ c. margarine, melted
¼ c. finely chopped nuts
2 T. sugar
2 env. unflavored gelatin
½ c. cold water
1 c. milk
1 7-oz. jar marshmallow creme
1 16-oz. can pumpkin
1½ tsp. pumpkin pie spice
½ tsp. salt
1 8-oz. container (3 c.) frozen whipped topping with real cream, thawed

Combine crumbs, margarine, nuts and sugar; press onto bottom of 9-inch square pan. Bake at 350° for 10 minutes. Cool. Soften gelatin in water; stir over low heat until dissolved. Add milk. Cool. Combine marshmallow creme, pumpkin and seasonings, mixing with wire whisk or electric mixer until well blended. Gradually add gelatin mixture, mixing until blended. Chill until thickened but not set; fold in 2 cups whipped topping. Pour over crust; chill until firm. Top with remaining whipped topping. Makes 6 to 8 servings.

FROSTED PUMPKIN SQUARES

Mark Ballard

2 c. all-purpose flour
1 tsp. ground cinnamon
1 tsp. baking soda
4 eggs
1½ c. granulated sugar
1 tsp. vanilla extract
1 tsp. baking powder
1 tsp. ground nutmeg
½ tsp. salt
1 16-oz. can pumpkin
1 c. vegetable oil

Sift together the flour, baking powder, cinnamon, nutmeg, soda and salt; set aside. In a large mixing bowl, beat together the eggs, pumpkin, sugar, oil and vanilla extract. Gradually add flour mixture to mixing bowl. Beat well. Spread batter into a 9 x 13 inch baking pan which has been sprayed with a no-stick cooking spray. Bake in a 350° oven for 25-30 minutes, or until a toothpick inserted in center comes out clean. Cool pan on a wire rack. Cool completely before frosting.

Cream Cheese Frosting:
6-oz. cream cheese, softened
½ c. butter
2 tsp. vanilla extract
1 16-oz. box confectioners' sugar
Halloween candy for decorating, if desired

Beat together the softened cream cheese, butter and vanilla extract until fluffy. Gradually add the sugar, beating until smooth. Spread over pumpkin cake directly in the pan. Cut into squares immediately and decorate, if desired with candy corn or Halloween candy creams. Serve directly from the pan or lift squares onto paper muffin cups and arrange on a serving tray. Recipe yields 35 squares.

GHOST AND GOBLIN BROWNIES

Mark Ballard

1 4-oz. pkg. sweet cooking chocolate
2 T. butter
3 eggs, divided
1½ vanilla extract, divided
1 c. granulated sugar, divided
½ c. self-rising flour
1 3-oz. pkg. cream cheese

Place chocolate and butter together in a sm. saucepan and melt over low heat, stirring occasionally. Cool. Beat 2 of the eggs and 1 teaspoon of vanilla extract until frothy. Gradually beat in ¾ cup of sugar and continue beating until thick and lemon colored. Stir in flour and beat well. Blend in chocolate mixture. Set chocolate mixture aside. Cream together the cream cheese and the remaining ¼ cup sugar until light and fluffy. Blend in the remaining egg and ½ teaspoon of vanilla extract. Spread half of the chocolate mixture in a greased and floured 8 x 8 x 2-inch baking pan. Pour cream cheese mixture over chocolate batter and top with remaining chocolate batter. Swirl lightly with the blade of a knife. Bake in a 350° oven for 40-45 minutes or until wooden toothpick inserted in the center comes out clean. Cool and cut into squares. Yields: 16 brownies.

GHOSTLY WHITE CHOCOLATE BROWNIES

Mark Ballard

½ c. butter
4 1-oz. sq. unsweetened chocolate
1¼ c. granulated sugar
½ tsp. almond extract
2 eggs, lightly beaten
¾ c. self-rising flour
1 3-oz. bar white chocolate, coarsely chopped
½ c. slivered almonds, toasted

Melt butter and chocolate together in a med. saucepan, stirring frequently until blended smooth. Remove from heat and stir in sugar and almond extract. Add lightly beaten eggs slowly, stirring constantly until blended. Stir in flour until just mixed. Fold in chopped white chocolate and toasted slivered almonds. Spread batter into a greased and floured 8 x 8 x 2-inch baking pan. Bake in a 350° oven for 25-30 minutes or until a wooden toothpick when inserted in the center of the pan comes out clean. Cool in pan on a wire rack. When cool, cut into squares and serve. Recipe yields 16 brownies.

PUMPKIN CHEESECAKE

Mark Ballard

8-oz. fat free cream cheese, soft
8-oz. reduced fat cream cheese, soft
¾ c. fat free egg substitute
½ c. granulated sugar
1 tsp. vanilla extract
1 c. canned pumpkin
¼ c. light brown sugar, packed
2 tsp. pumpkin pie spice
kumquats, sliced (optional)
mint sprigs (optional)

Graham Cracker Crust:
1 c. graham-cracker crumbs
3 T. orange marmalade, melted
1 T. granulated sugar

Beat cheeses with an electric mixer until smooth. Gradually beat in egg substitute, granulated sugar, and vanilla until smooth. Set aside 1 cup of cheese mixture. Add pumpkin, brown sugar, and pumpkin pie spice to remaining cheese mixture and beat. Preheat oven to 350°. Combine crumbs, marmalade, and sugar in a sm. bowl. Press crumb mixture into bottom and up sides of 9-inch pie plate. Bake until crust is set and lightly browned around edges, 8 to 10 minutes. Pour half of pumpkin mixture into crust. Top with reserved cheese mixture, then with remaining pumpkin mixture. Bake cheesecake until set, about 30 minutes. Cool on a wire rack. Refrigerate until chilled. Garnish with kumquats and mint. Serves 8.

PUMPKIN ROLL

Gail Harrison

3 eggs
1 c. sugar
¾ c. pumpkin
¾ c. self rising flour
1 tsp. lemon juice
2 tsp. cinnamon
1 tsp. ginger
½ tsp. nutmeg

Icing:
1 c. powder sugar
4 tsp. butter, melted
1 8-oz. cream cheese
1 tsp. vanilla

Beat eggs for 5 minutes gradually adding sugar. Add pumpkin, flour, lemon juice, cinnamon, ginger, and nutmeg and mix really well. Put in jelly roll pan and cook for 10 to 15 minutes. Take out and put powdered sugar on paper towel. Roll pumpkin roll up in paper towel until cool. Unroll. Spread icing onto inside of roll and roll back up in paper towel. Put in freezer until ready to eat.

PUMPKIN SQUARES

Mary McPeters

1 can pumpkin
½ tsp. cinnamon
1 c. sugar
1 c. chopped nuts
¾ c. Cool Whip
½ c. powdered sugar
1 can evaporated milk
3 eggs
1 box yellow cake mix
1 stick butter, melted
8-oz. cream cheese

Mix pumpkin, milk, cinnamon, eggs, and sugar and pour into sprayed 9 x 13-inch pan. Mix cake mix and chopped nuts together dry and sprinkle over first layer. Drizzle butter over top of cake mix and nuts. Bake at 350° for 50 to 60 minutes. Cool and invert. Mix Cool Whip, cream cheese and powdered sugar and top cake.

SPIDER CUPCAKES

Mark Ballard

1 18½-oz. pkg. white cake mix
2 12-oz. containers vanilla or chocolate ready-to-spread frosting
1 11¼-oz. pkg. red or black licorice
72 red cinnamon candies

Prepare and bake cake mix according to package directions for cupcakes. Spread frosting on top. Cut licorice into 192 (3- to 4-inch long) strips. Insert 4 strips into each side of cupcake to form legs, and add 3 red cinnamon candies for eyes and mouth.

BLACK CAT CAKE

Mark Ballard

½ c. shortening
2 c. granulated sugar
4 eggs
1 tsp. vanilla extract
2 sq. (1-oz. each) unsweetened chocolate, melted and cooled
2½ c. all-purpose flour
1½ tsp. baking soda
1 tsp. salt
1½ c. buttermilk

Cream shortening and sugar until light and fluffy. Add eggs, one at a time. Stir in vanilla extract. Add melted, cooled chocolate. Sift together the flour, baking soda and salt and add alternately to the batter along with the buttermilk. Grease and flour two 9-inch cake pans and divide batter evenly between the pans. Bake in a 325° oven about 40 minutes, or until a wooden toothpick inserted in the center of the cake comes out clean. Cool 10 minutes, remove from pans and cool completely before frosting.

Frosting:
½ c. butter, softened
1 8-oz.. pkg cream cheese
1 tsp. vanilla extract
dash salt
2 (1 lb. each) boxes confectioners' sugar, sifted
3 T. milk
3 (1-oz. each) sq. unsweetened chocolate, melted and cooled

Combine butter, cream cheese, vanilla and salt and beat until light and fluffy. Add confectioners' sugar slowly, beating on low speed. Stir in milk and melted chocolate. Beat until fluffy.

Assembly of Black Cat Cake:
Cut one layer of the cake to form the tail, head and ears of the cat. Arrange cake pieces to form the cat on a large tray. Frost and place candies on cat head to form eyes, nose and whiskers.

BUTTER AND NUT CAKE

Nell Lamb Holland

1 c. butter
2 c. sugar
3 c. cake flour
1 c. buttermilk
1 tsp. baking soda
¼ tsp. salt
3 eggs, separated
2 tsp. Butter and Nut flavoring

Cream butter and sugar thoroughly. Mix baking soda, salt, and buttermilk and add to butter/sugar mixture alternately with flour, mixing well. Add egg yolks one at a time, mixing well after each addition. Blend in flavoring. Beat egg whites until stiff and add to mixture. Pour into greased and floured 10-inch tube pan and bake 350° degrees for 1 hour or until it test done.

Butter and Nut Frosting:
½ c. softened butter
8-oz. cream cheese
1 box confectioners' sugar
1 tsp. Butter and Nut flavoring
1 c. chopped nuts

Cream butter and cream cheese well; add confectioners' sugar and flavoring, blending well. Stir in pecans and then spread on layers.

BEWITCHING COOKIES

Mark Ballard

1 c. butter
3 eggs
4½ c. all-purpose flour
½ tsp. salt
2 c. granulated sugar
1 tsp. vanilla extract
1 tsp. baking soda

Cream butter and sugar. Add eggs, 1 at a time. Stir in vanilla extract. Sift flour with baking soda and salt and stir into batter until just mixed. Cover and chill dough at least 2 hours. Roll ⅓ of dough at a time to a ⅛-inch thickness on a floured surface. Cut out cookies with a floured cookie cutter. Place on a baking sheet treated with a non-sticking cooking spray 1 inch apart and bake on the top rack of a 375° oven for 8-10 minutes or until lightly browned on the edges. Keep remaining dough chilled at all times. Re-chill scraps before rolling. Cool 2 minutes and loosen cookies from the sheet. Cool flat to room temperature before icing. Recipe yields 4 dozen large cookies.

Decorator's Icing:
⅓ c. butter, softened
½ tsp. vanilla extract
food coloring to tint
2 c. confectioners sugar
1 T. water

Cream butter until light and fluffy. Gradually beat in confectioners sugar. Stir in vanilla extract and water. Beat icing until fluffy. If icing appears too stiff, add more water a few drops at a time. Tint icing as desired with food coloring. This icing is easily spread over cooled cookies and can be piped through a pastry bag with decorating tips. Arrange iced cookies side-by-side on a serving tray. This icing will dry to the touch but will crush if cookies are piled on top of each other.

DIXIE CANDY APPLES

Mark Ballard

8 sm. red delicious apples
8 skewers
butter
1 c. water
2½ c. light brown sugar
½ c. light corn syrup
a few drops red food coloring

Wash and dry apples. Insert skewer part way through stem end of each apple. Butter a large cookie sheet and set aside. Combine water, sugar, and corn syrup in a medium, heavy saucepan. Place over heat and stir only until is dissolved. Cook without stirring, nearly to the hard-crack stage, 290°. This will take about 20 minutes. Immediately remove pan from heat. Add food coloring, if desired. Tip saucepan and swirl each apple in mixture to coat evenly. Lift out and swirl over saucepan to each drips. Reheat over low heat if mixture hardens. Place apples on buttered sheet.

DIXIE CARAMEL APPLES

Mark Ballard

2 c. light brown sugar, firmly packed
½ c. butter — **½ tsp. salt**
½ c. evaporated milk — **1 tsp. vanilla extract**
6-8 med. apples — **wooden sticks**

Combine light brown sugar, butter, salt and evaporated milk together in a heavy gauge saucepan. Bring mixture to a boil over medium heat, stirring constantly. Continue boiling until mixture forms a soft ball when dropped into cold water, about 240° on a candy thermometer. Remove from heat and add vanilla extract. Beat with a wire whisk about 10 minutes, or until mixture thickens and loses it gloss. Insert wooden sticks into washed and dried apples and dip into caramel syrup, coating entire surface of the apple. Place apples on a sheet of waxed paper which has been sprayed with a no-stick cooking spray. Dry thoroughly and store in a cool place. Recipe coats 6-8 medium apples.

GREAT PUMPKIN COOKIES

Mark Ballard

4 c. un-sifted all-purpose flour
2 c. quick or old-fashioned oats, uncooked
2 tsp. baking soda
2 tsp. ground cinnamon
1 tsp. salt
1½ c. butter or margarine, softened
2 c. firmly packed brown sugar
1 c. granulated sugar
1 egg
1 tsp. vanilla extract
1 can (16-oz.) solid pack pumpkin
1 c. real semi-sweet chocolate morsels
assorted icings or peanut butter
assorted candies, raisins, or nuts

Preheat oven to 350°. Combine flour, oats, soda, cinnamon and salt; set aside. Cream butter, gradually add sugars, beating until light and fluffy. Add egg and vanilla; mix well. Alternate additions of dry ingredients and pumpkin, mixing well after each addition. Stir in morsels. For each cookie, drop ¼ cup dough onto lightly greased cookie sheet; spread into pumpkin shape using a thing metal spatula. Add a bit more dough to form stem. Bake at 350° 20-25 minutes, until cookies are firm and lightly browned. Remove from cookie sheets; cool on racks. Decorate using icing or peanut butter to affix assorted candies, raisin or nuts. Yields about 32 large cookies.

JACK-O'-LANTERN COOKIES

Mark Ballard

2 20-oz. pkg. refrigerated sugar cookie dough
1 16-oz. container white ready-to-spread frosting
orange paste food coloring
1 4½-oz. tube green decorating frosting
1 4½-oz. tube brown decorating frosting
black licorice candy, milk chocolate kisses, assorted Halloween candy

Roll 1 package of cookie dough to ⅛-inch thickness on a lightly floured surface; cut with pumpkin-shaped cutter dipped into flour. Place cookies on greased baking sheets. Bake at 350° for 7 minutes or until lightly browned. Cool on baking sheet 1 minute; remove to wire racks to cool. Stir together white frosting and a small amount of food coloring until evenly colored; spread over each cookie. Decorate cookies with frostings and candies, as desired.

POPCORN GHOSTS

Mark Ballard

25 c. popped corn **1 c. granulated sugar**
¾ c. light corn syrup **pinch salt**
1 14-oz. can sweetened condensed milk
¼ c. butter **1½ tsp. vanilla extract**
waxed paper
orange or black ribbon or yarn
black construction paper and glue

Lightly butter a very large mixing bowl and measure popped corn into bowl. Watch closely for unpopped kernels. Allow popped corn to cool. In a heavy gauge saucepan, combine the sugar, corn syrup, salt and sweetened condensed milk and stir well. Cook over a medium heat source, stirring constantly, until a small amount dropped in cold water forms a soft ball (230° on a candy thermometer). Remove from heat and cool slightly. Stir in butter and vanilla extract. Gradually drizzle mixture over the popped corn, tossing popped corn to mix well. Shape coated popped corn into 3-inch balls with buttered hands. Place balls on buttered waxed paper to harden. When hard, wrap each ball in a 12-inch square sheet of waxed paper. Place in the center of the square; gather waxed paper around the ball and tie with ribbon or yarn. Cut small circles from construction paper and glue two "eyes" onto each ghost. Recipe yields 30 ghosts.

Every Halloween as a child, we looked forward to trick-or-treating at our neighbor Mrs. Baker's home. She treated us to homemade popcorn balls - something that's unheard of in these times. The popcorn ghost recipe brings back great memories for me. I hope you can create some wonderful Halloween memories for your kids and grandchildren.

Thanksgiving

Fall is definitely in the air and with it comes a special time for us to pause and be thankful for all that we have. We are truly blessed in the Middle Georgia area to be able to enjoy all of the four seasons. I just love it when we gracefully shift from one season to the next. Just when we are bored with the way things are, we are reminded of the fact that they are not always the same. Because of these changes that occur around us, we are forced to look at our landscape and our lives in a different way.

Just as the green leaves turn into beautiful shades of reds, golds, oranges and purples, we get ready to set aside time to be with the ones we love, to overeat and to offer thanks. Thanksgiving is always a special time for my family and me. It is a time when everyone cooks favorite dishes and desserts to sit along side the turkey. I always make my mother's wonderful dressing recipe. Although mine is not quite as good as hers, I was the one chosen to do her job when she died nine years ago. We never miss our loved ones who are gone more than at the holidays.

When I think of Thanksgiving, my first memories are of mounds of food and the wonderfully pleasant aromas that permeated the air. The home movies that my granddaddy took with one of the first home video cameras prove our enjoyment of this holiday. You know the cameras I'm talking about. They were huge and bulky, hard to maneuver and had a light as big as a car's headlight to illuminate the scene. Just as we were trying to break out our warm sweaters for the new season, we were kept hot under the camera lights as if we were food on a warming tray at a cafeteria. Eyes squinted and sweat popping out on our foreheads, we were photographed in living color on his moving pictures. We were stars and we thought we were so special!

Not only were we photographed, but our food table was as well. My granddaddy started at the head of the table and panned very slowly making absolutely sure that nothing edible was left out. There, caught on film was a smorgasbord in panoramic view. It was almost as if he was trying to chronicle everything we ate. Or perhaps, he was doing it for my granny's benefit to help with next year's food preparations. One thing is for sure. We were not allowed to touch one morsel until this ritual was complete and the blessing was asked.

In my constant quest to go out and create something beautiful, I have shown on many occasions how to construct a centerpiece. One thing that you may not know is that I was almost grown before I realized that a plate of biscuits was not supposed to be one. That's what we always had. And, to be completely honest with you, I think they still make a beautiful statement! I mean, when they are browned perfectly, mounded properly on a beautiful tray or plate, just out of the oven, what else could you possible ask for in a centerpiece?

If you should opt for a more traditional centerpiece, Autumn certainly has sufficient bounty to offer with a full pallet of fabulous colors just waiting to create a beautiful array. From rosy russets and bronzed golds to radiating reds and mellow tones of aubergine, the Autumn pallet is just about as rich as color gets. Because of that gift, you have a great start. Your color scheme is established and so are the many unique shapes and forms. From prickly cones of various sizes to lush chrysanthemums bursting into bloom, from the changing leaves to the berries, gourds, pumpkins, vegetables and fruits, there is literally a cornucopia of possibilities waiting to adorn your table this Thanksgiving. You need not look any further than your own yard to find most of these treasures. All you have to do is gather them together for a beautiful presentation.

It is amazing what a difference a colorful centerpiece can make to your family and friends. It easily and beautifully sets the mood for your thankful celebration. Whether you chose a ratan or vine horn of plenty that you fill to the brim with fruits and vegetables or opt for a more traditionally arranged centerpiece in an interesting container, using the bounty that surrounds us at this time of year takes a lot of the guess work out of the creative process. Your ingredients are already chosen, you just have to showcase them.

However, if cooking has taken up all of your time, you can simply take the biscuits out of the oven, arrange them on a plate, and make a mad dash to your Thanksgiving table with the realization that your biscuits alone can be centerpiece enough to set a mood. Butter will make it even better! After all, biscuits set my holiday mood for many years. Enjoy this special time of year and go out and create something beautiful.

GRANNY'S BISCUITS

Mark Ballard

4 cups self-rising White Lily flour
¾ cup butter-flavored Crisco
2 to 2¼ cups buttermilk

Using knives or a pastry cutter, cut shortening into flour until mixture is very grainy. (The finer you cut it in, the lighter the biscuit.) Add buttermilk starting with 2 cups. Using a spoon, stir the milk to combine and wet the mixture (do not overstir). The mixture should be moist - thick and gooey. If you need the additional milk, add at this time.

At this point, roll dough on floured surface and cut or using floured hands pinch and roll into biscuit-sized pieces. Place on greased baking sheet or biscuit pan. Top with a pat of butter on each biscuit. Bake at 475 to 500 degrees until golden brown.

CRANBERRY-PINEAPPLE SALSA

Mark Ballard

1 can (8-oz.) crushed pineapple, juice-packed
1 c. chopped onion
2 cloves garlic, minced
3 c. cranberries
½ c. packed light brown sugar
1 can. (4-oz.) chopped green chili peppers
½ tsp. hot-pepper sauce

Drain pineapple, reserving juice. Coat a large saucepan with nonstick spray. Heat over medium heat until hot, about 1 minutes. Saute onions and garlic in pan for 2 minutes. Add reserved pineapple juice, cranberries, and brown sugar. Cook, stirring occasionally, until cranberries begin to pop, about 5 minutes. Remove from heat. Stir in pineapple, peppers. And hot-pepper sauce. Cover and refrigerate for up to 3 days.

BACON CORN BREAD

Beverly Futch

2 c. yellow cornmeal	**2 c. all-purpose flour**
2½ c. milk	**½ c. real bacon bits**
½ c. butter, melted	**2 eggs**
2 T. baking powder	**2 tsp. salt**

Preheat oven to 425°. Coat a 9 x 13-inch baking pan with nonstick cooking spray. In a large bowl, combine all ingredients. Mix well and place in baking pan. Bake 30-35 minutes or until done. Cut into squares and serve warm.

BUTTERHORN ROLLS

Mark Ballard

1 c. butter
1 16-oz. small curd cottage cheese
2 c. flour
½ tsp. salt

Mix ingredients at room temperature. Then chill. Divide into 3 balls. Roll into circles. Cut into wedges. Roll up starting at wide end-point down on baking sheet. Bake for 20 minutes at 350°. Lightly frost and decorate with sprinkles.

CHICKEN AND BROCCOLI BREAD

Jo Ann Stephens

2 c. chopped cooked chicken
1 c. chopped broccoli
4-oz. Sharp Cheddar cheese, shredded (1 c.)
½ c. chopped red bell pepper
½ c. mayonnaise
1 tsp. dried dill weed
¼ tsp. salt
1 garlic clove, pressed
2 8-oz. cans Pillsbury Refrigerated Crescent Dinner Rolls
1 egg white, slightly beaten
2 T. slivered almonds

Heat oven to 375°. In large bowl, combine chicken, broccoli, cheese, bell pepper, mayonnaise, dill weed, salt and garlic; mix well. Unroll both cans of dough. Place dough with long sides together crosswise on large ungreased cookie sheet, forming 15 x 12-inch rectangle. Firmly press perforations and edges to seal. Spread chicken mixture in 6-inch strip lengthwise down center of dough. With scissors or sharp knife, make cuts 1½-inches apart to ½-inch of filling. Twisting each strip once, alternately cross strips over filling. Brush dough with egg white; sprinkle with almonds. Bake at 375° for 25 to 28 minutes or until deep golden brown. Cut into crosswise slices. Makes 8 servings.

EGGPLANT FRITTERS

Marion Page

1 med. eggplant, peeled and chopped into cubes
1 sm. onion, peeled and diced
1 egg, beaten
salt and pepper to taste
crushed cracker crumbs
oil for frying

Boil eggplant and onions together in salty water, drain and mash; add beaten egg and pepper. Mix in enough crushed cracker crumbs to make it the consistency of creamed potatoes. Drop by teaspoonfuls into hot oil and brown on both sides.

FULL-OF-CORN STICKS

Mark Ballard

5 ears fresh corn
¾ c. all-purpose flour
¾ c. yellow cornmeal
1 T. sugar
2 tsp. baking powder
½ tsp. salt
2 T. vegetable oil
2 egg whites
vegetable cooking spray

Cut whole kernels from 1 ear of corn, measure ½ cup. Grate corn from remaining 4 ears, reserving 1 cup pulp and aside. Arrange ½ cup cut corn in a vegetable steamer over boiling water. Cover and steam 5 minutes; drain and set aside. Combine flour and next 4 ingredients in a bowl; stir well. Make a well in center of mixture. Combine cut corn, grated corn, oil, and egg whites; stir well. Add to dry ingredients, stirring just until dry ingredients are moistened. Coat a cast-iron cornstick pan with vegetable cooking spray, and place in a 425° oven for 5 minutes. Spoon batter into prepared pan, filling two-thirds full. Bake at 425° for 15 minutes or until lightly browned. Cool 3 minutes in pan on a wire rack. Yield: 10 cornsticks.

POTATO SCONES

Mark Ballard

2 c. warm mashed potatoes
3 T. melted butter or bacon fat
⅔ c. flour
½ tsp. salt
butter, honey or pancake syrup

Blend the potatoes with the butter or bacon fat in a mixing bowl. Stir in as much as the potatoes will take without becoming too dry. Turn out on a floured surface; roll to ¼-inch thickness. Cut into circles; prick tops with a fork. Heat a greased cast-iron griddle or skillet over medium-high heat. Cook scones until brown on one side, about 5 minutes. Turn; cook to brown other side, 5 minutes. Serve warm with butter, honey or syrup. Makes 16 scones.

SWEET POTATO SCONES

Mark Ballard

½ c. whole wheat flour
½ c. unbleached flour
¼ c. corn bran or oat bran
1 tsp. cream of tartar
½ tsp. baking soda
⅛ tsp. cinnamon
⅛ tsp. nutmeg
¾ c. shredded raw sweet potatoes
¼ c. raisins
½ c. buttermilk
1½ tsp. canola oil

Preheat the oven to 475°. In a large bowl, whisk together flours, bran, cream of tartar, baking soda, cinnamon, and nutmeg. Stir in sweet potatoes and raisins. Add buttermilk and oil. Turn out onto a floured breadboard. With floured hands, knead mixture for 2 minutes. On the same board, roll dough ¼-inch thick. Cut out 1½-inch rounds. Transfer to a lightly oiled baking sheet. Use all dough by re-rolling leftovers. Bake for 6 to 8 minutes. Serve warm. Make 18 scones.

RAISIN SCONES

Mark Ballard

2 c. flour
4 tsp. baking powder
5 T. *each*: sugar, unsalted butter
⅛ tsp. salt
⅔ c. milk
½ c. golden raisins
1 egg, lightly beaten

Sift the flour and baking powder together into the container of a food processor with the metal table blade in place; add sugar and butter. Pulse until mixture resembles fine crumbs, about 30 pulses. Place the flour mixture in a medium bowl. Make a well in the center; add the milk and raisins. Gently stir, being careful not to overmix. Place dough on lightly floured surface; knead lightly 2 or 3 times. Roll dough to ⅜-inch thickness. Cut out scones with a 2½-inch round cookie cutter. Leftover dough scraps can be re-rolled for cutting. Place rounds on a greased baking sheet; brush egg on tops with pastry brush. Let stand 15 minutes. Heat oven to 400°. Bake scones until lightly browned, 15 minutes. Serve warm. Makes 12 scones.

YELLOW SQUASH GINGERBREAD

Mark Ballard

2 c. coarsely shredded yellow squash (about ¾ lb.)
2½ c. all-purpose flour
⅓ c. firmly packed brown sugar
2 tsp. baking soda
2 tsp. ground ginger
1 tsp. ground cinnamon
½ tsp. ground allspice
½ tsp. ground cloves
⅔ c. molasses
3 T. vegetable oil
1 tsp. vanilla extract
1 egg, lightly beaten
1 egg white, lightly beaten
vegetable cooking spray
1 T. powdered sugar

Place squash on several layers of paper towels; cover with additional paper towels. Let stand 15 minutes, pressing down occasionally to remove moisture; set aside. Combine flour and next 6 ingredients in a large bowl; stir well. Add squash; stir well, and make a well in center of mixture. Combine molasses and next 4 ingredients in a bowl; stir well. Add to dry ingredients, stirring just until moistened. Pour batter into a 9 x 5 x 3-inch loaf pan coated with cooking spray. Bake at 350° for 55 minutes or until a wooden pick inserted in center comes out clean. Cool in pan 10 minutes on a wire rack; remove from pan, and cool completely on a wire rack. Sprinkle with powdered sugar. Yield: 18 servings.

BISCUIT BREAD

Judy Harris

2 c. self-rising flour
1 c. milk
⅓ c. cooking oil
extra oil for oiling pan

Oil a cast-iron frying pan and place in 400° over to heat slightly. While oven is heating, stir flour, milk, and oil together. Spread in frying pan and bake 15-20 minutes until top is golden. Flip bread onto thin paper plate or paper towels to prevent sweating . This has the same taste and texture as homemade biscuits.

COUNTRY GRIT CAKES

Mark Ballard

4 c. chicken stock
salt and pepper to taste
½ c. semolina flour
1 c. grated asiago cheese
2 c. heavy cream
½ c. yellow cornmeal
1 c. coarse ground grits
½ c. country ham (Virginia)

Combine stock, cream, salt and pepper in a large heavy gauge pot. Bring to a boil, then add cornmeal, semolina flour and grits gradually while stirring. Cook over medium-high heat while constantly stirring. Grits are ready when it begins to pull away from the sides of the pot (10-15 minutes). Remove from heat, add in cheese and ham - incorporate well. Spread grits onto oiled sheet pans (approximately ½ thick). Cool to room temperature, then refrigerate. Allow to cool for a few hours. Cut into desired shapes/sizes. Saute in olive oil until golden brown.

D's BREAKFAST CASSEROLE

Debra Montford

1 lb. ground sausage, browned and drained
1 pkg. Crescent rolls or canned biscuits
2 c. cheese
6-8 eggs
⅓ c. milk
salt and pepper to taste

Beat eggs, salt and pepper, and milk together with fork in bowl. Press rolls or biscuits out flat by hand on wax paper and then in bottom of greased casserole dish. Layer cooked sausage then cheese and finally egg and milk mixture on top. Cook 20-25 minutes at 350° until golden brown. May be made the night before.

FRIED COUNTRY HAM WITH REDEYE GRAVY

Mark Ballard

Country ham **coffee**

Fry one ¼-inch thick slice of country ham in a large skillet (preferably cast-iron) over medium heat, turning once, until golden browned on both sides, about 10 minutes. Transfer ham to a warm plate. Add ½ cup boiling coffee to skillet and stir with a wooden spoon, scraping up any brown bits on bottom of pan. Pour gravy over ham. Serve with fried eggs, grits, and biscuits.

SWEET POTATO WAFFLES

Mark Ballard

2¼ c. all-purpose flour
¼ c. firmly packed brown sugar
4 tsp. baking powder
1½ tsp. ground cinnamon
½ tsp. ground ginger
4 lg. eggs, separated
2 lg. eggs
2 c. milk
1 tsp. vanilla extract
1 c. mashed cooked sweet potato (about 1 lb.)
1 c. chopped pistachio nuts
Apricot Syrup (optional)
Garnish: chopped pistachio nuts

Combine first 5 ingredients in a bowl; make a well in center. Stir together 4 egg yolks, 2 whole eggs, milk, vanilla, and sweet potato; stir in flour mixture until moistened. Beat 4 egg whites at high speed with an electric mixer until soft peaks form; gently fold into batter. Sprinkle 1 tablespoon chopped pistachios on a preheated, lightly greased waffle iron; cover with batter, and bake until crisp. Repeat procedure with remaining pistachios and batter. Serve with Apricot Syrup, and garnish, if desired.

YAM PANCAKES

Mark Ballard

1 c. sifted all-purpose flour
½ tsp. baking soda
¼ tsp. salt
1 egg, separated
1 c. buttermilk
1 T. butter or margarine, melted
1 med. yam, pared and shredded (¾ c.)
2 tsp. grated fresh orange peel

Sift flour together with baking soda and salt. In a medium mixing bowl beat egg yolk and buttermilk until well blended. Stir in flour mixture, melted butter, yam and orange peel. In a small mixing bowl beat egg white until stiff; fold into batter. Using 2 tablespoons batter for each pancake, drop batter onto a hot greased griddle. Cook until cakes are puffy, full of bubbles and edges are cooked. Turn and cook other side. Serve with maple syrup. Makes 25 medium pancakes.

CAJUN TURKEY GUMBO

Debra Ballard

1 c. cooked ham, diced
1 c. onion, finely chopped
¼ c. margarine
2 (1 lb.) cans whole tomatoes, drained
1 (6-oz.) can tomato paste
2 cloves garlic, crushed
2 tsp. salt
1 bay leaf
½ tsp. black pepper
½ tsp. crumbled basil
¼ tsp. hot pepper sauce
¼ tsp. chili powder
¼ tsp. leaf thyme
1 (10-oz.) pkg. frozen okra, sliced
½ lb. (1 c.) shelled shrimp, fresh or frozen
2 c. cooked turkey, cut into bite size pieces
4 c. cooked rice

Saute onion and ham in butter for 4 minutes. Remove from heat. Combine tomatoes, tomato paste, garlic, salt, bay leaf, pepper, basil, hot pepper sauce, chili powder and leaf thyme. Add tomato mixture to onion and ham in large, heavy pan. Bring to a boil. Stir in okra and shrimp. Reduce heat and cook covered, stir once or twice, for 10 minutes. Add turkey and cook 2 minutes longer. Serve in soup bowl with a large spoonful of cooked rice in each bowl.

CRANBERRY CHUTNEY

Mark Ballard

1 16-oz. pkg. fresh cranberries
¾ c. packed brown sugar
½ c. light raisins
½ c. chopped celery
½ c. chopped apple
½ c. water
¼ c. coarsely chopped walnuts
2 T. finely snipped candied ginger
2 T. lemon juice
1 tsp. onion salt
¼ tsp. ground cloves

In a large saucepan combine cranberries, brown sugar, raisins, celery, apple, water, walnuts, ginger, lemon juice, onion salt, and cloves. Bring to boiling, stirring constantly. Simmer, uncovered, 15 minutes, stirring occasionally. Store covered, in the refrigerator. Serve chilled. Top with walnut half, if desired. Makes 3 cups.

CRANBERRY SALAD

Mildred Gossett

1 can sweetened condensed milk **¼ c. lemon juice**
1 16-oz. can whole cranberry sauce
1 20-oz. can crushed pineapple, drained
½ c. chopped nuts **1 8-oz. Cool Whip**

Combine milk and lemon juice. Stir in cranberry sauce, pineapple and nuts. Fold in Cool Whip. Freeze until firm.

FRESH SWEET POTATO SALAD

Betty Jones

4 c. shredded raw sweet potatoes
1 med. apple, chopped
½ c. chopped pecans
½ c. sour cream
½ c. mayonnaise
2 T. lemon juice
2 T. honey
¼ tsp. salt
¼ tsp. pepper

Combine first 3 ingredients in a bowl; stir well. Combine remaining ingredients; mix well. Pour dressing over salad and mix well. Chill. May add pineapple chunks, if desired. Serves 6 to 8.

TURKEY CHILI

Mark Ballard

vegetable cooking spray
1 c. chopped green bell pepper
¾ c. chopped celery
½ c. chopped carrots
½ c. chopped onion
1 lb. ground raw turkey
2 tsp. chili powder
1 tsp. dried Italian seasoning
1¼ c. vegetable cocktail juice
1 (8-oz.) can no-salt-added tomato sauce

Coat a large nonstick skillet with cooking spray; place over medium-high heat until hot. Add next 4 ingredients; saute 8 minutes or until tender. Add turkey and next 2 ingredients; cook 2 minutes or until turkey is browned, stirring to crumble. Add remaining ingredients; reduce heat, and simmer, uncovered, 30 minutes or until thickened, stirring occasionally. Yield: 4 servings.

BEETS WITH ORANGE GLAZE

Fran Bragg

Use Shoestring or Tiny Whole Beets (cooked)

Sauce:
1 c. orange juice
2 T. corn starch
⅓ c. sugar
⅛ T. salt
1 T. margarine

Combine sugar, cornstarch and salt and mix well. Add orange juice and margarine and cook in top of double boiler for five minutes or until thick. Pour over cooked beets.

CREAMED CORN

Mark Ballard

4 ears fresh corn
2 c. 2% low-fat milk, divided
¾ c. coarsely chopped onion
½ tsp. black peppercorns
¼ c. all-purpose flour
½ tsp. salt

Cut off tops of corn kernels; scrape "milk" and remaining pulp from cobs using the dull side of a knife blade. Set corn pulp aside, and reserve one cut cob. Cut reserved cob in half. Combine cob halves, 1¾ cups milk, chopped onion, and peppercorns in a medium saucepan; bring to a boil. Reduce heat, and simmer, uncovered, 5 minutes. Strain mixture; discard cob, onion, and peppercorns. Combine ¼ cup flour and remaining ¼ cup milk in a saucepan, stirring with a wire whisk until blended. Add warm milk mixture; cook over low heat 3 minutes or until thickened, stirring constantly. Add corn pulp and salt; stir well. Cook over medium-low heat 15 minutes or until corn is tender, stirring frequently. Yield: 6 servings.

CORN PUDDING

Mark Ballard

5 ears fresh corn
2 tsp. sugar
2 c. half-and-half
1 pinch nutmeg
3 eggs
2 T. melted butter
salt and pepper to taste

Preheat oven to 350°. Remove and reserve kernels from 5 ears of corn, discarding cobs. Put half of the corn in a blender or food processor; set aside remaining corn. Add sugar, eggs, half-and-half, butter, nutmeg and salt and pepper to blender. Process for 1-2 minutes, then pour into greased 5 x 9-inch loaf pan. Gently mix in the remaining corn, and bake until golden and a toothpick inserted in the middle of the pudding comes out clean, about 1 hour. Serves 8.

CURRIED GREEN BEANS

Mark Ballard

1 16-oz. pkg. of frozen green beans
2 T. margarine or butter
⅓ c. roasted peanuts, coarsely chopped
1 tsp. curry powder

Cook green beans according to package directions. In the meantime, melt margarine or butter over medium heat. Add peanuts and curry powder and saute, stirring constantly, until peanuts are coated and warm. Stir peanuts into drained green beans and serve warm. Yields: 6 servings.

INDIAN CORN CASSEROLE

Mark Ballard

4 ears of fresh corn with husks
3 c. grated zucchini
1 c. minced onion
1 4-oz. can chopped green chiles, drained
½ c. all-purpose flour
1 tsp. ground cumin
1 tsp. chili powder
¼ tsp. salt
½ tsp. freshly ground pepper
¼ ground red pepper
2 15-oz. cans black beans, drained

Husk corn, reserving 12 husks; rinse husks thoroughly. Bring 1 quart water to a boil in a saucepan; add husks. Remove from heat. Cover; let stand 15 minutes. Drain; pat dry with paper towels. Line a 2-quart baking dish with softened husks, allowing excess to extend over sides. Cut whole kernels from 2 ears of corn; set aside. Grate corn from remaining ears, pressing firmly to remove pulp. Add grated corn to cut corn; set aside. Combine zucchini, onion, and chiles in a large nonstick skillet. Cover and cook over medium-low heat 10 minutes, stirring occasionally. Add flour and next 5 ingredients; stir well. Add corn and beans; stir. Cook, uncovered, over medium heat 4 minutes, stirring frequently. Spoon mixture into prepared dish. Fold extended ends of husks toward center, overlapping. Bake at 325° for 25 minutes. Yield: 6 servings.

MACARONI AND CHEESE

Mark Ballard

2 c. elbow macaroni, cooked
2 c. (8-oz.) shredded sharp Cheddar cheese
1 c. cottage cheese
¾ c. sour cream
½ c. skim milk
2 T. grated onion
½ tsp. salt
¼ tsp. pepper
1 lg. egg, lightly beaten
vegetable cooking spray
¼ c. fine, dry breadcrumbs
1½ T. butter, melted
¼ tsp. paprika

Stir together cooked macaroni and next 8 ingredients; spoon into a 2-quart baking dish coated with vegetable cooking spray. Stir together breadcrumbs, margarine, and paprika. Bake, covered, at 350° for 20 minutes. Uncover, sprinkle with breadcrumb mixture, and bake 5 more minutes or until set. Makes 6 servings.

OVEN-FRIED SWEET POTATOES

Mark Ballard

3 lg. sweet potatoes, unpeeled (about 2 lb.)
⅔ c. fine, dry breadcrumbs
¾ tsp. dried rosemary, crushed
⅓ c. skim milk
vegetable cooking spray

Cut potatoes crosswise into ⅜-inch thick slices. Stir together breadcrumbs and rosemary. Dip potato slices in milk, and dredge in breadcrumb mixture. Place in a single layer on a baking sheet coated with cooking spray; spray slices lightly with cooking spray. Bake at 450° for 15 minutes; turn and bake 10 more minutes or until potatoes are tender. Makes 6 servings.

SWEET POTATO CRISP

Mark Ballard

6 med. sweet potatoes
½c. butter
¼ c. all-purpose flour
½ c. brown sugar, firmly packed
1½ tsp. black pepper
¼ c. evaporated milk
¼ c. pecans, finely chopped

Boil potatoes in skins until tender. Peel and slice crosswise into one-half inch pieces. Spread into a shallow, buttered 1½ quart casserole dish. Cut butter into flour and brown sugar until mixture resembles coarse crumbs. Add pepper, milk and nuts. Mix well and spread over potatoes. Broil until bubbly.

SQUASH CASSEROLE

Debra Ballard

3 c. squash, cooked and drained
2 eggs
1 T. butter, melted
2 c. crushed Ritz crackers
1 med. onion, chopped
2 c. grated sharp cheddar cheese
1 T. milk
1 sm. can cream of chicken soup

Mix squash with beaten eggs, onion, cheese, milk and soup. Place in greased pan. Mix butter and crackers. Use to top squash mixture. Bake 30 to 40 minutes at 350 degrees or until bubbly and topping is golden brown.

SWEET FRIED APPLES

Mary Ballard

6-8 slices bacon
4 T. bacon drippings
6 c. apples slices, unpeeled
½-1 c. brown sugar, firmly packed

Cook bacon until crisp; drain and keep hot. Leave about 4 tablespoons dripping in skillet. Add apples; brown lightly. Sprinkle brown sugar over apples. Cover. Cook slowly until tender. Remove cover and let apples brown, cooking off excess juice. Add crumbled bacon. Serve immediately.

YELLOW RICE CASSEROLE

Mark Ballard

1 5-oz. pkg. yellow rice
1 12-oz. can Mexicorn, drained
1 med. onion, chopped
1 8-oz. can tiny English peas, drained
1 2-oz. jar diced pimento, drained (optional)
1 10½-oz. can undiluted cream of chicken soup
1 8-oz. ctn. sour cream
½ stick melted margarine
1 can water chestnuts, drained and sliced
1 c. grated cheddar cheese

Cook yellow rice according to package directions. Blend soup, sour cream, and melted margarine. Combine all other ingredients except grated cheese. Pour into a 7 x 11-inch baking dish and cook for 25 minutes in a 350° oven. Top with grated cheese and return to oven 5 more minutes or until melted. Serves 8.

CHICKEN AND DRESSING CASSEROLE

Edith Sullivan

6 boneless-skinless chicken breasts
8-oz. sour cream
½ c. milk
⅓ c. spicy mustard
1 can cream of chicken soup
1 box of chicken-flavored Stove Top stuffing

Bake chicken breasts 1 hour for 350°; cool and cut in small pieces. Place in bottom of casserole dish. Mix sour cream, milk, spicy mustard and cream of chicken soup. Pour this over chicken that has been cut up. May add salt and pepper. Cook a box of chicken-flavored Stove Top stuffing as directed. Add to top of chicken and mixture. Bake at 350° for 1 hour. Note: Chicken can be cooked day before or use leftover chicken, just make certain chicken is deboned and skinless and cut into small pieces.

SLOW COOKER TURKEY AND DRESSING

Jo Ann Stephens

1 (8-oz.) pkg. herb-seasoned stuffing mix
1 onion, chopped — **2 celery ribs, chopped**
1 c. dried cranberries — **¾ c. chicken broth**
3 T. butter or margarine, melted
1 (3 lb.) frozen boneless turkey breast, thawed
¼ tsp. salt — **½ tsp. pepper**
¼ tsp. dried thyme — **1 (.88-oz.) pkg. turkey gravy mix**

Coat inside of a 4-quart electric slow cooker with cooking spray. Add stuffing mix, onion, celery, and cranberries. Combine broth and melted butter. Pour over stuffing, and stir gently. Remove string from turkey breast. Rinse turkey breast. Place turkey in slow cooker on top of stuffing. Combine salt, pepper, and thyme; sprinkle over turkey. Cover and cook on HIGH 1 hour. Reduce to LOW, and cook 5 to 6 hours or until a meat thermometer inserted in turkey registers 170°. Remove turkey to a serving platter. Stir stuffing gently in slow cooker; cover and let stand 3 to 4 minutes. Spoon stuffing around turkey on platter. Yield: 5 to 6 servings.

SPICY CHICKEN AND RICE

Mark Ballard

4 garlic cloves, halved
kosher salt
3 T. extra-virgin olive oil
One 3½ lb. chicken, cut into 8 pieces
¼ c. plus 2 T. chopped cilantro
2 lg. poblano chiles
2-oz. lean, smoky bacon, cut into ¼-inch dice
1 med. onion, finely chopped
1 lg. jalapeño, seeded and minced
1½ c. med.-grain Spanish rice, such as Valencia or Bomba
½ c. dry sherry
1 can (14-oz.) whole peeled tomatoes, crushed, juices reserved
2 c. chicken stock or canned low-sodium broth
lime wedges, for serving

In a small bowl, mash the garlic to a paste with ½ teaspoon of salt. Stir in 1 tablespoon of the olive oil. In a large bowl, combine the chicken pieces with the garlic paste and ¼ cup of the cilantro; toss to coat. Let stand at room temperature for 30 minutes. Roast the poblanos over an open flame or under the broiler until charred all over. Transfer to a bowl, cover with plastic wrap and let steam for 5 minutes. Stem, peel and seed the poblanos, then cut them crosswise into ½-inch wide strips. Preheat the oven to 350°. Heat the remaining 2 tablespoons of olive oil in a medium enameled cast-iron casserole. Add half of the chicken pieces and cook over moderate heat until golden brown. Transfer to a plate. Repeat with the remaining half of the chicken. Add the bacon to the casserole and cook over moderately low heat until the fat begins to melt, about 2 minutes. Add the onion and jalapeño and cook, stirring until softened, about 5 minutes. Add the rice and stir over moderate heat until well coated with fat, about 3 minutes. Add the sherry and boil, stirring, until absorbed, about 2 minutes. Add the tomatoes and their juices, the poblanos, stock and 1 teaspoon of salt, then bring to a boil. Tuck the chicken into the rice, cover and bake for 35 minutes, or until the rice is tender and the stock absorbed. Let stand, covered, for 10 minutes. Sprinkle with the remaining 2 tablespoons of cilantro; serve with lime wedges.

ALMOND PEAR PIE

Mary McPeters

Pastry for a 9-inch pie crust
5 Bosc pears, peeled, cored, and thickly sliced
6 T. ground almonds
⅓ c. firm butter
1 c. sugar
⅓ c. all-purpose flour
unsweetened whipped cream, as a garnish

Preheat the oven to 400°. Roll the pastry into a 12-inch circle and fit it into a pie pan. Set aside. In a medium bowl mix sliced pears with ground almonds. Heap the fruit in the unbaked pie shell. Cut the butter into small pieces and dot it over the fruit. In a small bowl mix the sugar and flour and sprinkle it over the pie. Bake in a 400° oven for 15 minutes. Reduce the heat to 350° and bake for 1 hour more. If the edges start to brown too soon, cover them with strips of foil. Serve with unsweetened whipped cream. Yield: 6 to 8 servings.

BAKED FIGS

Betty Jones

fresh figs
brown Sugar
lemon juice
sour cream

Fill baking dish tight with fresh figs - stems down. Sprinkle with brown sugar and lemon juice. Pick figs with fork and bake 1 hour at 300°. Serve hot in a bowl with syrup and a spoonful of sour cream. Use 6 to 7 figs per serving.

BUTTERMILK PECAN PIE

Mark Ballard

1½ c. sugar
1 T. cornstarch or 2 T. flour
1 stick margarine, melted
3 eggs
¼ c. buttermilk
1 tsp. vanilla
1 c. pecans

Mix flour and sugar, add beaten eggs, melted margarine, vanilla, buttermilk and pecans. Place in unbaked pie shell and bake at 350° F. for 45 minutes. Bake until center is set. Doubles nicely.

CURRIED FRUIT

Mildred Gossett

1 lg. can plums, drained well
1 No. 2 can cling sliced peaches, drained well
1 No. 2 can firm pears, drained well
1 No. 2 can peeled apricots, drained well
1 No. 2 can crushed pineapple, drained well
1 pkg. seedless prunes, drained well
1 box light brown sugar (divided)
2 tsp. curry powder
1 stick of butter
1 med. can applesauce
1 pinch of salt
cinnamon
Cherries on top

Mix ½ package light brown sugar, 2 teaspoons curry powder, and pinch of salt. Place fruit in casserole dish. Cover with sugar mixture and lumps of butter on top. Cook until done at 350°. Melt a stick of butter with ¾ cup light brown sugar and 1 medium can of applesauce. Mix until hot. Pour over fruit and sprinkle with cinnamon.

SPICED CARROT CAKES

Mark Ballard

2¼ c. sifted cake flour
1 tsp. baking powder
1 tsp. baking soda
1 tsp. salt
2 tsp. cinnamon
2 c. granulated sugar
3 c. grated carrots (5-6 minutes)
4 eggs
1¼ c. vegetable oil
2 tsp. vanilla extract
1 c. chopped pecans

Sift flour, baking powder, soda, salt and cinnamon together. Stir sugar into flour mixture and blend well. Beat eggs well with vegetable oil and vanilla. Stir grated carrots into dry ingredients and mix with wet ingredients. Fold chopped pecans into batter. Spoon batter into muffin tins which have been lined with paper baking cups. Only fill ⅔ full. Bake in a 325° oven for 20-30 minutes or until cupcakes spring back when lightly pressed in the center with fingertips. Cool completely before frosting. Recipe yields: 3 dozen.

Frosting:
1 (8-oz.) pkg. cream cheese, softened
¼ c. butter, softened **1 tsp. vanilla extract**
1 (1 lb.) box confectioners' sugar, sifted

Beat cream cheese and butter until light and fluffy. Stir in vanilla extract. Gradually beat in sifted confectioners' sugar. Cover tops of cupcakes with frosting and garnish with Halloween candies.

SWEET POTATO COBBLER

Barbara Rouse

5 med. sized sweet potatoes
1 stick of butter
2 T. vanilla extract
nutmeg (if desired)
sugar (approximately 2 c. or to taste)
Pie Crust strips or refrigerated pie crust, cut into strips

Peel, rinse and slice sweet potatoes. Place in a 2-quart boiler with water level up to the top of potatoes. Simmer on medium heat for approximately 20 minutes or until potatoes are soft or juice thickens, add other ingredients while potatoes simmer. Place pie crust strips on bottom of 2-quart casserole dish, pour in sweet potatoes (and juice), then place pie crust strips on top. Bake at 350°, until crust is golden brown, approximately 20 minutes.

SWEET POTATO PIE

Rachel G. Branch

2 med. potatoes
1 stick butter
1 tsp. vanilla
1 c. sugar
½ c. condensed milk or
½ c. sour cream or
½ c. whipping cream

Boil potatoes with small amount of water. When almost done, mash and add butter, sugar, milk, and vanilla. Bake 225° for 1½ hours. Makes 2 pies.

SWEET POTATO PUDDING

Mark Ballard

2 cans mashed sweet potatoes
½ tsp. *each*: nutmeg, cinnamon, and allspice
1 tsp. vanilla
1 beaten egg
½ c. butter
1 c. milk
1 c. sugar
½ c. Karo syrup
2 T. bourbon
1 c. chopped pecans

Mix together and pour into greased iron skillet (or Pyrex dish). Cook at 350° 30 to 45 minutes. Stir several times. Serve warm with whipped cream.

BUTTERMILK CARAMEL ICING

Connie Howard

3½ c. sugar
3 T. white Karo syrup
2½ sticks butter
¾ c. buttermilk
1½ tsp. baking soda
1 c. chopped pecans

In large saucepan, combine all ingredients (except nuts), mixing soda with buttermilk before adding to other ingredients. Cook until mixture reaches 236° on candy thermometer. Immediately add nuts and beat hot icing on high speed with electric mixer to spreading consistency. (About 3 to 5 minutes.)

MARK'S FAMOUS CARAMEL CAKE

Mark Ballard

¾ c. Crisco
2 c. sugar
pinch salt
1 c. milk
5 eggs
1 c. plain flour
1 c. self-rising flour
1 tsp. vanilla

Cream Crisco and sugar. Add eggs one at a time. Blend in flours and salt alternating with milk. Add vanilla. Grease 3 layer pans with Crisco or butter and coat with flour. Bake at 300° until brown but still very moist. Allow to cool on racks for no more than 5 minutes. Turn out onto racks and leave until ready to ice.

Caramel Icing:
3½ c. sugar
½ c. boiling water
1 c. canned milk
½ c. butter
1 T. white Karo syrup
1 tsp. vanilla

In an iron or Teflon coated skillet, brown ½ cup sugar over low to medium heat. When sugar liquefies and turns dark brown, pour boiling water into pan and allow to boil until mixture is bubbly and is consistency of thin syrup (about 3 to 5 minutes). While this is taking place, combine remaining 3 cups of sugar with other ingredients (except vanilla). Bring mixture to a boil. Continue boiling while adding syrup mixture. Cook until mixture reaches soft boil stage. Remove from heat, add vanilla and beat mixture with a wooden spoon while it cools slightly to spreading consistency. Do not allow to begin to harden in the pan before icing the cake.

This HAS to be my signature cake! I've made so many of these that I could probably make one in my sleep. This cake takes some practice and some time to master, but let me tell you – the taste of warm, moist cake layers with warm, luscious caramel icing is well worth the trouble!

EASY CREAM CARAMEL CAKE

Dorothea Stewart

1 c. butter
3 c. sugar
6 eggs
2⅔ c. plain flour
¼ tsp. baking soda
1 tsp. salt
8-oz. sour cream
1 T. vanilla

Preheat oven to 350°. Cream butter and sugar until light and fluffy. Add eggs, one at a time, beating well after each addition. Sift dry ingredients together. Add to creamed mixture, alternating with sour cream. Add vanilla extract. Pour into three 9-inch greased and floured cake pans. Cook 15-25 minutes, check for doneness. Remove from oven. Cool on racks 10 minutes. Carefully remove from pans to racks. Cool completely.

Frosting:
1 c. butter
2 c. light brown sugar
½ c. evaporated milk
½ tsp. vanilla extract
1 lb. powdered sugar

Melt butter, add brown sugar and evaporated milk. Cook 2 minutes over medium heat. Stir constantly. Remove from heat. Add vanilla extract and pour over powdered sugar. Beat until smooth. Cool slightly. Frost layers.

SWEET POTATO SURPRISE CAKE

Thelma McCoy

1 c. vegetable oil
2 c. sugar
4 eggs (separated)
¼ c. hot water
2½ c. sifted cake flour
¼ tsp. salt
1 tsp. nutmeg
1 T. baking powder
1 T. ground cinnamon
1½ c. grated uncooked sweet potatoes
1 c. pecans or walnuts (chopped)
1 tsp. vanilla flavoring

Combine oil, sugar, egg yolks and water. Beat at medium speed until just combined. Combine dry ingredients and add to oil mixture; mix until just moistened. Stir in sweet potatoes, nuts and vanilla. Beat egg whites until stiff but not dry; fold into batter. Spoon batter into 3 greased 9-inch cake pans. Bake at 350° for 25-30 minutes or until cake tests done. Immediately invert layers on wire cooling racks. Cool 5 minutes and remove from pans. Cool completely. Spread Creamy Coconut Frosting between layers and on top and sides of cake. Garnish with pecan halves.

Creamy Coconut Frosting:
1 (13-oz.) can evaporated milk
½ c. butter or margarine
1 tsp. vanilla flavoring
½ c. pecans
1 c. sugar
3 egg yolks
1½ c. flaked coconut

Combine milk, sugar, butter, egg yolks and vanilla in a heavy saucepan. Cook over medium heat, stirring constantly, about 12 minutes or until thickened. (Mixture will have consistency of pudding.) Remove from heat and stir in coconut and pecans. Cool completely. Makes frosting for 1 (9-inch) layer cake.

Winter

Old Man Winter gives us a chill as he blows in to visit us during this season. For warmth, we turn up the heat, build fires and bundle up in heavy coats, woolen mittens and scarves. Our thoughts turn to the holiday season that so quickly approaches and visions of sugar plums certainly dance in our heads. Parties and other celebrations become daily occurrences while we try to stay focused on school or on our jobs. This is an exciting and wonderful season as trees magically become decorated with colorful lights that glow in the night. Families and friends come together to exchange beautifully wrapped gifts, partake of homemade confections and make sincerely spoken toasts. The new year bounds in to the sounds of horns, laughter and Auld Lang Syne and it's out with the old and in with the new. In January we gather to watch the game of all games and then we celebrate a day of love with paper hearts and our real national favorite - chocolate. The season ends with the "wearin' o' the green" in a celebration of St. Patrick's Day.

53231E-sg-4

Christmas

I learned so many things over the years from my grandparents. After all, they had been on this earth much longer than me. My grandmother and I used to spend a lot of time together planting, cooking and flower arranging. She also taught me to respect the value of a dollar. Sometimes I take my everyday blessings for granted, but she never did. I owe a lot of my cooking skills to her and many recipes in my cookbooks are hers.

One of my favorite memories of my grandmother is the making of her annual fruitcake. You could count on her, just like clockwork, to bake one right before Thanksgiving every year. Because the candied fruit was so expensive, it had to last from Thanksgiving to Christmas. Being raised Southern Baptist, she certainly did not put any kind of "spirits" on her cake to keep it moist. That would have been unacceptable! You know some of us Southern Baptists justify using a little wine in cooking. We rationalize that it cooks out in the cooking process! However, you could not use that excuse for a glaze over an already baked cake. Granny would begin by chopping pecans and cutting up all the candied fruit. It took a whole day to prepare. She had to get everything cut up into the perfect little cubes and dusted with flour so they wouldn't sink to the bottom of the cake. She mixed up the batter and combined it with the dusted fruit and nuts. She poured it into a tube pan (which I still use today) and into the oven it went. I loved the way her kitchen would smell when the cake was baking.

Granny always put the finished cake in this old tin that had a little scene of Christmas on top. Each year this was the tin the fruitcake lived in. We all knew what was in it and where it was kept, but you didn't dare touch it because she was the only one who could cut it. She methodically cut these teeny little wedges of cake. She had a serrated knife and I don't, to this day, know how she cut that cake so thin. She would go back and forth in a sawing motion, slicing the cake so thin that I remember thinking that you were lucky if you could even taste that there was fruit involved. I also remember being fascinated by the fact that it was so colorful. I would hold it up to the light and look through. It was almost like stained glass windows as the light passed through all the colorful candied fruit. Thanksgiving Day the cake made its debut. We all had our first piece - or should I say bite? Then it was taken away and wrapped.

Now Granny, having gone through the Great Depression, never threw away a single thing. She kept bread wrappers, twisty-ties, pie pans and anything else you could possibly think of. She flat out saved everything because she was sure that she was going to need it one day. This included any kind of gift you gave her. She always wore the rattiest slips, hose, gowns and robes because she was "just going to be around the house." Every year we would put a beautiful new gown or robe under the tree for her and she would tell us that it was pretty and then just tuck it away in a drawer. That is after she got it unwrapped. As we tore into our gifts, Granny very carefully took her fingernail or a knife and cut the gift wrap away from the box. She then folded it into a neat square and laid it beside her before she opened her present. I cannot tell you how many times we got that same gift wrap back on one of our packages the next year - even if the creases didn't match the box she was wrapping!

Granny also believed that real Christmas trees were a waste so she had one of those silver trees. You know what I'm talking about. It was made of a silvery, metallic material. There was a main metal trunk and then all the metal branches went into the color-coded matching holes on the trunk. Granny's was small enough to sit on a table. They were extremely flammable. You could not get near it with any kind of heat. To give it some pizzazz, a light shone on it. This light was connected to a disk with four quadrants of red, green, yellow and blue that rotated in front of the light. During Christmas time, I can remember watching as the tree went from a beautiful glow of yellow, to red, then green and finally blue. Even during home movies you can tell which color the tree is by the shadow of color on our faces. It was so beautiful. At least it was until the tree got too close to the whirling kaleidoscope of color and caught fire. My granddaddy had to rush it outside. The rainbow tree died then and there. The next year was just not the same.

Getting back to the fruitcake, Granny went through an embalming process with that fruitcake every time she stored it between servings. She would get one of her saved bread wrappers, slide the cake into it and tie it off with one of her saved twisty-ties. The end that was tied off would go first into the next bread wrapper. It was then wrapped in some sort of cloth that Granny had saved and placed into the tin to be stored to last throughout the holiday season. There had to be a special occasion or party for that cake to be disturbed because it took 20 minutes to get into it. You just didn't decide in the afternoon that you wanted a piece of fruitcake. Without any spirits on it, by the time Christmas day came around, it was everything you could do to choke down a piece because it had dried out so badly. No one ever told Granny though.

Here's the recipe - made so it won't dry out. Enjoy and think of Granny and Christmases past!

GRANNY'S FRUITCAKE

1 lb. butter, softened
2¼ c. sugar
10 eggs, slightly beaten
1 tsp. salt
¼ c. orange juice
4 c. flour
½ lb. candied cherries
½ lb. candied mixed fruit
½ lb. candied pineapple
1 lb. white raisins
1 lb. pecans
whiskey or extra orange juice

Chop all the candied fruits and nuts into small cubes. Combine and dust them with flour and set aside. Cream butter and sugar. Add eggs gradually, mixing well after each addition. Beat in salt and orange juice. Add flour 1 cup at a time; mix well. Mix fruits and nuts into the batter. Grease tube pan and cut a piece of waxed paper to fit the bottom of pan. Cook at 275 degrees approximately 2½ hours. Cool thoroughly; remove from pan.. Yields a 7½ lb. cake. Pour good whisky *(Granny's turning over in her grave!)* or orange juice over cake to keep moist or wrap in a cloth soaked in whisky or juice before placing in an airtight container.

CHRISTMAS PARTY PINWHEELS

Jo Ann Stephens

2 pkg. (8-oz. each) cream cheese, softened
1 pkg. (.4-oz) ranch salad dressing mix
½ c. minced sweet red pepper
½ c. minced celery
¼ c. sliced green onions
¼ c. sliced stuffed olives
3 to 4 flour tortillas (10-inches)

In a mixing bowl, beat cream cheese and dressing mix until smooth. Add red pepper, celery, onions, and olives; mix well. Spread about ¾ cup on each tortilla. Roll up tightly; wrap in plastic wrap. Refrigerate for at least 2 hours. Slice into ½-inch pieces. Yield: 15-20 servings.

HOLIDAY CHEESE LOG

Mark Ballard

2 8-oz. pkg. cream cheese, softened
1 small can crushed pineapple
½ c. canned coconut
1 small jar maraschino cherries, drained & chopped
½ c. walnuts, chopped
1½ c. walnuts, crushed (for rolling)

Drain pineapple. Mix all ingredients except crushed walnuts. Form mixture into 2 log shapes or balls. Roll in crushed nuts. Serve with butter crackers or Hawaiian bread.

HOLIDAY MIX

Edith Sullivan

2 c. red and green M & M's candy
2 c. dry roasted peanuts
2 c. raisins
2 c. chocolate chips
2 c. dried bananas

May add or leave out anything you wish. Place in mason pint jars or small cleaned pickle jars decorate lids, may give as gifts.

SPICED NUTS

Mildred Gossett

1 c. sugar
⅓ c. evaporated milk
1 tsp. cinnamon
1 T. butter
1 tsp. vanilla
dash of salt
3 c. pecan halves

In saucepan, combine sugar, evaporated milk, cinnamon and butter. Bring to a rolling boil over medium heat and boil 1 minute. Stir in vanilla, salt and pecan halves. Pour onto lightly buttered baking sheet. Cool and separate pecan halves.

FROSTED CRANBERRIES & GRAPES

Mark Ballard

Cranberries or Grapes **1 egg white**
granulated sugar
raspberry flavored gelatin or lime flavored gelatin (optional)

Wash cranberries or bunches of grapes and dry thoroughly. Add a little water to one egg white and beat slightly. Brush fruit with egg white mixture, then sprinkle liberally with granulated sugar. For more color, after brushing fruit with egg white mixture, sprinkle cranberries with dry raspberry flavored gelatin and grapes with dry lime flavored gelatin. Use frosted fruits for garnishing desserts, fruit salads, meats, and poultry.

CRANBERRY PERCOLATOR PUNCH

Mark Ballard

2 c. cranberry juice cocktail
2½ c. unsweetened pineapple juice
½ c. water
⅓ c. brown sugar, firmly packed
1½ tsp. whole cloves
1½ tsp. whole allspice
3 2-inch cinnamon sticks, broken

Combine liquid ingredients and brown sugar in 6 to 8 cup percolator. Place basket in position with spices inside. Cover. Heat over medium heat until mixture comes to a full perk. Reduce heat to low and perk 3 minutes. Remove basket of spices before serving. Makes 8 servings.

CRANBERRY TEA

Jo Ann Stephens

6 oz. can frozen orange juice
1 qt. cranberry juice
½ c. red hots (cinnamon hearts)
¼ tsp. ground cloves
1 qt. water
1 c. sugar

Mix together all ingredients and simmer on stove.

CRANBERRY TODDY

Mark Ballard

1 c. cranberry juice
½ c. unsweetened pineapple juice
½ c. water
1 T. light brown sugar
1 2-inch stick cinnamon
6 whole allspice

Combine all ingredients in a small saucepan; heat just to boiling. Reduce heat; simmer 5 minutes; remove spices. (A few drops of red food coloring may be added if you like). Pour into warm mugs; trim edge of mug with a wedge of pineapple or a stick of cinnamon. Yield: 2 servings.

HOLIDAY CRANBERRY PUNCH

Mark Ballard

2 c. orange juice
½ c. lemon juice
½ c. sugar
1 48-oz. bottle cranberry juice cocktail
2 pt. raspberry sherbet
2 46-oz. bottles ginger ale, chilled

Combine orange juice, lemon juice and sugar; stir until sugar dissolves. Add cranberry juice; mix well. Chill. Spoon scoops of sherbet on top of punch. Add ginger ale; gently stir to blend. Yield: 3½ quarts.

HOLIDAY ORANGE EGGNOG

Mark Ballard

6 eggs
¾ c. sugar
¼ tsp. cinnamon
½ tsp. nutmeg
1 c. chilled evaporated milk
3 c. cold milk
1 c. chilled fresh orange juice
grated orange peel
nutmeg

In large bowl beat eggs until light and fluffy; add sugar, cinnamon and nutmeg. Stir in milk, blending well. Gradually stir in orange juice. Serve in small mugs or cups; sprinkle each serving with a little grated orange peel and a dash of nutmeg. Yield: 24 cups.

OLD-TIMEY EGG NOG

Judy Harris

2 c. sugar
8 pasteurized eggs, separated
1 pt. whipping cream
¾ c. high quality bourbon

Mix egg yolks and sugar until well blended. Beat egg whites until stiff. Add yolk mixture and bourbon to this. Whip cream until stiff and stir into sugar mixture. Add extra bourbon if desired. Serve cold.

POINSETTIA SIPPER

Mark Ballard

2 c. cranberry juice cocktail
2 c. apple juice
½ c. sugar
2 T. unsweetened orange juice
3 whole cloves
2 3-inch cinnamon sticks
2 c. water
orange rind curls (optional)

Combine first 7 ingredients in a saucepan, stirring until sugar dissolves. Bring to a simmer; cover and cook 30 minutes. Remove cloves and cinnamon sticks from pan with a slotted spoon. Serve warm or chilled. Garnish with orange rind curls, if desired. Yield: 6 cups

CINNAMON FRENCH TOAST

Mark Ballard

1 lg. egg
2 egg whites
¼ c. skim milk
½ tsp. vanilla extract
½ tsp. ground cinnamon
⅛ tsp. ground nutmeg
8 1-inch-thick diagonally cut slices French or Italian bread
cinnamon sugar and reduced calorie maple syrup (optional)

In a shallow bowl, using a wire whisk or a fork, beat the egg and egg whites until foamy. Add the milk, vanilla, cinnamon, and nutmeg. Beat well; set aside. Preheat the oven to 200°. Lightly spray a large nonstick skillet with vegetable cooking spray; heat over medium heat. Dip 4 of the bread slices into the egg mixture, turning to coat and draining excess back into the dish. Place bread slices in prepared skillet. Cook until golden brown, turning once, about 1 to 2 minutes per side. Transfer cooked slices to a plate; keep warm in oven. Dip remaining slices in egg mixture; cook as directed. Spay skillet with vegetable cooking spray as needed. Divide French toast among serving plates. Sprinkle lightly with cinnamon sugar and top with maple syrup. Serve immediately.

CHRISTMAS STRATA

Mark Ballard

4 2-inch slices of French Bread, cubed
2 tablespoons butter, melted
1 lb. bulk sausage
6 eggs
2 c. milk
1 tsp. salt
1 tsp. dry mustard
1½ c. sharp Cheddar cheese, grated

Saute bread in butter. Set aside. Brown and drain sausage. In medium-sized bowl, beat together eggs, milk, salt and mustard. Layer bread, cheese, and sausage in greased 2-quart casserole. Pour egg mixture over all. REFRIGERATE OVERNIGHT. Bake in preheated 350° oven for 45-50 minutes. Allow to set a few minutes before cutting. Yield: 6-8 servings

PINEAPPLE CASSEROLE

Mary Ballard

¾ c. margarine, softened
1½ c. sugar **dash of salt**
2 qt. soft bread cubes (8-10 slices)
3 eggs, beaten
2 T. milk
1 20-oz. can unsweetened crushed pineapple, undrained

Cream margarine, sugar and salt. Add bread cubes, eggs, milk and pineapple. Pour into a greased 2-quart casserole. Bake at 350° for 45 minutes.

CHRISTMAS RICE

Mark Ballard

½ c. finely chopped onion
3 celery stalks, chopped
½ med. sweet red pepper, chopped
½ med. green pepper, chopped
1 T. butter
2 c. chicken broth
2 c. uncooked instant rice
½ tsp. salt
¼ tsp. pepper

In a skillet, saute onion, celery and peppers in butter over medium heat for 2 minutes or until crisp-tender. Remove from heat and set aside. In a saucepan, bring broth to a full boil. Remove from heat and quickly stir in rice, vegetable mixture, salt and pepper. Cover and let stand for 6 to 7 minutes. Stir before serving.

BEEF TENDERLOIN

Jo Ann Stephens

¾ c. vegetable oil
½ c. soy sauce
⅓ c. firmly packed brown sugar
¼ c. red wine vinegar
2 cloves garlic, crushed
2 tsp. ground ginger
½ tsp. ground coriander
1 (5 to 6 lb.) beef tenderloin, trimmed
2 tsp. pepper
commercial cocktail rolls
horseradish spread

Combine first 7 ingredients; stir well. Place tenderloin in a large shallow dish; add marinade. Cover; refrigerate up to 8 hours, turning tenderloin occasionally. Remove tenderloin from marinade, reserving marinade. Place marinade in a saucepan. Bring to a boil; reduce heat, and simmer 5 minutes. Place tenderloin on a rack in a roasting pan; sprinkle with pepper. Insert meat thermometer into thickest portion of tenderloin. Bake at 425° for 30 minutes. Reduce heat to 375°; bake 25 minutes or until thermometer register 140° (rare) or 160° (medium), basting frequently with marinade. Cool. To serve, thinly slice tenderloin across grain. Serve warm or cold with cocktail rolls.

BRAISED BEEF IN CREAM

Cele Minshew

1 4-lb. chuck roast
salt and pepper to taste
new potatoes
carrots
2 c. heavy cream
¼ c. lemon juice
¾ tsp. pepper
2 T. shortening
½ c. water
onions
½ c. butter
2 lg. cloves of garlic
1½ tsp. salt

Slowly brown meat on all sides in hot shortening. Season generously with salt and pepper. Add water, cover and simmer for 2½ to 3 hours, or until meat is tender. Add new potatoes, onions and carrots about half of the way through the cooking time. Remove from pan and allow to stand 20 minutes. Slice beef thinly and pour off pan juices. Heat butter in the same pan until it bubbles and browns. Add remaining ingredients. Cook over medium heat, stirring about 3 minutes or until sauce reduces slightly. Spoon sauce over meat and vegetables.

CURT'S MARVELOUS LASAGNA

Mark Ballard

Meat Sauce:

3 lbs. ground beef
2 cloves garlic, minced
3 T. parsley flakes
2 tsp. salt
2 c. chopped onions
3 6-oz. cans tomato paste
5 T. sugar
2 tsp. crushed basil

Cook ground beef, onion and garlic until meat is brown and onion tender. Drain off any fat. Add remaining ingredients and simmer uncovered one hour or until mixture is thick.

Filling:

1 lg. carton cottage cheese
1 c. grated Parmesan cheese
2 tsp. salt
6 eggs, well beaten
2 T. parsley flakes
2 tsp. Italian Seasoning

Mix all ingredients as listed together very well.

Remaining Ingredients:

16 oz. lasagne noodles, cooked and drained
1½ lbs. Mozarella cheese, sliced
1½ lbs. sharp cheddar cheese, grated
1 c. Parmesan cheese, grated

Preheat oven to 350 degrees. In two oblong baking pans (13x9½x2) each, layer half of the drained noodles, meat sauce, mozzarella cheese and cottage cheese mixture. Repeat, reserving enough sauce for a thin top layer. Spread the sauce over the top, sprinkle with Parmesan cheese. Bake covered 45 minutes. Let stand for 15 minutes prior to serving.

Why is Lasagna in the Christmas section? Many times, this is what our children request for Christmas dinner! It works for us!

POTATOES AU GRATIN

Mark Ballard

Irish Potatoes, enough to fill a 9 x 13 inch baking dish
½ stick butter
1 can cream of chicken or mushroom soup
1 8-ounce carton sour cream
1 cup shredded sharp cheddar cheese
½ cup chopped green onions

Slice and parboil potatoes. Drain and place in dish. Cut butter into pats and place on top of potatoes. Combine remaining ingredients in separate bowl. Pour over the potatoes and butter. Bake at 350 degrees for 35 to 45 minutes until bubbly.

APPLE FRUITCAKE

Mark Ballard

½ c. butter, softened
1 c. (firmly packed) light brown sugar
1 egg
1 tsp. vanilla extract
1¾ c. flour
1 tsp. baking powder
½ tsp. *each*: soda, cinnamon, nutmeg and salt
¼ c. milk
1½ c. peeled chopped apples
1 c. raisins
1 c. mixed candied fruit
1 c. chopped nuts

Cream butter in large bowl. Add brown sugar gradually, beating until light and fluffy. Add egg and vanilla; mix well. Sift dry ingredients together. Add to creamed mixture alternately with milk, beginning with dry ingredients. Fold in apples, raisins, candied fruit and nuts. Spread evenly in waxed paper-lined 9 x 5 x 3-inch loaf pan. Bake at 275° for 2 hours and 30 minutes to 3 hours or until cake tests done. Cool in pan. Remove paper. Wrap well before storing in cool place.

JAPANESE FRUIT CAKE

Sharlene Brantley

1 c. butter
2 c. sugar
4 eggs
3¼ c. plain flour
2 T. baking powder
1 tsp. vanilla
1 tsp. allspice
1 tsp. cinnamon
¼ lb. raisins (dark)
1 c. milk or water

Cream butter and sugar. Add eggs, flour and liquid alternately. Add vanilla. Divide the batter evenly into two bowls. To one bowl, add the spices and raisins and bake in **two** layers. Divide the other batter into **two** layers and bake. Bake at 325° for 20 minutes or until done. After the layers cool, prepare the filling.

Japanese Fruit Cake Filling:
juice of 2 lemons
rind of 1 lemon (grated)
1 coconut grated (2 6-oz. pkg., if frozen)
2 c. sugar
1 c. boiling water
2 T. cornstarch
sm. can crushed pineapple (optional)

Mix all together in saucepan and cook over medium heat until thick. This can be used as filling and icing, or filling only and iced with white icing. Layer the following; spice layer, icing, white layer, icing, spice layer, icing, white layer. Then spread the remaining icing around the sides.

LANE CAKE

Mark Ballard

8 egg whites
1 c. butter
1 c. sweet milk
2 c. sifted sugar
3¼ c. sifted flour
2 tsp. baking powder
1 T. vanilla

Sift flour and baking powder together three times. Cream the butter and sugar until perfectly light. Add milk and sifted flour alternately and a little at a time to the creamed mixture until all are used, beginning and ending with flour. Last, beat in the well whipped egg whites and vanilla. Bake in four layers, using medium-sized pans, with one layer of ungreased wax paper in the bottom of each pan.

Filling:

8 egg yolks	**1 wineglass of good whisky or brandy**
1 lg. c. sugar	**1 tsp. vanilla**
½ c. butter	**1 c. seeded and finely clipped raisins**

Beat together well the egg yolks, sugar, and butter. Pour into a small deep stew pan and cook on top of stove until quite thick, stirring all the time. If you don't stir, it will burn. When done and while still hot, put in the raisins, liquor and vanilla. Spread thickly between layers and ice. Cake is better if made a day or two before serving.

This is the original Lane Cake recipe as it appeared in SOME GOOD THINGS TO EAT by Mrs. Emma Rylander Lane in Clayton, Alabama in 1898. She won a prize for the cake and it has been called Lane cake ever since.

Suggested Icing for Lane Cake
4 lg. egg whites
1 lb. (2 cups) sugar
9 T. water

Combine egg whites, sugar and water in the top pan of a double boiler or in heavy pot. Beat until the sugar is dissolved and the mixture is smooth. If you're using a double boiler, have the bottom pan ready with boiling water. When you place the top pan onto the double boiler, be sure that the water isn't touching the top pan at any point. If using the heavy pot, place over low heat. Cook the mixture for 7 minutes or until the icing will stand in soft peaks. Remove it from heat and use it immediately or it will crust over. This icing may be flavored by using the juice of 1 lemon or orange in place of the water. You can also add zest from either fruit to it to flavor it even more.

RED VELVET POUND CAKE

Judy Harris

1 c. butter
½ c. shortening
3 c. sugar
7 eggs
1 c. milk
1 T. vanilla
1-oz. red food coloring
3 c. cake flour
¼ tsp. salt

Cream butter, shortening, and sugar until light and fluffy. Add eggs one at a time, beating well after each. Stir in vanilla and food coloring. Combine cake flour with salt. Beginning with flour-salt mixture, add alternately with milk to creamed mixture, beating well after each. Pour into greased and floured tube pan and bake at 325° for about 1-1¼ hours or cake tests done. Remove from pan and cool to room temperature. Glaze with vanilla or almond glaze or ice with cream cheese frosting.

RUM CAKE

Carolyn Pompei

1 pkg. yellow cake mix, 2 layer size
1 c. sour cream
1 pkg. vanilla flavor instant pudding & pie filling (4 serving size)
3 eggs
½ c. orange juice
½ c. oil
½ c. Bacardi Dark or Light Rum
1 c. chopped pecans

Sprinkle nuts even in bottom of greased and floured 10-inch tube or fluted tube pan. Combine cake mix, pudding mix, eggs, oil and rum in large mixer bowl. Blend, then beat at medium speed for 4 minutes. Pour into pan. Bake at 325°or 1 hour or until cake tester inserted in center of cake comes out clean and cake begins to pull away from sides of pan. Do not under bake. Cool in pan for 15 minutes.

Glaze:
1 c. sugar
½ c. margarine
¼ c. water
½ c. Bacardi Rum

Combine sugar, butter and water in sauce pan. Cook and stir until mixture comes to a boil. Boil 5 minutes stirring constantly. Remove from heat. Stir in ½ cup rum. Bring just to a boil. Invert cake onto serving plate and prick with tester or wooden pick. Carefully spoon warm syrup over warm cake. Garnish if desired.

CHRISTMAS SQUARES

Mildred Gossett

½ box brown sugar
1 stick margarine
2 eggs
½ lb. candied cherries
1 c. flour, self-rising
1 tsp. vanilla
2 c. chopped nuts
3 slices candied pineapple

Cream margarine and sugar. Add eggs, flour and vanilla. This makes stiff batter. Grease shallow pan. Spread 2 cup nuts in pan. Spread batter over nuts. Put cut up fruit on top of batter. Cook at 300° for about 45 minutes. Cut in squares while warm.

FRUIT BARS

Mary Ballard

1 box brown sugar
4 eggs
2 c. self-rising flour
1 tsp. vanilla
½ stick butter
½ lb. candied fruit
1 c. nuts

Mix and bake at 350° for 30 minutes. The temp and time may vary with each oven. Cut into bars and dust with confectioners' sugar.

HOLLY COOKIES

Traci Freeman

6 c. corn flakes
2 tsp. green food coloring
3½ c. mini-marshmallows
1 stick butter
red hots

Melt butter and dump in marshmallows until melted. Add food coloring, pour corn flakes 1 cup at a time, then grease fingers and spoon onto wax paper. Place 2-3 red hots on top and cool.

CHRISTMAS PIE

Mildred Gossett

1 stick margarine, melted
3 eggs, beaten
½ c. coconut
½ c. raisins
½ tsp. cinnamon
½ tsp. allspice
¼ tsp. cloves
1 c. sugar
½ tsp. orange flavoring

Mix well in the same pot used to melt margarine. Pour in unbaked pie shell and cook 45 minutes at 350°.

COCONUT BALLS

Gail Harrison

2 boxes powdered sugar
1 stick butter
1 lg. bag coconut
1 c. chopped nuts
1 can condensed milk
1 pkg. almond bark (vanilla)

Mix sugar, milk, butter, coconut and nuts. Roll in small balls and place in ice box until cool. Melt chocolate. Dip balls in chocolate and place on wax paper until cool. Makes about 130 balls.

DIVINITY

Mark Ballard

½ c. light corn syrup
¼ tsp. salt
2 egg whites
1 c. chopped nuts
2½ c. sugar
½ c. water
2 tsp. vanilla

Beat egg whites until stiff. Mix syrup, sugar, salt and water. Bring to a boil at 248° (use candy thermometer). Pour one-half of syrup slowly into egg whites beating as you pour. Bring the remaining one-half of syrup to 272°. Then pour this syrup into mixture, beating slowly until mixture thickens. Add nuts and flavoring. Stir until firm and spoon by teaspoons quickly onto wax paper. Allow to completely cool and harden before removing paper. Store in airtight containers.

Every time I make this candy, I think of my dear, departed friend DeLora and miss the adventures we had making this delicious divinity.

DIVINITY CLOUDS

Linda G. Jones

2½ c. sugar
½ c. light corn syrup
½ c. water
⅛ tsp. salt
2 egg whites
1 tsp. vanilla
¾ - 1 c. chopped nuts (optional)
cherry and pecan halves (optional)

Combine sugar, syrup, water and salt in a 3-quart (large) casserole or mixing bowl. Microwave on high 5 minutes. Microwave thoroughly. Cook on high 9-12 minutes, or until mixture reaches hard-ball stage (260°). Start with 9 minute and work in 1 minute intervals. Drop mixture in cold water to test. Meanwhile, beat egg whites until stiff peaks form. Slowly, pour syrup over egg whites beating at high speed with electric mixer. Add vanilla. Continue beating 3-5 minutes or until mixture holds it's shape and begins to lose some of it's gloss. Stir in nuts. As soon as it gets a little stiff, quickly drop heaping teaspoons onto wax paper. Top with pecan or cherry halves. If you desire, you may drop half of mixture at top with cherries and then use about ½ teaspoon cherry juice in candy (makes it pink) and top with pecan half.

MICROWAVE DIVINITY

William C. Kitchens

3 c. sugar
½ c. light corn syrup
⅔ c water
¼ tsp. salt
1 egg white
¼ tsp. vanilla
1 c. chopped pecans

In a 3-quart glass bowl, microwave sugar, syrup, and water on FULL POWER for 12 to 18 minutes, or until mixture spins a fine thread. In another bowl, add salt to egg whites, beating constantly until whites are stiff and form peaks. Slowly pour a thin stream of syrup mixture into egg whites, beating constantly until mixture loses shine and thickens. Stir in vanilla and nuts. Immediately drop by teaspoonsful on waxed paper. 30 servings

SISTER'S RUM BALLS

Vicki Brantley

2½ c. finely crushed vanilla wafers
1 c. confectioners' sugar
2 tablespoons baking cocoa
1 c. finely chopped pecans
6 tablespoons light corn syrup
⅓ c. light rum confectioners' sugar

Combine first 4 ingredients in bowl; mix well. Add corn syrup and rum; mix well. Shape into walnut sized balls. Roll in confectioners' sugar. Store in tightly covered container

BUCKEYES

Debra Ballard

2 c. peanut butter (smooth or chunky)
1 stick butter, softened but not melted
2 c. powdered sugar
1 12-oz. pkg. sweet chocolate chips
½ bar paraffin wax

Combine the first three ingredients in a large mixing bowl. Mix these very well. The consistency should be such that you can roll and form the dough into a ball. You may want to refrigerate the dough for 15 to 20 minutes as this makes it easier to work with. Roll into 1-inch balls. Return to the fridge and chill until firm. Melt chocolate and paraffin wax over water in a double boiler or over very low heat in a saucepan. Dip the balls into the chocolate. They can be partially or completely covered. Use a toothpick or spoon to submerge and remove them from the chocolate mixture onto wax paper to dry. If in a hurry, place the chilled balls on wax paper and drizzle the chocolate over the balls. Can be stored in the refrigerator, frozen or eaten immediately.

It is not Christmas without these wonderful treats that Debra and the kids make each year. Our friend Bill Terry expects to find some of these on the table each time he comes over and usually brings his own container to take a few home!

WINTER PEACH PIE

Claire Strawn

1 9-inch unbaked pie shell
1 c. dried peaches that have been stewed, mashed, and sweetened. (Measured after cooking)

Custard:
½ c. sugar
2 T. flour
3 egg yolks
2 T. butter
1 c. scalded milk
1 tsp. vanilla
dash nutmeg

Meringue:
3 egg whites
¼ tsp. cream of tartar
6 T. sugar

Spread peaches in bottom of pie shell. Set aside. Beat egg yolks, add sugar, flour, then scalded milk, butter, vanilla, and nutmeg. Pour carefully over peaches and bake until custard is firm (approximately 45 minutes) at 325°. Beat egg whites and cream of tartar. Gradually add sugar, beat until stiff. Top custard with meringue and bake at 325° until brown.

Paper Camellias

Paper. We have used it in some form or another for most of our lives. Early on, it was placed in our hands as a way to communicate our thoughts and feelings. We learned to scribble on it with our chubby, uncoordinated hands as a infant. We drew colorful masterpieces on it with crayons as a child. And as we matured and became students, we used it to diligently and carefully answer our homework questions. Or, at least, most of us did when our dog wasn't eating it! How many times have we been asked to put on paper everything from a recipe, to a phone number, to the answers we weren't sure of on the day our teacher surprised us with a pop quiz? We have folded it, cut it, bound it, drawn on it, wrapped in it and even glued it to our walls. It has saved us , on many festive occasions, in the form of plates and napkins, when we were in a pinch and didn't want to use the "good china."

There is no doubt that paper has many uses. It would be hard to exist without it. You are even holding it in your hand right now! But, have you ever made a beautiful flower out of it? During these months filled to the brim with these flowering blossoms, let me show you how to create your own everlasting paper camellia.

I have always been fascinated with camellias. You know the ones. Those beautiful and wonderful Southern flowers in various shades of white, pink and red. My love of them may stem from the fact that when most everything else is dormant and lifeless, these beauties burst forth with such brilliance and grace they command your attention. They have been placed on the earth to bloom at just the right time to brighten our lives during the cold and dreary winter months. How dull our winters would be without them.

Let me share with you how I first learned to construct a paper camellia. No, I didn't go to the Orient on an exchange program. I learned right here in Middle Georgia. I saw in the paper where Donna and Bill Shepherd from Charleston, South Carolina, would be at the American Camellia Society Headquarters teaching how to make paper camellias. Massee Lane, as it is referred to, is located between Fort Valley and Marshallville and is truly an amazing place. If you have never gone for a visit, you must. You will not be disappointed.

It was the mid-eighties and I, a much younger artist, decided to go take the course. Now let me tell you a little secret about myself. I have a very short attention span! I didn't realize this until I became older. I always have fun creating the first thing, but then the fun diminishes before you can say, glue gun! I came to this realization when I was painting eight dining room chairs for a client. I had the time of my life on the first one and was in tears by the eighth. I decided that I had to trick myself into doing multiples.

I now paint one thing on each of the chairs and continue until they all end up finished at the same time. Sort of like an assembly line. You will NEVER see me working on an automobile assembly line. I just could not do it! After a day of putting on bumpers, I would go insane! I would have to ask them to please let me put steering wheels on for a while. I chose to look at this as a sign of creativity in order to accept it. Whatever it takes, you know!

I headed down the road all prepared to learn. I walked into a room with several tables filled with older women. They looked at me as if to ask, "What are YOU doing here?" A little intimidated, I found the only seat left. The class was supposed to take all day. I could not imagine what we were going to do the WHOLE day. I figured in that time we could plant some real camellias and watch them bloom. The teachers were very laid back and began to show us what to do. This is when the fun began.

I forgot to tell you that along with having Attention Deficit Disorder, I am also a little hyper and impatient. Other creative characteristics, I presume! I wanted my flower yesterday, and intended to make it lickety-split. The other ladies were nervous and attentive as they watched the teachers take ten minutes for each petal. Bored with this process, I did what I have always done in this situation. I jumped ahead! I know, teachers hate it when students do that. I didn't know how much until I stated teaching. I'm sure that everything that I have done to my teachers is coming home to haunt me now.

Beady eyes and strange stares were being fired in my direction like bullets from a gun. The already nervous group of ladies were shaking because I had almost finished my flower. Finally, the lady to my left had as much as she could stand, and get this, TOLD on me! She pointed to my flower and told the teacher that I had jumped ahead, giving me a glare mixed with a little smirk. I was embarrassed as every eye looked in my direction with disgust. I tried to quickly hide my flower as I smiled back at the lady beside me. I was thinking to myself that she probably should had hidden hers. Oh well!

That is how it all began. By the way, I left before lunch with two things. My beautiful camellia and a splitting headache. I went home and over the next few days developed what I feel is a quick and simple way to create these wonderful copies. I have since held many classes all over this area teaching this art. All of my students have done well. I'm sure that you can do the same if you follow these simple steps.

Supplies

8½ x 11 Onionskin Paper, 9 lb, 25% Cotton Fiber Content, Plain Cockle Finish

1 to 1½ inch Circle cut from cardboard or heavy poster board

Silk Flower "stamen" and leaves

Tools
Glue Gun and glue sticks
Prismacolour Pencils or Design Magic Markers
in shades of pink or red

Instructions
Count 16 sheets or layers of paper. Trace the pattern onto the top sheet for each of the two different sizes of petals. Taking care to keep the paper stacked together, Cut 16 of each size. Keep the sizes separated into two piles. If you are going to color your petals, do so now. To do this, begin at the smaller end of the petal and use even strokes to color out to the petal's edge. It helps to look at an actual camellia when doing this so that your paper camellia looks authentic.

To form the actual petal shape that will be attached to the circle base, place a dot of glue in the center of the small end of the petal and pinch together. (Remember that if you have colored your petals to glue 8 of the large petals with the fold or pinch down to the white side and 8 of the large petals with the fold up to the colored side.)

When all the petals are "pinched", take your circle base and squirt glue onto the entire surface, leaving a margin around the outside of the circle of about ⅛ to ¼ of an inch. Spacing evenly, place 8 of the large petals on the circle, with the pinched side down. Then attach the remaining 8 of the large petals, placing a dot of glue on the petals one at a time and placing on top of and "between" the bottom layer. These petals are attached with the pinched side up. Then begin with the smaller petals, making two layers with the pinched side up. When you get to the top layer, they may overlap each other. Again, look at an actual camellia for authenticity. When the petal phase is finished, glue your "stamen" in the very center, nestling it into the middle of the top petals.

Attach your leaves to the bottom side of the circle base. Remove any glue "strings".

Display in a variety of ways. In a shadowbox, on a Christmas Tree, in a centerpiece......

Patterns:

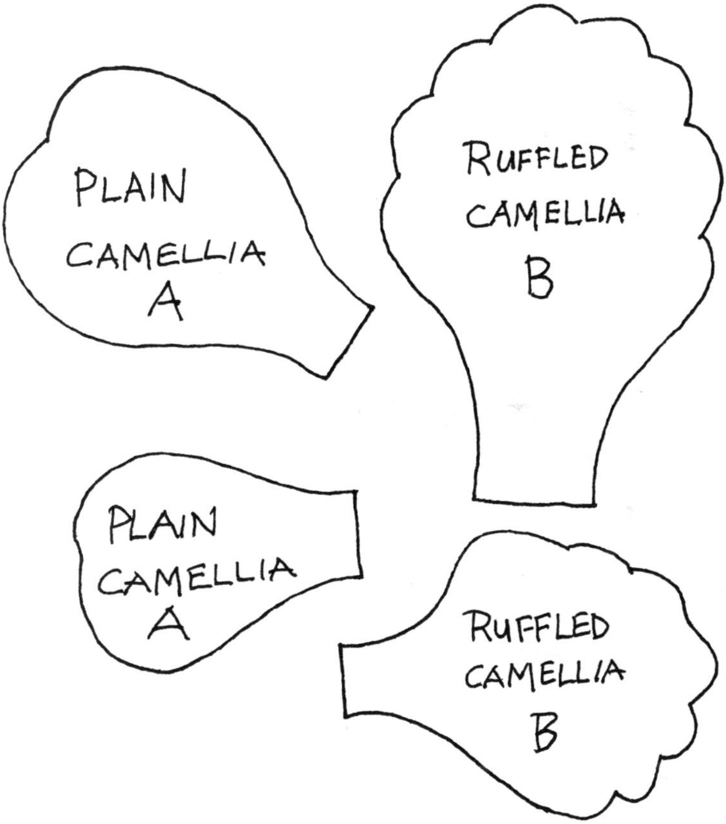

New Years

CHEESE FRUIT BALLS

Jo Ann Stephens

2 8-oz. cream cheese, softened
1 can fruit cocktail, drained
1 3-oz. pkg. vanilla instant pudding

Combine all together. Make two balls, and roll each in almonds.

SUGARED PEANUTS

Diane E. Nickels

1 c. water
1 tsp. vanilla
2 c. sugar
4 c. peanuts

Dissolve sugar in water and vanilla. Cook until liquid begins to sugar, stirring frequently. Spray a cookie sheet with Pam and put sugared nuts on cookie. Sprinkle with salt. Bake 1 hour at 200° stirring after 30 minutes.

BLOODY CAESAR

Debra Ballard

¾ c. clam juice-flavored tomato juice
¼ c. vodka
2 T. lemon juice
pinch celery salt
2 dashes Worcestershire sauce
dash hot pepper sauce
freshly ground pepper
lime wedge, optional

Pour tomato juice, vodka and lemon juice over ice in a highball glass. Stir in celery salt, Worcestershire sauce and pepper sauce. Top with black pepper to taste. Garnish with lime wedge, if desired.

HOT SPICED CIDER

Mark Ballard

1 lg. can apple cider
1 lg. can pineapple juice
¼ c. lemon juice
1 lg. can frozen orange juice
cinnamon, cloves and sugar to taste

Mix all ingredients and heat to boiling. Serve warm

KAHLUA

Carolyn Pompei

3 c. water
1½ c. sugar
10 tsp. instant coffee
4 tsp. vanilla
1 qt. of vodka

Simmer water, sugar and instant coffee for 1 hour. Let cool, add vanilla and vodka. Note: use cheap vodka and best coffee.

CITRUS STREUSEL QUICK BREAD

Mrs. J. B. Franklin

1 pkg. (18¼-oz.) lemon or orange cake mix - Divided
2 T. brown sugar
1 tsp. ground cinnamon
1 tsp. finely grated orange (or lemon) rind
1 T. cold butter
½ c. chopped pecans
1 pkg. (3.4-oz.) instant vanilla pudding mix
1 T. finely grated orange (or lemon) rind
4 eggs
1 c. (8-oz.) sour cream
⅓ vegetable oil

Glaze:
1 c. confectioners' sugar
2 T. milk

In a small bowl combine 2 tablespoons cake mix, brown sugar, and cinnamon; cut in butter until crumbly. Add grated rind. Stir in pecans. Set aside. In a mixing bowl, combine the pudding mix, rind, eggs, sour cream, oil and remaining cake mix. Beat on medium speed for 2 minutes. Pour into 2 greased 8 x 4 x 2-inch loaf pans. Sprinkle with pecan mixture. Bake at 350° for 45-20 minutes, or until a toothpick inserted near center comes out clean. Cool in pans for 10 minutes before removing to wire racks. Combine glaze ingredients; drizzle over warm bread. Yield: 2 loaves.

CRANBERRY PECAN BREAD

Mark Ballard

3 c. all-purpose flour — **1 c. sugar**
1 T. baking powder — **¼ tsp. salt**
2 slightly beaten egg whites
1¼ c. skim milk — **¼ c. vegetable oil**
2 tsp. grated orange peel
1½ c. coarsely chopped cranberries
½ c. pecans

Preheat oven to 350° degrees. Spray 9 x 5 x 3-inch loaf pan with non-stick coating; set aside. In large bowl stir together flour, sugar, baking powder, and salt. In a small bowl combine egg white, milk, oil and orange peel. Add liquid mixture to the flour mixture; stir just till combined. Stir in cranberries and pecans. Pour batter into prepared pan. Bake for 1 to 1¼ hours or till a wooden toothpick inserted near the center comes out clean. Cool the bread in the pan for 10 minutes. Remove bread from pan and cool completely on a wire rack. Yield: 1 large loaf.

HOPPIN' JOHN

A New Year's Day Requirement from an old Southern cook

2 c. dried black-eyed peas or 4 c. fresh or frozen peas
½ lb. dry-cured salt pork or country ham
1 lg. onion, finely chopped
2 garlic cloves, minced (optional)
1 pod cayenne pepper
½ tsp. dried thyme
1 bay leaf
Black pepper to taste
Salt to taste
1 c. rice, cooked

Wash and drain the peas. If you are using dried peas, put them in a bowl that will hold twice their volume and add enough water to cover by 3 inches. Soak the peas for 4 hours or overnight. Drain the soaked peas and put them in a large pot with 3 pints of water. Do not add salt at this point. Bring the peas to a boil over medium heat. Reduce heat to a slow simmer and then cover the pot and simmer for 30 minutes. Add pork, onion, optional garlic, and other seasonings (still no salt though). Cover the pot again and let the peas simmer until tender, usually about 2 hours. If using fresh or frozen peas, bring 3 pints of water to a boil in a pot that will hold all ingredients. Add the pork and seasonings (except the salt) first and allow to simmer for about 45 minutes. Raise the heat, add the peas and let the mixture come to a boil. You may want to skim off any "scum" from the top of the water and then reduce the heat to a simmer and cook for about 30 minutes or until the peas are tender.

To finish the Hoppin' John, taste the broth and correct for salt. If the pork you used was very salty, it may not be necessary to add

additional salt. Keep in mind though that the broth should be highly seasoned as it will flavor the rice.
Take 2 cups of broth in a separate pot and bring to a boil over medium heat. Add the rice and let it come to a boil. Reduce the heat, cover the pot and let cook until the rice is ready (see package directions). When the rice is ready, drain the broth from the peas but don't discard it yet. Fluff the rice with a fork and gently mix in the peas, tossing them with a fork rather then stirring with a spoon. If the mixture is a little too dry, add a bit of the reserved broth. Don't add too much though. This isn't a soup. Place a piece of pork on top of each serving or cut it up and mix it in with the rice and peas.
Serve immediately

SOUTHERN GREENS

Jo Ballard

8 c. stock
4 lbs. mixed greens (or favorite green)
salt and freshly ground pepper to taste

Stock: Can use smoked, cured pork to flavor. Cook a good sized slice in 6 cups of water for ½ hour, tightly covered. Substitutes include chicken stock, vegetable stock or lightly salted water (about 2 tsp. salt per quart of water).

Preparation: Buy greens that are fresh and young. If leaves are fresh and young, simply cut away the thick base of the stem. For collards or if leaves are a little older, cut the entire stem and central rib from the leaf. Leave smaller leaves whole; larger ones can be cut or torn in pieces. Wash all types of greens carefully in a least two changes of clean water. Fill a sink full of water and

immerse a few leaves at a time, swishing around to clean off any grit. Place the washed leaves in a colander, clean the sink and repeat until there is no longer any dirt or sand settling in the bottom of the sink. This can be done a day or so ahead of time. Place clean greens in the fridge until you're ready to cook.
Cooking: Brink the stock to a boil in a large Dutch oven or heavy saucepan. Add the prepared greens, waiting for one batch to wilt down into the water before adding the next batch. This will seem like a lot of greens, but they cook down. Cook, uncovered over high heat until the greens are just tender, about 15 to 20 minutes. Do NOT overcook. They should be tender and still vibrant green in color. During cooking, season with salt and pepper. When done, use slotted spoon to remove from the pot; draining off excess liquid (reserve this as "pot likker" to be eaten with cornbread for a great Southern supper) and serve hot! Enjoy!

EASY WONTON SOUP

Beverly Futch

1 1¼-lb. ground pork **½ tsp. ground ginger**
½ tsp. black pepper
3 cans (14½-oz.) ready to use chicken broth
1 c. water **2 T. soy sauce**
2½-oz. (1 c.) fresh mushrooms, sliced
6 scallions, sliced
1 pkg. (6-oz.) wonton skins, cut into ½ strips

In a soup pot, brown the pork over medium-high for 3 to 5 minutes or until no pink remains. Drain off excess liquid. Reduce heat to medium and add the remaining ingredients except the wonton strips. Bring to a boil. Separate the wonton strips and stir into the soup. Cook for 8-10 minutes or until the strips are cooked. Serves 4 to 6.

NEW YEARS DAY BLACK EYE PEA SOUP

Matilen Sheram

2 cans black eyed peas (undrained)
2 cans diced tomatoes with onions and green peppers
2 c. chopped celery
2 c. chopped onion
chopped hams
Juice of one lemon
Salt and Pepper to taste

Saute celery and onion in butter - but not too long as the celery should still be crunchy. Mix all ingredients together and cook until done.

TOMATO-RICE SOUP

Mark Ballard

½ c. chopped onion
½ c. chopped celery
½ c. chopped carrots
1 tsp. olive oil
8 c. diced plum tomatoes
1 c. cooked quick-cooking rice
1 c. reduced-fat chicken broth
¼ c. fresh parsley or 1 T. dried
1 T. fresh basil or 1 tsp. dried
1 tsp. fresh thyme or ½ tsp. dried
1 clove garlic, minced
1 strip (½-inch by 1-inch) orange peel

In a 4-quart pot, combine onions, celery, carrots, and oil. Cover pot and cook over medium-low heat for 10 minutes, stirring often to prevent sticking. Process tomatoes in a blender or food processor until smooth. Press through a coarse sieve. Add to pot, and bring to a boil over medium heat. Reduce heat to medium-low, partially cover pot, and simmer for 20 minutes. Add rice and broth. Partially cover and simmer until thick, about 20 minutes. Mince parsley, basil, thyme, garlic, and orange peel. Ladle soup into individual bowls. Stir a generous spoonful of the minced herbs into each bowl. Serves 6.

"EXTRA SPECIAL" RICE CASSEROLE

Mary Ballard

1 c. long grain rice, uncooked
1 15½-oz. can chicken broth
water
1 lb. Monterey Jack cheese, grated
1 16-oz. carton sour cream
⅓ c. creamy Italian dressing
1 4-oz. can green chili peppers, chopped
1 8-oz. can water chestnuts, sliced and drained

Combine rice, chicken broth, plus enough water to make 2 cups liquid. Cook rice until tender. Add cheese, sour cream, dressing, chili peppers and water chestnuts; stir until well blended. Pour into 9 x 13-inch dish. Bake, uncovered at 350° for 25 minutes. Can be made the day before. Freezes well.

MUSHROOM RICE CASSEROLE

Jeannie Cox

2 c. rice
1 stick butter
2 cans French Onion soup
1 can water
1 can Beef broth
1 jar mushroom pieces and stems, liquid also

Mix all ingredients together. Cover and bake at 375° for 50 minutes. Serves 6-8 .

MUSHROOM IN PUFF PASTRY

Betty Jones

3 T. butter	**3 T. flour**
1 lb. mushrooms	**¼ c. parsley, chopped**
2 sheets Frozen Puff Pastry	
1 egg, beaten	**1 c. milk**
1 tsp. salt	**pepper to taste**

Melt butter and mix in flour. Cook for a few minutes. Add seasonings and mushrooms. Simmer 1-2 minutes; add parsley and cool. Thaw pastry sheets. Cut in half, crosswise on floured board. Roll out each sheet 1-inch wider and 1-inch longer. Spread mushroom mixture in center of 2 pieces, leaving ½-inch around edges. Top with second sheet. Seal edges with fork. Prick holes in top and brush with egg. Bake in preheated over 400° for 20 minutes or until golden brown. Serves 4.

RUTABAGAS

Debra Ballard

1 large rutabaga (about 2¼ lbs.), peeled and cut into chunks
Meat for seasoning **Salt to taste**

Put rutabaga pieces and meat into a large saucepan. Cover with salted water. Bring to a boil, reduce the heat, simmer until the pieces are fork tender. About 30 to45 minutes. Remove from heat, drain serve. If you're going to mash or whip the rutabagas, add 2 to 4 T. of butter and more salt to taste if necessary.

My mother always whipped or mashed her rutabagas (not one of my personal favorites). When my wife Debra came into the picture, she preferred hers left in whole slices or pieces. Mother would always take Debra some out once they were cooked and then mash the rest. Oh, what we will do for loved ones!

POTATO CASSEROLE

Carolyn Pompei

1 32-oz. frozen Southern Style Ore-Ida Hash Brown potatoes
1 c. melted margarine **1 tsp. salt**
¼ tsp. pepper **½ c. chopped onion**
1 can cream of chicken soup
1 8-oz. or 10-oz. Velveeta Shredded cheese
2 c. corn flakes, crushed **¼ c. melted margarine**

Defrost potatoes. Mix ingredients. Bake in 13 x 9 or 2 smaller pans. Top with 2 cups corn flakes crushed and ¼ cup melted margarine. Bake at 350° for 1 hour.

CHICKEN CASSEROLE

Jo Ann Stephens

1 can cream of celery soup
1 can cream of chicken soup
1 c. sour cream
6 chicken breasts, cooked and chopped
1 bag stuffing mix
1 stick butter, melted
1 c. chicken broth

Mix soups, sour cream and cooked, chopped chicken breast. Put in baking dish. Mix stuffing mix, butter and chicken broth and pour over chicken. Bake at 350° for approximately 45 minutes.

HERB-SEASONED CHICKEN BREASTS

Betty S. Ragland

8 skinned and boned chicken breast halves
1½ c. herb seasoned stuffing mix
1 T. margarine, melted
¼ c. orange juice
hot cooked wild rice
Sweet Orange Sauce

Arrange chicken in a lightly greased 13 x 9-inch baking dish. Sprinkle with stuffing mix, and drizzle with butter. Pour orange juice over chicken; cover and bake at 350° for 1 hour. Serve over wild rice with sauce. Yield: 8 servings.

Sweet Orange Sauce:
1 (6-oz.) can frozen orange juice concentrate, thawed and diluted
½ c. orange marmalade
2 T. steak sauce

Combine all ingredients in a microwave-safe container. Microwave on high 6 minutes or until hot and bubbly, stirring once. Yield: 1⅓ cups.

QUICKIE CHICKEN DIVAN

Traci Freeman

1 (10-oz.) pkg. frozen broccoli, cooked
3-4 lg. cooked chicken breasts
1 can cream of chicken soup
⅓ c. milk
1 c. grated cheddar cheese

Place cooked broccoli in greased 10 x 7-inch baking dish. Top with cooked chicken breasts. Combine soup and milk in small bowl and stir until well blended. Pour soup mixture over chicken. Sprinkle with cheese. Bake uncovered at 350° for 30 minutes.

SOUR CREAM CHICKEN CASSEROLE

Gladys Aaron

4-6 chicken breasts, cooked
1 c. sour cream
1 can cream of chicken soup
1 stick melted margarine
17 Ritz crackers

Cut chicken into small pieces. Place in bottom of casserole. Mix soup and sour cream. Spread over soup. Put cracker - melted margarine on top. Bake at 425° for 30 minutes. Serves 6.

SPAGHETTI SAUCE AND MEATBALLS

Gloria Sikes

4 29-oz. cans tomato sauce
2 12-oz. cans tomato paste
1½ tsp. granulated garlic
1½ tsp. season salt
1 tsp. paprika
1 tsp. red pepper
1 lg. chopped onion

Mix all ingredients together in a 5-6 quart pot. Simmer while making meatballs.

Meatballs:
4-5 lb. ground beef
1 lg. chopped onion
3 eggs
1½ tsp. granulated garlic
1 tsp. Season All
1 tsp. paprika
1 tsp. red pepper
40 saltines, crushed

Mix all ingredients together. Shape into meatballs. Drop in sauce. Cook about 4 hours on low heat. Makes 40-50 meatballs.

FROZEN PECAN PIE

Mark Ballard

1 (8-oz) pkg. cream cheese
¾ c. corn syrup
¼ c. brown sugar
¾ c. milk
1 tsp. vanilla
½ c. pecans, chopped
graham cracker crust
caramel sauce
whipped topping and pecan halves

Bring cream cheese to room temperature. Whip in mixer until light. Add corn syrup, sugar, milk, and vanilla. Blend well. Add chopped pecans and pour into cooled crust. Freeze overnight. Remove from freezer 10 minutes before serving. Arrange on serving plate and garnish with whipped cream or topping and a pecan half. Makes 10 servings.

Graham Cracker Crust:
11 whole graham crackers (⅓ lb.)
¼ c. pecans, chopped
¼ c. margarine, melted
2 T. sugar

Preheat oven to 350°. Place crumbled crackers and pecans in food processor. Pulse several times until fine crumbs are formed. Slowly add sugar and melted margarine while processor is running. Blend until crumbs are coated. Spray a 9-inch pie plate with pan spray. Press crumb mixture evenly into pie plate. Place into preheated oven for 5 to 10 minutes until set. Remove and cool before filling.

Super Bowl

4-CHEESE CHEESE BALL

Traci Freeman

1 (8-oz.) pkg. cream cheese, softened
1 c. (4-oz.) 4-cheese blend, shredded
¼ c. minced onion
2 T. minced parsley
1 tsp. Worcestershire sauce
¼ tsp. salt
1 tsp. granulated garlic
2 tsp. chives
⅓ c. chopped pecans, toasted
Extra chopped and toasted pecans for rolling

Blend cream and mixed cheeses. Add remaining ingredients and blend well. Shape into a ball and roll in extra pecans. Chill and serve with crackers. VARIATIONS: Use cheddar instead of cheese blend. Add well drained 8¼ ounces can crushed pineapple for a fruit and nut cheese ball. Add crushed red peppers, green onions, pickle relish, or whatever pleases your taste. Roll in crisp chopped bacon or bacon and nut mix. Toasting pecans before using adds a different flavor but plain is okay also.

QUICK PARTY MIX

Mark Ballard

¼ c. butter or margarine, melted
1 12-ounce can mixed nuts ¼ cup grated Parmesan cheese
Dash of ground celery seeds Dash of garlic powder
¼ teaspoon dried whole oregano
4 cups honey graham cereal

Combine all ingredients in a a large mixing bowl and stir well. Place mixture in a 15 x 10 x 1 inch jelly roll pan. Bake at 300 degrees for 15 minutes or until mixture begins to lightly brown. Stir or shake so that none of mixture burns. Cool completely in pan or pour onto wax paper. Store in airtight container. Keeps indefinitely. Make 5½ cups.

CHEESE STRAWS

Mark Ballard

1 pkg. frozen puff pastry, defrosted according to directions
¾ c. grated Parmigiano-Reggiano grated cheese

Preheat oven to 375°. Dust work surface with ¼ cup grated parmigiano-reggiano. Lay unfolded sheet of puff pastry on top of cheese, then sprinkle with ¼ cup more grated cheese. Gently roll dough out with a rolling pin, pressing cheese into dough, to a thickness of about ⅛-inch. Dust with more cheese as needed. Cut pastry into long ½-inch wide strips. Give each strip several twists, then lay ½ inch apart on a parchment-lined baking sheet. Bake until golden, about 10 minutes. Allow to cool slightly, then remove from paper and serve. Makes 24 14-inch straws.

CIRCLE OF GOODNESS

Judy Harris

1 (10-oz.) can chicken breast
1 (8-oz.) pkg. cream cheese, softened to point of almost melted
½ c. Miracle Whip
2 c. spinach leaves, torn into small pieces
2 c. shredded or grated cheddar cheese
½ tsp. red pepper flakes
2 8-count cans crescent rolls

Optional Glaze:
1 egg white, lightly beaten
poppy seeds

Put chicken in a large bowl and break into small pieces. Add cheeses, Miracle Whip, spinach, and pepper flakes and combine well. Set aside. Unroll crescent rolls and separate into triangles. Arrange rolls into two circles with wide ends of roll in center, overlapping slightly, and points towards outside of pans. Circle in center should be 4-5 inches in diameter. Place large spoonful of chicken mixture in center of each roll and pull points back over mixture, overlapping at an angle to fill in gaps. May bake as is or brush tops with egg white and sprinkle with poppy seeds. Bake at 375° for 15-28 minutes or lightly browned. Cut into slices and serve.

PIZZA DIP

Betty S. Ragland

1 8-oz. light cream cheese, softened
½ c. light sour cream
¼ tsp. dried oregano
¼ tsp. garlic powder
¼ tsp. red pepper
¾ c. pizza sauce
½ c. pepperoni chopped
¼ c. green onions, chopped
1 c. Mozzarella cheese, shredded

Beat cream cheese, sour cream, oregano, garlic and red pepper until well blended. Spread in lightly greased 9-inch pie plate. Spread pizza sauce evenly over top. Sprinkle with chopped pepperoni and top with chopped green onions. Bake at 350° for 10 minutes. Sprinkle with mozzarella cheese and bake 10 more minutes or until cheese melts. Serve with tortilla chips.

SALMON CHEESE BALL

Barbara Rouse

1 can (14-16-oz.) salmon
2 pkg. (8-oz.) cream cheese
2 T. horseradish sauce
2 tsp. grated onion
½ c. chopped pecans

Mix first 4 ingredients together. Form into a ball. Roll in chopped nuts. Serve with crackers. Mixture can prepared ahead and frozen.

MARINATED CHICKEN WINGS

Martha Armstrong

½ c. chicken broth
⅓ c. soy sauce
3 T. sugar
3 T. brown sugar
3 T. vinegar
¼ tsp. ground ginger
garlic to taste
3 lbs. chicken wings

Combine all ingredients except garlic and chicken wings. Place chicken wings in a baking dish and sprinkle with garlic. Pour marinade mixture over wings and marinate overnight. Bake uncovered at 325 degrees for two hours.

CRUSTY GARLIC BREAD

Mark Ballard

2 cloves garlic, minced
2 tsp. olive oil
2 T. chopped fresh parsley
2 T. chopped fresh thyme or 2 tsp. dried thyme
2 tsp. chopped fresh marjoram or ¾ tsp. dried marjoram
½ tsp. paprika
2 T. grated Parmesan cheese (optional)
2 sm. loaves (4-oz.) Italian or French bread

Preheat oven to 350°. In a small bowl, combine the garlic and oil; mix well. In another small bowl, combine parsley, thyme, marjoram and paprika. Add Parmesan; mix well. Cut each loaf crosswise into diagonal slices, without cutting all the way through. Brush cut sides of slices with garlic oil. Sprinkle herb mixture between slices. Wrap each loaf in foil; place on a baking sheet. Bake until heated through, about 10 to 15 minutes. Unwrap the loaves and place them on a breadboard or in a basket. Serve immediately. May freeze for up to 1 month. Freeze unbaked. Bake 25 to 30 minutes.

BLACK-AND-RED CHILI

Mark Ballard

½ lb. 93% ultra-lean ground beef
2 c. diced onion
1 c. chopped green bell pepper
1½ T. chili powder
2 tsp. ground cumin
1½ tsp. dried whole oregano
1 tsp. sugar
¼ tsp. celery seeds
3 (8-oz.) cans no-salt-added tomato sauce
1 (15½-oz.) can black beans, undrained
1 (14½-oz.) can no-salt-added whole tomatoes, undrained and chopped

Cook meat in a large saucepan over medium heat until browned, stirring to crumble. Add onion and bell pepper; saute 3 minutes or until tender. Add chili powder and remaining 8 ingredients; bring to a boil. Reduce heat, and simmer, uncovered, 30 minutes, stirring occasionally. Yield: 6 servings.

CHICKEN SOUP

Edith Sullivan

1 whole chicken cooked in water 1 hour, deboned
(use 3 c. of chicken, freeze remainder)
6 c. chicken broth
4 ribs of celery
5 bouillon cubes
1 onion, chopped
1 can sliced carrots
1 can (28-oz.) tomatoes
½ tsp. oregano
½ tsp. thyme
½ tsp. garlic salt
1 can red kidney beans
1 lb. bag yolk-free noodles

Take 3 cups chicken and add to 3 cups broth, water, onions, and celery and cook for 10 minutes. Add tomatoes, carrots, spices. While this is cooking, boil noodles in the other 3 c. of broth for 10 minutes and drain. Add noodles to chicken/vegetable pot. Stir in drained can of light red kidney beans. Heat for 5 minutes. Total cooking time is usually 20 to 25 minutes.

CHICKEN-VEGETABLE SOUP

Mark Ballard

1 can (13-oz.) reduced-fat chicken broth
1 c. frozen mixed vegetables
½ c. elbow macaroni, cooked
⅛ tsp. dried oregano or dried thyme
½ c. diced cooked chicken
snipped fresh parsley or slice scallions

Bring broth to a boil in a medium saucepan. Add vegetables, macaroni, oregano, and chicken. Reduce heat. Simmer for 3 to 4 minutes. Garnish with parsley or scallions. Serves 2.

SALMON STEW

Mrs. J. B. Franklin

1 16-oz. can (high quality) salmon, undrained
1 qt. milk
1 can cream of chicken soup
1 can cream of celery soup

Remove bones from salmon. Mix all ingredients together and cook over low heat until very hot.
A few slices of cooked and crumbled bacon may be sprinkled over each serving.

CRISPY POTATO WEDGES

Mark Ballard

4 med. russet potatoes, cut into lg. wedges
1 T. vegetable oil
¼ tsp. freshly ground black pepper
⅛ tsp. salt
2 cloves garlic, minced (optional)
reduced-sodium ketchup (optional)

Place potatoes in a large bowl; add cold water to cover. Let stand for 15 minutes. Preheat oven to 425°. Spray a nonstick baking sheet with vegetable cooking spray. Set aside. Drain potatoes in a colander. Spread on a double layer of paper towels. Cover with a second layer of paper towels. Press down on the towels to dry potatoes. Transfer potatoes to a clean large bowl. Sprinkle with oil, pepper, and salt; toss gently to combine. Arrange seasoned potatoes in a single layer on prepared baking sheet. Bake potatoes for 20 minutes. Using a spatula, turn potatoes; sprinkle with garlic. Bake until golden, about 20 minutes, turning baking sheet after 10 minutes for even browning. Serve immediately with ketchup on the side.

HASH BROWN CASSEROLE

Mildred Gossett

2 lb. bag frozen hash browns
16-oz. sour cream
1 can creamy chicken mushroom soup
½ c. chopped onion
1 stick margarine
2 c. grated cheese
salt and pepper

Mix potatoes, sour cream, soup, onion, margarine, salt and pepper. Cook 1 hour at 350°. After 30 minutes, cover with foil. Add cheese last 5 minutes.

BAKED SALMON CROQUETTES

Jackie Johnson

1 (7¾-oz.) can salmon
½ tsp. salt
cheese sauce
2 T. grated lemon peel
buttered cracker crumbs
2 T. chopped green onion
1 T. water
1½ c. cooked rice
2 eggs

Combine salmon, including liquid, with rice, onion, lemon peel, salt and 1 egg. Shape into croquettes. Beat remaining egg with water. Roll croquettes in egg and then in cracker crumbs. Chill 30 minutes. Bake at 375° for 25 to 30 minutes or until delicately browned. Pour cheese sauce over croquettes and serve. Make 8 croquettes.

Cheese Sauce:
2 T. butter or margarine
1 T. flour
¼ tsp. salt
dash of white pepper
1 c. milk
¾ c. grated cheddar cheese

In a saucepan, melt 2 tablespoons butter or margarine and blend in 1 tablespoon flour, ¼ teaspoon salt and a dash of white pepper. Add 1 cup milk and heat until thickened. Add ¾ cups grated cheese, stirring until melted.

ITALIAN FIESTA BRUNCH BAKE

Mark Ballard

1 lb. spicy hot bulk sausage, browned and drained
1 jar (4-oz.) diced pimentos, drained and divided
10-oz. frozen spinach, thawed and drained
1 c. all-purpose flour
1 c. freshly grated Parmesan cheese
1 T. minced onion
1½ tsp. crushed and dried Italian herb seasonings
½ tsp. hot and spicy season salt
8 eggs
2 c. skim milk
2 T. finely chopped fresh basil leaves
1 c. (4-oz.) Provolone cheese, shredded

Heat oven to 350°. Sprinkle cooked sausage in bottom of non-stick sprayed 9 x 13-inch baking dish. Top with half of pimento and all of spinach. In a small bowl, whisk together the flour, cheese, onion, herbs and season salt. In a large bowl, beat eggs and milk, until blended; whisk in flour mixture, beating well. Pour over spinach and bake for 35-45 minutes or until just set. Sprinkle with basil and remaining pimento and top with the shredded cheese. Bake 2-3 minutes or until cheese is melted. Garnish with basil. Cut into squares and serve. Serves 10 or more.

KING RANCH CHICKEN

Mark Ballard

1 can (10½-oz.) cream of chicken soup
1 can (10¾-oz.) cream of mushroom soup
2 c. chicken broth
1 can (10-oz.) Ro-Tel tomatoes
12 tortillas, cut in pieces
3-4 lb. chicken, cooked in pieces
1 lg. onion, chopped
2 c. grated American cheese

Combine soups, chicken broth and tomatoes and set aside. Oil a 3-quart casserole. Layer half of tortilla pieces, half of chicken and half of cheese in the casserole. Pour half of chicken broth mixture over layers. Repeat layers of tortillas, chicken and onion, then pour remaining chicken broth over and top with remaining cheese. Bake 350° for 20 minutes. This may be frozen and reheated and will still taste great.

OVEN-BAKED CHICKEN PARMESAN

Betty S. Ragland

4 boneless, skinless chicken breasts
1 egg, beaten
¾ c. Italian seasoned dry bread crumbs
1 jar (26-oz.) Ragu pasta sauce
1 c. shredded mozarella cheese (4-oz.)

Preheat oven to 400°. Dip chicken in egg, then in bread crumbs. In 13 x 9-inch dish, arrange chicken. Bake uncovered 20 minutes. Pour sauce over chicken, top with cheese and bake 10 minutes or until chicken reaches 170° or is no longer pink in the center. Serve, if desired, with hot cooked pasta.

RUSTIC LASAGNA

Mary Ballard

9 lasagna noodles
2 cans (8-oz. each) low-sodium tomato sauce
1 clove garlic, minced
1 tsp. fresh oregano or ¼ tsp. dried oregano
1 pkg. (10-oz.) frozen chopped broccoli, thawed and squeezed of excess liquid
1 c. shredded carrots
1 container (15 to 16-oz.) part-skim ricotta cheese
¼ c. grated Parmesan cheese
1 c. shredded part-skim mozzarella cheese

Cook lasagna noodles according to package directions, but not add salt. While noodles are cooking preheat oven to 350°. Spray a 13 x 9-inch baking dish with vegetable cooking spray; set aside. In a small bowl, combine tomato sauce, garlic, and oregano. Mix well. In a medium bowl, combine broccoli, shredded carrots, ricotta, and Parmesan. Mix well. Drain noodles in a colander. Spread ½ cup of tomato sauce in bottom of prepared dish. Place 3 noodles on top of tomato sauce. Spread half of broccoli mixture over noodles. Spoon ½ cup of tomato sauce over broccoli; place 3 noodles on top. Spread with remaining broccoli mixture; top with ½ cup of tomato sauce. Top with remaining noodles and tomato sauce; sprinkle mozzarella over top. Bake until bubbling, about 45 minutes. Place on a wire rack and cool for about 15 minutes; cut into squares.

SAUSAGE NOODLE BAKE

Mark Ballard

1 large bag of wide egg noodles, cooked
1 pound ground sausage, fully cooked
1 can, cream of chicken soup
1 to 1½ c. sharp cheddar cheese
1 large jar, pimentos

Cook egg noodles, drain well and set aside. Brown sausage, drain well and set aside. Combine soup, ½ of cheese and pimentos. Stir in noodles and sausage, mixing well. Pour into baking dish that has been sprayed with coating. Top with remaining cheese. Bake at 450 degrees for approximately 20 minutes until mixture is bubbly and top is browned.

BRICKLE CRUNCH

Maryann Hall

35 saltine crackers (about 1 sleeve from a 16-oz. box)
2 sticks butter
1 c. sugar
10 or 11-oz. bag of Milk Chocolate Chips (about 2 c.)
10 or 11-oz. bag of Peanut Butter Chips (about 2 c.)

Preheat oven to 375°. Line a 10 x 15 cookie sheet with aluminum foil. Lay out the crackers on the cookie sheet, packing tightly. In a medium-sized saucepan, melt the butter, then add the sugar and boil, stirring frequently for 2 to 3 minutes until sugar is completely dissolved. Immediately pour the mixture over the crackers, spread evenly, bake for 7 minutes. Remove from oven and immediately sprinkle the chocolate and peanut butter chips over the crackers, spreading evenly as they melt. Spread carefully. Refrigerate for at least an hour or longer then break into sm. pieces. Serve immediately or refrigerate until ready to serve. If desired you may sprinkle a few chopped peanuts (roasted) on top of melted chips before refrigerating.

QUICK PRALINE BARS

Beverly Futch

24 graham cracker squares
½ c. brown sugar, packed
½ c. (1 stick) butter, melted
½ tsp. vanilla
½ c. chopped pecans

Heat oven to 350°. Arrange graham crackers in single layer in an ungreased jelly roll pan, 15½ x 10½ x 1-inch. Heat brown sugar and butter to boiling in 2 quart saucepan. Boil 1 minute, stirring constantly, remove from heat, stir in vanilla. Pour sugar mixture over crackers; spread evenly. Sprinkle with pecans. Bake 8-10 minutes or until bubbly. Cool slightly. Break into pieces. Makes about 2 dozen.

HI-PROTEIN ENERGY BARS

William C. Kitchens

½ c. butter or margarine
1⅓ c. brown sugar
2 eggs **1 tsp. vanilla**
⅓ c. cocoa or carob powder
¼ c. milk **¼ c. nonfat dry milk**
¼ c. wheat germ **1 c. whole wheat flour**
½ tsp. baking powder **¼ tsp. baking soda**
2 c. (12-oz.) peanut butter chips
½ c. raisins

Cream butter, sugar, eggs, and vanilla in large bowl until light and fluffy. Blend in cocoa and milk; add dry milk, wheat germ, flour, baking powder and baking soda. Beat until ingredients are thoroughly combined. Fold in peanut butter chips and raisins. Spread mixture evenly in a greased 13 x 9 x 2-inch baking pan. Bake at 350° for 30 to 35 minutes. Cool. Cut into bars.

Valentine's Day

The Day of X's and O's

Fancy and intricately cut out paper hearts. Handmade cards diligently put together with glue, construction paper and glitter. Beautiful silk ribbons in shades of reds, pinks and lavenders tied into bows. Dozens of roses creatively arranged in glass vases or bundled up with string. Colorful boxes filled to the brim with chocolates and other confections in assorted sizes, flavors and shapes. Plush teddy bears and other stuffed animals with cute and cuddly expressions. Quiet and romantic candle lit dinners. Four little letters that spell LOVE. These are the images that come to my mind when I think of Valentine's Day.

These tokens of affections serve as vehicles for us to show the ones closest to us how much they are appreciated and loved. It is the one day of the year that we pause to simply say, "I love you!" Holidays were established to serve as reminders during the year of how important the people around us really are. In our hectic schedules, they are there to gently nudge us into doing something special for the ones we love and adore.

In these startling and uncertain times, it is more critical than ever to take stock of our relationships as well as take inventory of what people mean to us. Taking people for granted is truly an unfortunate and sad deed. Life and people are precious and we need to treat them as such.

How can we really show someone we care? Over the years, I have demonstrated ways to go out and create something beautiful for the ones we love. We have tied bows and created wreaths, made cookies, brownies and fudge, arranged roses and even folded cloth napkins into the shape of a heart. These creations will certainly make someone feel special for the day, but how can we make them feel special for the year? Do we only need to express love on February 14?

The answer is no. We need to commit to a daily expression of love – to allow our feelings to spill out on regular days instead of just on holidays. In my opnion, there is nothing more tragic than not speaking directly from your heart. If it takes a card, flower or box of candy to do it, then that is what you should do. But it may be as simple as a kiss, a kind word, a hug, a phone call, or gently holding someone else's hand. It is a fact of life that no matter what background we come from, we all need positive reinforcement.

Now, I love a gift as well as the next person, but it need not be elaborate or expensive to get the message across. Some of the most precious gifts from the heart are handmade. My wife and I still cherish the valentines that our children created years ago with chubby hands, dull scissors and thick paste. They may be old, tattered and faded, but they are still filled to the brim with love. Just remember, strive to make each and every day a special one. It doesn't necessarily take diamonds or roses to say "I love you!" A simple gift or kind word from the heart will do just fine!

HOT CHOCOLATE MIX

Mark Ballard

8½ c. nonfat dry milk (25.6 pkg.)
1½ c. Coffeemate (6-oz. jar)
3 c. Instant Chocolate Drink mix for milk (16-oz.)
1½ c. confectioners' sugar
1½ c. mini-marshmallow

Mix all ingredients. Store in airtight container. Mix ½ cup of mixture with 9 ounces of water and heat.

CAPPUCCINO

Betty Jones

1 c. powdered non-dairy creamer
1 c. chocolate milk mix
⅔ c. instant coffee
½ c. sugar
½ tsp. ground cinnamon
½ tsp. ground nutmeg

Combine all ingredients. Mix well. Store in airtight container. To serve, place 1 tablespoon plus 1 teaspoon mix in cup. Add boiling water. Stir well. Yield: 33 servings.

HONEY ALMOND FRENCH TOAST

Mark Ballard

6 lg. eggs
1 c. milk
2 T. granulated sugar
1 T. honey
2 tsp. pure vanilla extract
1 tsp. *each*: grated orange zest and ground cinnamon
⅛ tsp. *each*: salt and black pepper
1 (12-oz.) day-old loaf challah or country-style bread, cut into 8 ¾-inch-thick slices
1⅔ c. sliced almonds
4 T. unsalted butter
confectioners' sugar
warm maple syrup, fresh fruit or marmalade

Preheat oven to 200°. In bowl, whisk eggs, milk, sugar, honey, vanilla, zest, cinnamon, salt and pepper. Put 4 slices bread into egg mixture, submerging. Let soak until slices have absorbed egg mixture and are very soft but still hold their shape; transfer to plate. Scatter both sides with half the almonds, pressing gently to adhere. In 12-inch nonstick skillet, heat 2 tablespoons butter over medium-low heat. Add soaked slices; cook 3 to 4 minutes per side, until golden-brown. Transfer slices to baking sheet; keep warm in oven. Wipe skillet clean with paper towels. Soak remaining bread in egg mixture, and press sides with almonds. Cook in 2 tablespoons butter. Dust toast with confectioners' sugar. Serve with syrup, fruit or marmalade.

BON-BON'S TEA CAKES

Mark Ballard

1¾ cups sugar
1 teaspoon vanilla
2 eggs
1 cup butter
4 cups plain flour
4 teaspoons baking powder

Combine all ingredients as listed. Roll out the dough on a floured surface. It should be thin. Cut using a cookie cutter. Place on cookie sheet. Bake at 350 degrees until lightly browned.

Use different "seasonal" cookie cutters and appropriately colored icing to make these cookies during any season of the year. Courtney and I still make these - for all the major holidays!

CHOCOLATE PIE

Jo Allen Ballard

3 eggs, separated
6 tablespoons flour
2 cups milk
3 tablespoons butter
1¾ cup sugar
4 tablespoons cocoa
2¼ teaspoons vanilla
1 9 inch pie crust

Cream yolks (retain whites for meringue) and sugar. Add flour and cocoa. Mix well. Add milk. Cook on low to medium heat in a sauce pan until thick. Add butter and vanilla. Pour into pie shell. Beat egg whites until stiff to make meringue and top pie. Cook at 400 degrees until meringue is golden brown.

CHOCOLATE FONDUE

Mark Ballard

3-4 Toblerone Candy bars
2-3 T. Brandy
whipping cream, enough to make chocolate dipping consistency

Melt Toblerones in double boiler. Add brandy, the chocolate will clump. Add enough whipping cream to make it dipping consistency. Will keep forever in refrigerator.

CHOCOLATE SAUCE

Olga Lien

½ c. sugar
1½ T. cornstarch
1 1-oz. square unsweetened chocolate, melted
dash of salt
½ c. cold water
1½ tsp. vanilla

Mix sugar and cornstarch in saucepan. Add melted chocolate, salt and water. Cook until thickens. Remove from heat and add butter and vanilla. This is one serving. The recipe can easily be doubled, tripled and so on to make more. Spoon over just about anything and top off with crushed Heath Bars for a great taste.

CHOCOLATE STUFF

From *The Sweet Potato Queens' Book of Love*

2 eggs
½ c. flour
1 stick butter
1½ tsp. vanilla
1 c. sugar
¼ tsp. salt
2 T. Hershey's Cocoa
nuts

Beat the eggs and combine with the sugar and flour. Add the salt and set aside. Melt the butter and combine with the cocoa. Dump the butter-cocoa mixture in to the other mixture and stir real good. Add vanilla and nuts (which are optional). Pour into a greased loaf pan. Set this pan into a pan of water and bake at 300 degrees for 40 to 50 minutes. When top is crunchy, it is done. Do not overcook. Eat with ice cream or whipped topping.

Absolutely fabulous! Our choc-o-holic friend Sharon introduced this to us and we've been in a sugar coma ever since!

CHOCOLATE NUT BALLS

Gloria Sikes

2 sticks margarine
1 c. coconut
2 c. crushed graham crackers
1 c. chopped nuts
1½ c. crunchy peanut butter
1 tsp. vanilla
1 box powdered sugar
2 pkg. chocolate flavored bark coating

Mix first 7 ingredients thoroughly. Form mixture into small balls. Melt bark coating in microwave, then dip balls until covered. Place on wax paper until cool. Makes about 50 pieces.

FUDGY BONBONS

Daphne Sides

1 12-oz. pkg. semi-sweet chocolate chips (2 cups)
¼ c. butter
1 14-oz. can sweetened condensed milk (not evaporated)
2 c. flour
1 tsp. vanilla
60 milk chocolate candy kisses, unwrapped
2 oz. white baking bar or white candy coating
1 tsp. shortening or oil

Heat oven to 350 degrees. In a medium saucepan, combine chocolate chips and butter; cook and stir over very low heat until chips are melted and smooth. Add sweetened condensed milk and mix well. Lightly spoon flour into measuring cup and level off. In medium bowl, combine flour, chocolate mixture and vanilla; mix well. Shape 1 tablespoon dough (use a measuring spoon) around each candy kiss, covering completely. Place 1 inch apart on ungreased cookies sheets. Bake for 6 to 8 minutes. DO NOT OVERBAKE. Cookies will be soft and appear shiny but will become firm as they cool. Remove from the cookie sheets carefully to cool. In a small saucepan, combine the white baking bar and shortening or oil. Cook and stir over low heat until melted and smooth. Drizzle over cookies. Store in tightly covered container. Makes 5 dozen.

CREME DE MENTHE BARS

Lucille Wientzen

Crust:
1 stick butter, melted
1 square unsweetened chocolate
½ c. sugar
1 c. flour

Mix all together, pour into a 9" square pan and bake at 350 degrees for 10 minutes.

Filling:
1 can sweetened condensed milk
1½ c. coconut
½ c. chopped pecans
1 T. creme de menthe

Pour over baked crust and bake for additional 25 to 30 minutes.

Topping: 12-oz. pkg. mint chocolate chips

Remove from oven and, while still hot, pour mint chocolate chips over the top and swirl with a pastry knife. If mint chocolate chips are unavailable, use chocolate mint wafer or mini mint patties.

Our "Yankee" friend Lucille Wientzen won $250 and Second Grand Prize for this recipe in the Cincinnati Enquirer Recipe Contest. You go, girl!

MISS NORA'S FUDGE

Mark Ballard

4½ c. sugar
1 tall can milk
2 T. butter
½ tsp. salt
12-oz. semi-sweet chocolate morsels
1 pkg. German chocolate squares
1 pt. marshmallow cream
2 c. nuts

Mix sugar, milk, butter and salt together and bring to a boil. Boil 6 minutes stirring constantly. Remove from heat and add chocolate morsels, German chocolate squares, marshmallow cream and nuts. Pour into buttered pan and allow to cool before cutting.

LUMPS CANDY

Mary McPeters

12-oz. Almond Bark or White Chocolate
1½ c. Captain Crunch
1½ c. Rice Krispies
1½ c. mixed nuts

Heat oven to 350°, turn oven off. In oven-proof bowl add almond bark or white chocolate, put in oven for 15 to 20 minutes or until melted. Add Captain Crunch, Rice Krispies and mixed nuts and drop by spoonful on to waxed paper.

MICROWAVE CREAMY FUDGE

William C. Kitchens

1½ c. sugar
12-oz. evaporated milk
¼ c. butter or margarine
2 c. miniature marshmallows
12-oz. chocolate chips (2 c.)
1 tsp. vanilla
1 c. chopped nuts (optional)

Mix sugar, milk, butter and a dash of salt in a 3 quart microwave safe bowl. Cover loosely with wax paper. Microwave on high 4 minutes. Uncover, continue to microwave 10 minutes more, stirring every 3 minutes. Continue cooking, stirring every 2 minutes, until candy thermometer reads 234 to 240 degrees (soft ball stage). Stir in marshmallows and chocolate chips and nuts if using. Stir vigorously until creamy and slightly glossy. Spread in a buttered 11 x 7 pan. Refrigerate 2 hours or until set.

PEANUT BUTTER CUPS

Mark Ballard

2 c. peanut butter
2½ c. confectioners' sugar
½ c. margarine, melted plus 1 T. margarine
12-oz. chocolate chips or semi-sweet chocolate

Mix peanut butter, ½ cup margarine and confectioners' sugar and put in greased and floured pan or paper lined muffin pans. Melt chocolate and margarine and pour on top. Chill in refrigerator and cut into squares.

CHOCOLATE-PEANUT BARS

Mark Ballard

1 c. butter, softened
1 c. softened peanut butter
1 16-oz. box powdered sugar
1½ c. vanilla wafers, crushed (about 45 cookies)
1 12-oz. pkg. semisweet chocolate morsels
½ c. whipping cream

Beat butter and peanut butter at medium speed with an electric mixer until blended. Add powdered sugar and vanilla wafer crumbs; beat until blended. Press mixture evenly into a lightly greased 13 x 9-inch baking pan lined with wax paper. Stir together chocolate morsels and whipping cream in a medium saucepan over low heat until melted and smooth. Spread evenly on top of peanut butter mixture. Chill 1 hour or until firm. Remove from refrigerator and let stand at room temperature 10 minutes or until slightly softened. Cut into 48 bars.

CHOCOLATE TOFFEE TRIFLE

Mark Ballard

Duncan Hines Cake Mix
Chocolate pudding (not instant), lg. size
2 Heath bars (5-oz.) **2¼ c. milk**
¾ c. Kahlua
lg. ctn. Cool Whip

Bake cake in sheet pan, as it is easier to slice in half. Let cool completely. Cook pudding using 2¼ cup milk and ¾ cup Kahlua and stir slowly until it bubbles for a couple minutes. Cool pudding completely. Crush Heath bars up. In trifle bowl or large size bowl layer cake, pudding, Cool Whip, Heath bars and repeat. If you want to end up with cool whip on top, layer Heath bars and then cool whip.

YUMMY MICROWAVE PEANUT BUTTER FUDGE

Sharon Freeman

1 12-oz. bag semi-sweet chocolate chips
1 12-oz. jar crunchy peanut butter
1 14-oz. can sweetened condensed milk

Line a 8x8-inch baking pan with wax paper. Set aside. In 1½ quart bowl, melt chocolate and peanut butter in a microwave on high (100%) about 3 minutes. Remove and stir well. Add milk gradually, stirring until well blended. Pour mixture into prepared pan and refrigerate at least 4 hours to chill well. Cut into 1-inch pieces when firm. Makes 64 squares.

TOFFEE BARS

Mark Ballard

2 c. flour
1 c. light brown sugar
½ c. butter
1 c. chopped pecans
1 c. butter, no substitute
¾ c. light brown sugar
1 6-oz. pkg. semi-sweet chocolate morsels

Preheat oven to 350°. Mix together the flour and 1 cup brown sugar. Cut in ½ cup butter. Press mixture into a 9 x 13-inch ungreased metal pan. Sprinkle pecans over the mixture. Bring to a boil the butter and remaining sugar and boil exactly one minute, stirring constantly. Pour over pressed mixture and bake in preheated 350° oven exactly 20 minutes. Let sit a minute, then sprinkle with the chocolate morsels. When completely softened, spread the chocolate with a spatula. Cut while still hot. Chill thoroughly but return to room temperature before cutting. Freezes well.

TREE BARK

Gayle Fox

2 sticks butter
1 c. light brown sugar
1 lg. bag semi-sweet chocolate morsels
saltines

Line a baking sheet with aluminum foil. Place saltines side by side to form a layer on top of foil. Boil sugar and butter for 3 minutes. Pour over saltines. Bake at 400° for 7 minutes. Immediately sprinkle with chocolate chips and gently spread to cover the saltine/butter mixture with a spatula. Allow to cool/harden. Break into pieces and put in airtight container.

WHITE CHOCOLATE-ORANGE DREAM COOKIES

Jo Ann Stephens

1 c. butter or margarine, softened
⅔ c. firmly packed light brown sugar
½ c. granulated sugar
1 lg. egg
1 T. grated orange zest
2 tsp. orange extract
2¼ c. all-purpose flour
¾ tsp. baking soda
½ tsp. salt
1 pkg. (12-oz.) white chocolate chips

Preheat oven to 350°. In a mixing bowl, beat first 3 ingredients at medium speed of an electric mixture until creamy. Add egg, orange zest, and orange extract, beating until blended. Combine flour, baking soda, and salt; gradually add to sugar mixture, beating just until blended after each addition. Stir in chips. Drop dough by rounded tablespoonfuls onto ungreased baking sheet. Bake 10 to 12 minutes until edges are lightly browned. Cool on baking sheets 2 minutes; transfer to wire racks to cool completely. Yield about 3½ dozen cookies.

CHOCOLATE CARAMEL PECAN BARS

Denise Chambers

Crust
½ c. powdered sugar
½ c. butter, softened
1 T. whipping cream
1 c. plain flour

Heat oven to 325 degrees. Grease a 9-inch square pan. In medium bowl, combine powdered sugar, butter and whipping cream. Blend well. Add flour, mix until crumbly. With floured hands, press evenly into greased pan. Bake for 15 to 20 minutes or until firm to the touch.

Filling
24 caramels, unwrapped
⅓ c. whipping cream
2 c. pecan halves

While the crust is baking, in a medium sauce, over low heat, combine caramels and cream, stirring frequently until caramels are melted and the mixture is smooth. (This can be done in a microwave. Heat the mixture for 1 minute and stir; for 1 minute and stir; keep repeating until the mixture is smooth. Do not burn.) Remove from heat or the microwave and add pecans. Stir well to coat the nuts. Immediately spoon over the baked crust. Spread evenly to cover.

Topping
1 tsp. butter
½ c. milk chocolate chips
2 T. whipping cream

In a small sauce pan over low heat, melt butter and chocolate chips, stirring constantly. (This melting can be done in a microwave very carefully as mentioned in the filling.) Stir in whipping cream. Drizzle this mixture over the filling.

Refrigerate for 1 hour or until filling is firm. Cut into bars. Makes approximately 24 bars.

BUTTERFINGER COOKIE BARS

Jo Ann Stephens

1 c. sugar
1 c. light corn syrup
1½ c. peanut butter
5 c. Special K cereal
1 6-oz. pkg. chocolate chips
1 6-oz. pkg. butterscotch chips

Mix sugar and syrup and bring to boil. Add peanut butter and Special K. Put in buttered jelly roll pan. Melt chocolate chips and butterscotch chips and spread on top. Allow to cool and cut into bars.

CHOCOLATE CHIP CHEESECAKE BARS

Vicki Brantley

2 (20-oz.) rolls of refrigerated chocolate chip cookie dough
2 (8-oz.) packages cream cheese, softened
2 c. sugar
3 eggs

Freeze rolls of cookie dough; slice one roll into 40 (⅛ inch) slices. Arrange cookie slices in a well-greased 15 x 10 x 1-inch jellyroll pan. Press cookie dough together to form bottom crust. Set aside. Beat cream cheese at high speed of an electric mixer until light and fluffy; gradually add sugar, and mix well. Add eggs, one at a time, beating well after each addition. Pour mixture onto cookie layer. Slice remaining dough into (⅛ inch) slices; arrange over cream cheese mixture. Bake at 350° for 45 minutes. Cool and cut into squares.

St. Patrick's Day

ST. PATRICK'S FRUIT PLATTER

Mark Ballard

1 can (16-oz.) Bartlett-pear halves
leaf lettuce
2 c. shredded iceberg lettuce
2 or 3 California kiwi fruit, pared and sliced
Poppy Seed dressing

Drain pears; reserve 1 tablespoon liquid for Poppy Seed dressing. Cut pear halves in half lengthwise. Line platter with leaf lettuce; arrange shredded lettuce in center. Place pears and kiwi fruit on lettuce. Drizzle with Poppy Seed Dressing; pass extra dressing. Makes 6 servings.

Poppy Seed Dressing:
¼ c. oil
2 T. lime juice
1 T. reserved pear liquid
1 tsp. sugar
⅛ tsp. dry mustard
dash salt
1 tsp. poppy seeds

Combine ¼ cup oil, 2 tablespoons lime juice, 1 tablespoon reserved liquid, 1 teaspoon sugar, ⅛ teaspoon dry mustard and dash salt. Add 1 teaspoon poppy seeds; use wire whisk to blend well. Makes about ½ cup.

WATERGATE SALAD

Jo Ballard

1 3½-oz. pkg. instant pistachio pudding mix
1 15½-oz. can crushed pineapple
1 12-oz. carton Cool Whip
1 c. miniature marshmallows (optional)
½ c. chopped nuts

Pour undrained pineapple over pudding mix and stir. Fold in remaining ingredients. Serve 8 to 10.

This is one of my very favorite congealed salads of all time!

GREEN BEANS WITH ALMONDS

Gladys Aaron

½ c. slivered almonds
½ c. butter
2 T. lemon juice
2 cans French Green beans
salt to taste

Cook ½ cup slivered almonds in ½ cup butter over low heat until golden looking. Remove from heat; add 2 tablespoons lemon juice and salt to taste. Pour over 2 cans of heated and drained French green beans.

GLORIFIED HASH BROWNS

Mrs. J. B. Franklin

2 can (10¾-oz. each) condensed cream of celery soup
2 ctn. (8-oz each) spreadable chive and onion cream cheese
1 pkg. (2 lb.) frozen cubed hash brown potatoes, thawed
1 c. (4-oz.) shredded cheddar cheese, divided

Combine soup and cream cheese in large (Dutch-oven size) pan, and heat over very low heat until cream cheese is melted, stirring frequently. Add potatoes and ½ cup of the sharp cheddar cheese and stir until coated. Spoon into a greased 13 x 9 x 2-inch baking dish. Bake, uncovered, at 350° for 35-40 minutes, or until potatoes are tender. Sprinkle with remaining ½ cup cheddar cheese. Bake 3-5 minutes longer or until cheese is barely melted. Yield: 10 servings.

END-OF-THE-RAINBOW MACARONI AND CHEESE

William C. Kitchens

1 T. vegetable oil
1 lb. elbow macaroni
8 T. (1 stick) plus 1 T. butter
½ c. (2-oz.) shredded Muenster cheese
½ c. (2-oz.) shredded mild Cheddar cheese
½ c. (2-oz.) shredded sharp Cheddar cheese
½ c. (2-oz.) shredded Monterey Jack cheese
2 c. half-and-half
1 c. (8-oz.) Velveeta, cut into small cubes
2 lg. eggs, lightly beaten
¼ tsp. seasoned salt
⅛ tsp. freshly ground black pepper

Preheat the oven to 350°. Lightly butter a deep 2½-quart casserole. Bring the large pot of salted water to a boil over high heat. Add the oil, then the elbow macaroni, and cook until the macaroni is just tender, about 7 minutes. Do not overcook. Drain well. Return to the cooking pot. In a small saucepan, melt eight tablespoons of the butter. Stir into the macaroni. In a large bowl, mix the Muenster, mild and sharp cheddar, and Monterey Jack cheeses. To the macaroni, add the half-and-half, 1½ cups of the shredded cheese, the Velveeta, and the eggs. Season with salt and pepper. Transfer to the buttered casserole. Sprinkle with the remaining ½ cup of the shredded cheese and dot with the remaining one tablespoons of butter. Bake until it's bubbling around the edges, about 35 minutes. Serve hot.

SPICY STEWED CABBAGE

Audrey and Veronica Hevican

1 med. size cabbage
1 med. bell pepper, chopped
1 med. onion, chopped
6 slices bacon
¼ c. vinegar
¼ c. water
1 T. lemon juice
1 T. sugar
½ tsp. garlic salt
½ tsp. cayenne pepper
1 tsp. dry mustard
salt and pepper to taste

In a large skillet, fry 6 slices of bacon. Remove bacon, leaving grease in frying pan. Set bacon aside. Add vinegar, water, lemon juice, sugar, garlic salt, red pepper and dry mustard. Bring to a boil, add cabbage, peppers, onions and bacon pieces and stir in. Remove from heat and let sit for 3 hours, stirring occasionally, then finish cooking over low heat until done.

BARBARA'S BRISKET

Elizabeth "Bebe" Wahlsand

1 whole brisket (first cut and well trimmed of fat)
¾ bottle of med. size ketchup
pinch or 2 of garlic salt
1 pkg. dry onion soup mix
½ c. brown sugar

Mix together the dry soup mix, ketchup, brown sugar and garlic salt. Spread over meat. Wrap tightly in 2 sheets of aluminum foil being careful to prevent any juice from leaking out. Bake at 325° for 2 hours or longer if desired. This makes its own gravy and can be sliced like London Broil. Great with rice and a salad. Serves 12.

CORNED BEEF & CABBAGE DELIGHT

Debra Ballard

4 to 5 lb. corned beef
water to cover
2 bay leaves
6 peppercorns
1 lg. head green cabbage

Tie beef into shape with cord. Place it in large heavy pot and cover with cold water. Bring water to boil; drain off. Cover beef with fresh water; add bay leaves and peppercorns. Cook over low heat for 3 to 4 hours or until meat is tender. About 12 to 15 minutes prior to serving, add cabbage cut into wedges and cook uncovered until cabbage is tender. Remove string from beef and slice. Serve with horseradish cream. Serves 8 to 10.

Horseradish Cream:

1 c. sour cream	**1 tsp. salt**
1 T. fresh horseradish, grated	**1 tsp. pepper, freshly ground**
1 T. heavy cream	**1 tsp. hot mustard**

Combine ingredients and serve hot or cold.

SHAMROCK COOKIES

Mark Ballard

1 pkg. (16-oz.) white angel food cake mix
½ c. water
1 tsp. vanilla
½ c. chopped nuts
1 pkg. (7-oz.) shredded coconut
1 c. ready-to-spread vanilla frosting
2 or 3 drops green food color
12 to 15 spearmint gumdrop leaves
sugar

Heat oven to 350°. Cover cookie sheet with aluminum foil or heavy brown paper. Beat cake mix (dry), water and vanilla on low speed, scraping bowl constantly, 30 seconds. Beat on medium speed, scraping bowl occasionally, 1 minute. Fold in nuts and coconut. For each shamrock, drop batter by three ½ teaspoonfuls with edges touching (place each shamrock about 2 inches apart). Bake until set and edges are brown, 12 to 15 minutes. Slide foil onto wire rack; cool cookies completely before removing from foil. Mix frosting and food color; frost cookies. Flatten gumdrop leaves on sugared surface with rolling pin. Cut flattened leaves lengthwise into halves. Place 1 half between 2 leaves of each shamrock to form stem. Makes 2 to 2½ dozen cookies.

BUTTER COOKIES

Emma Richardson

1 lb. (4 sticks) butter, room temperature
1 c. sugar
2 whole eggs
1 T. flavoring - any combination of favorites to make 1 T. (vanilla, lemon, almond, etc.)
¼ to ½ tsp. red or green color (Green for St. Patrick's Day!)
5½ c. plain all-purpose flour
1 tsp. *each*: baking powder and salt

Cream together butter and sugar with blending fork or large spoon; then add eggs 1 at the time, mixing thoroughly, then add flavoring and color (if used). Always put the coloring in before the flour, because it is almost impossible to get the color mixed properly after the flour has been added Sift together flour, baking powder and salt. Begin adding this mixture until all is blended into the dough. You will have to use your hands to finish this because it gets rather stiff. If you use a cookie press, you can begin at this point, because if the dough gets too cold it will be too stiff to go through the cookie press. You can place cookies fairly close together on the ungreased baking sheet because they do not spread much. Bake at 375° for 10 to 12 minutes. When done, remove from sheets and cool on a paper towel-covered rack. Then store in a can with a good top. (If you like to roll and cut out cookies with different cutters, you should chill the dough first but not too long, it gets too stiff. Then roll out on a lightly floured surface, cut out and place on a ungreased baking sheet and bake the same as above.)

Index of Recipes

53231E-sg-5

Appetizers

Beverages

Breakfast

Cakes

Candies and Cookies

Casseroles and Main Dishes

Desserts, Pastries and Pies

Meats

Salads and Soups

Vegetables and Side Dishes

How to Order

Get your additional copies of this cookbook or order Mark's other books:

- by returning this order form and your check or money order to

Mark Allen Ballard
P O Box 4232
Macon, GA 31208

- by signing on to www.markballard.com and clicking on Mark's Merchandise (details and ordering instructions)

- by calling (478)757-6877 and leaving a message for Mark

Order Form
(clip and mail)

Please send me :

______ copies of *The Four Seasons* cookbook at $19.95 per copy plus $4.00 for shipping and handling per book.

______ copies of *Blossoms & Bees, Peaches & Poundcakes* cookbook at $14.95 plus $3.00 for shipping and handling per book.

______ copies of *Colorful Comedies and Creative Celebrations* short story book at $12.95 plus $3.00 for shipping and handling per book.

Enclosed is my check or money order for $________.

Mail books to:

Name ____

Address ____

City____________________ State ______ Zip ________

Please personalize book(s) to: __________________________

Mark Allen Ballard, The Artist

Since childhood, Mark Allen Ballard, known to television viewers as THE ARTIST™, has combined his incredible artistic talent with a marvelous sense of humor to amaze and entertain.

Entertainer

In 1996, at the urging of friends and clients who had attended fabulous parties and tours that Mark organized for area charities, he held a seminar on holiday entertaining and decorating. The "fans" called for more and Mark now combines his artistic talent, wonderful sense of humor and story-telling ability to entertain standing-room only crowds at frequent seminars and speaking engagements, at public appearances and on regional television several times a week. His one-man comedy shows are standing room only affairs that benefit non-profit organizations in his hometown.

Author/Columnist

Mark's first book, a cookbook, *Blossoms & Bees, Peaches & Poundcakes,* was published in the fall of 1999 and is now in its sixth printing. His second book featuring stories of growing up and living in the South, *Colorful Comedies and Creative Celebrations, A Lighter Look at Life as Told by a Raised Right Southern Gentleman,* was published in the fall of 2000. Mark's advice column on decorating, entertaining and crafts is featured weekly in *The Macon Telegraph* and in each issue of *Macon Magazine.*

Artist/Designer

At an early age, Mark focused his talent on the visual arts, graduating with honors from the Atlanta College of Art at the High Museum in Atlanta. Mark's paintings have found their way into private, corporate and public collections all over the United States and in several foreign countries. In addition to one-dimensional paintings and murals, Mark is also known for his exquisite painted furniture, lamps, porcelains and fabrics. In recent years, he has also been in demand in the areas of floral and interior design. His line of note cards, limited edition prints and porcelain plates are carried in finer frame, gift and stationary shops nationwide.

PANTRY BASICS

A WELL-STOCKED PANTRY provides all the makings for a good meal. With the right ingredients, you can quickly create a variety of satisfying, delicious meals for family or guests. Keeping these items in stock also means avoiding extra trips to the grocery store, saving you time and money. Although everyone's pantry is different, there are basic items you should always have. Add other items according to your family's needs. For example, while some families consider chips, cereals and snacks as must-haves, others can't be without feta cheese and imported olives. Use these basic pantry suggestions as a handy reference list when creating your grocery list. Don't forget refrigerated items like milk, eggs, cheese and butter.

STAPLES

Baker's chocolate
Baking powder
Baking soda
Barbeque sauce
Bread crumbs (plain or seasoned)
Chocolate chips
Cocoa powder
Cornmeal
Cornstarch
Crackers
Flour
Honey
Ketchup
Lemon juice
Mayonnaise or salad dressing
Non-stick cooking spray
Nuts (almonds, pecans, walnuts)
Oatmeal
Oil (olive, vegetable)
Pancake baking mix
Pancake syrup
Peanut butter
Shortening
Sugar (granulated, brown, powdered)
Vinegar

PACKAGED/CANNED FOODS

Beans (canned, dry)
Broth (beef, chicken)
Cake mixes with frosting
Canned diced tomatoes
Canned fruit
Canned mushrooms
Canned soup
Canned tomato paste & sauce
Canned tuna & chicken
Cereal
Dried soup mix
Gelatin (flavored or plain)
Gravies
Jarred Salsa
Milk (evaporated, sweetened condensed)
Non-fat dry milk
Pastas
Rice (brown, white)
Spaghetti sauce

SPICES/SEASONINGS

Basil
Bay leaves
Black pepper
Bouillon cubes (beef, chicken)
Chives
Chili powder
Cinnamon
Mustard (dried, prepared)
Garlic powder or salt
Ginger
Nutmeg
Onion powder or salt
Oregano
Paprika
Parsley
Rosemary
Sage
Salt
Soy sauce
Tarragon
Thyme
Vanilla
Worcestershire sauce
Yeast

HERBS & SPICES

DRIED VS. FRESH. While dried herbs are convenient, they don't generally have the same purity of flavor as fresh herbs. Ensure dried herbs are still fresh by checking if they are green and not faded. Crush a few leaves to see if the aroma is still strong. Always store them in an air-tight container away from light and heat.

BASIL Sweet, warm flavor with an aromatic odor. Use whole or ground. Good with lamb, fish, roast, stews, beef, vegetables, dressing and omelets.

BAY LEAVES Pungent flavor. Use whole leaf but remove before serving. Good in vegetable dishes, seafood, stews and pickles.

CARAWAY Spicy taste and aromatic smell. Use in cakes, breads, soups, cheese and sauerkraut.

CELERY SEED Strong taste which resembles the vegetable. Can be used sparingly in pickles and chutney, meat and fish dishes, salads, bread, marinades, dressings and dips.

CHIVES Sweet, mild flavor like that of onion. Excellent in salads, fish, soups and potatoes.

CILANTRO Use fresh. Excellent in salads, fish, chicken, rice, beans and Mexican dishes.

CINNAMON Sweet, pungent flavor. Widely used in many sweet baked goods, chocolate dishes, cheesecakes, pickles, chutneys and hot drinks.

CORIANDER Mild, sweet, orangy flavor and available whole or ground. Common in curry powders and pickling spice and also used in chutney, meat dishes, casseroles, Greek-style dishes, apple pies and baked goods.

CURRY POWDER Spices are combined to proper proportions to give a distinct flavor to meat, poultry, fish and vegetables.

DILL Both seeds and leaves are flavorful. Leaves may be used as a garnish or cooked with fish, soup, dressings, potatoes and beans. Leaves or the whole plant may be used to flavor pickles.

FENNEL Sweet, hot flavor. Both seeds and leaves are used. Use in small quantities in pies and baked goods. Leaves can be boiled with fish.

HERBS & SPICES

GINGER A pungent root, this aromatic spice is sold fresh, dried or ground. Use in pickles, preserves, cakes, cookies, soups and meat dishes.

MARJORAM May be used both dried or green. Use to flavor fish, poultry, omelets, lamb, stew, stuffing and tomato juice.

MINT Aromatic with a cool flavor. Excellent in beverages, fish, lamb, cheese, soup, peas, carrots and fruit desserts.

NUTMEG Whole or ground. Used in chicken and cream soups, cheese dishes, fish cakes, and with chicken and veal. Excellent in custards, milk puddings, pies and cakes.

OREGANO Strong, aromatic odor. Use whole or ground in tomato juice, fish, eggs, pizza, omelets, chili, stew, gravy, poultry and vegetables.

PAPRIKA A bright red pepper, this spice is used in meat, vegetables and soups or as a garnish for potatoes, salads or eggs.

PARSLEY Best when used fresh, but can be used dried as a garnish or as a seasoning. Try in fish, omelets, soup, meat, stuffing and mixed greens.

ROSEMARY Very aromatic. Can be used fresh or dried. Season fish, stuffing, beef, lamb, poultry, onions, eggs, bread and potatoes. Great in dressings.

SAFFRON Aromatic, slightly bitter taste. Only a pinch needed to flavor and color dishes such as bouillabaisse, chicken soup, rice, paella, fish sauces, buns and cakes. Very expensive, so where a touch of color is needed, use turmeric instead, but the flavor will not be the same.

SAGE Use fresh or dried. The flowers are sometimes used in salads. May be used in tomato juice, fish, omelets, beef, poultry, stuffing, cheese spreads and breads.

TARRAGON Leaves have a pungent, hot taste. Use to flavor sauces, salads, fish, poultry, tomatoes, eggs, green beans, carrots and dressings.

THYME Sprinkle leaves on fish or poultry before broiling or baking. Throw a few sprigs directly on coals shortly before meat is finished grilling.

TURMERIC Aromatic, slightly bitter flavor. Should be used sparingly in curry powder and relishes and to color cakes and rice dishes.

Use 3 times more fresh herbs if substituting fresh for dried.

BAKING BREADS

HINTS FOR BAKING BREADS

- Kneading dough for 30 seconds after mixing improves the texture of baking powder biscuits.
- Instead of shortening, use cooking or salad oil in waffles and hot cakes.
- When bread is baking, a small dish of water in the oven will help keep the crust from hardening.
- Dip a spoon in hot water to measure shortening, butter, etc., and the fat will slip out more easily.
- Small amounts of leftover corn may be added to pancake batter for variety.
- To make bread crumbs, use the fine cutter of a food grinder and tie a large paper bag over the spout in order to prevent flying crumbs.
- When you are doing any sort of baking, you get better results if you remember to preheat your cookie sheet, muffin tins or cake pans.

3 RULES FOR USE OF LEAVENING AGENTS

1. In simple flour mixtures, use 2 teaspoons baking powder to leaven 1 cup flour. Reduce this amount 1/2 teaspoon for each egg used.
2. To 1 teaspoon soda, use 2 1/4 teaspoons cream of tartar, 2 cups freshly soured milk or 1 cup molasses.
3. To substitute soda and an acid for baking powder, divide the amount of baking powder by 4. Take that as your measure and add acid according to rule 2.

PROPORTIONS OF BAKING POWDER TO FLOUR

biscuits ....to 1 cup flour use 1 1/4 tsp. baking powder
cake with oil ....to 1 cup flour use 1 tsp. baking powder
muffins ....to 1 cup flour use 1 1/2 tsp. baking powder
popovers ....to 1 cup flour use 1 1/4 tsp. baking powder
waffles ....to 1 cup flour use 1 1/4 tsp. baking powder

PROPORTIONS OF LIQUID TO FLOUR

pour batter ....to 1 cup liquid use 1 cup flour
drop batter ....to 1 cup liquid use 2 to 2 1/2 cups flour
soft dough ....to 1 cup liquid use 3 to 3 1/2 cups flour
stiff dough ....to 1 cup liquid use 4 cups flour

TIME & TEMPERATURE CHART

Breads	Minutes	Temperature
biscuits	12 - 15	400° - 450°
cornbread	25 - 30	400° - 425°
gingerbread	40 - 50	350° - 370°
loaf	50 - 60	350° - 400°
nut bread	50 - 75	350°
popovers	30 - 40	425° - 450°
rolls	20 - 30	400° - 450°

BAKING & DESSERTS

PERFECT COOKIES

Cookie dough that must be rolled is much easier to handle after it has been refrigerated for 10 to 30 minutes. This keeps the dough from sticking, even though it may be soft. If not done, the soft dough may require more flour and too much flour makes cookies hard and brittle. Place on a floured board only as much dough as can be easily managed. Flour the rolling pin slightly and roll lightly to desired thickness. Cut shapes close together and add trimmings to dough that needs to be rolled. Place pans or sheets in upper third of oven. Watch cookies carefully while baking in order to avoid burned edges. When sprinkling sugar on cookies, try putting it into a salt shaker in order to save time.

PERFECT PIES

- Pie crust will be better and easier to make if all the ingredients are cool.
- The lower crust should be placed in the pan so that it covers the surface smoothly. Air pockets beneath the surface will push the crust out of shape while baking.
- Folding the top crust over the lower crust before crimping will keep juices in the pie.
- When making custard pie, bake at a high temperature for about 10 minutes to prevent a soggy crust. Then finish baking at a low temperature.
- When making cream pie, sprinkle crust with powdered sugar in order to prevent it from becoming soggy.

PERFECT CAKES

- Fill cake pans two-thirds full and spread batter into corners and sides, leaving a slight hollow in the center.
- Cake is done when it shrinks from the sides of the pan or if it springs back when touched lightly with the finger.
- After removing a cake from the oven, place it on a rack for about 5 minutes. Then, the sides should be loosened and the cake turned out on a rack in order to finish cooling.
- Do not frost cakes until thoroughly cool.
- Icing will remain where you put it if you sprinkle cake with powdered sugar first.

TIME & TEMPERATURE CHART

Dessert	Time	Temperature
butter cake, layer	20 - 40 min.	380° - 400°
butter cake, loaf	40 - 60 min.	360° - 400°
cake, angel	50 - 60 min.	300° - 360°
cake, fruit	3 - 4 hrs.	275° - 325°
cake, sponge	40 - 60 min.	300° - 350°
cookies, molasses	18 - 20 min.	350° - 375°
cookies, thin	10 - 12 min.	380° - 390°
cream puffs	45 - 60 min.	300° - 350°
meringue	40 - 60 min.	250° - 300°
pie crust	20 - 40 min.	400° - 500°

VEGETABLES & FRUITS

COOKING TIME TABLE

Vegetable	Cooking Method	Time
artichokes	boiled	40 min.
	steamed	45 - 60 min.
asparagus tips	boiled	10 - 15 min.
beans, lima	boiled	20 - 40 min.
	steamed	60 min.
beans, string	boiled	15 - 35 min.
	steamed	60 min.
beets, old	boiled or steamed	1 - 2 hours.
beets, young with skin	boiled	30 min.
	steamed	60 min.
	baked	70 - 90 min.
broccoli, flowerets	boiled	5 - 10 min.
broccoli, stems	boiled	20 - 30 min.
brussels sprouts	boiled	20 - 30 min.
cabbage, chopped	boiled	10 - 20 min.
	steamed	25 min.
carrots, cut across	boiled	8 - 10 min.
	steamed	40 min.
cauliflower, flowerets	boiled	8 - 10 min.
cauliflower, stem down	boiled	20 - 30 min.
corn, green, tender	boiled	5 - 10 min.
	steamed	15 min.
	baked	20 min.
corn on the cob	boiled	8 - 10 min.
	steamed	15 min.
eggplant, whole	boiled	30 min.
	steamed	40 min.
	baked	45 min.
parsnips	boiled	25 - 40 min.
	steamed	60 min.
	baked	60 - 75 min.
peas, green	boiled or steamed	5 - 15 min.
potatoes	boiled	20 - 40 min.
	steamed	60 min.
	baked	45 - 60 min.
pumpkin or squash	boiled	20 - 40 min.
	steamed	45 min.
	baked	60 min.
tomatoes	boiled	5 - 15 min.
turnips	boiled	25 - 40 min.

DRYING TIME TABLE

Fruit	Sugar or Honey	Cooking Time
apricots	1/4 c. for each cup of fruit	about 40 min.
figs	1 T. for each cup of fruit	about 30 min.
peaches	1/4 c. for each cup of fruit	about 45 min.
prunes	2 T. for each cup of fruit	about 45 min.

VEGETABLES & FRUITS

BUYING FRESH VEGETABLES

Artichokes: Look for compact, tightly closed heads with green, clean-looking leaves. Avoid those with leaves that are brown or separated.

Asparagus: Stalks should be tender and firm; tips should be close and compact. Choose the stalks with very little white; they are more tender. Use asparagus soon because it toughens quickly.

Beans, Snap: Those with small seeds inside the pods are best. Avoid beans with dry-looking pods.

Broccoli, Brussels Sprouts and Cauliflower: Flower clusters on broccoli and cauliflower should be tight and close together. Brussels sprouts should be firm and compact. Smudgy, dirty spots may indicate pests or disease.

Cabbage and Head Lettuce: Choose heads that are heavy for their size. Avoid cabbage with worm holes and lettuce with discoloration or soft rot.

Cucumbers: Choose long, slender cucumbers for best quality. May be dark or medium green, but yellow ones are undesirable.

Mushrooms: Caps should be closed around the stems. Avoid black or brown gills.

Peas and Lima Beans: Select pods that are well-filled but not bulging. Avoid dried, spotted, yellow or limp pods.

BUYING FRESH FRUITS

Bananas: Skin should be free of bruises and black or brown spots. Purchase them slightly green and allow them to ripen at room temperature.

Berries: Select plump, solid berries with good color. Avoid stained containers which indicate wet or leaky berries. Berries with clinging caps, such as blackberries and raspberries, may be unripe. Strawberries without caps may be overripe.

Melons: In cantaloupes, thick, close netting on the rind indicates best quality. Cantaloupes are ripe when the stem scar is smooth and the space between the netting is yellow or yellow-green. They are best when fully ripe with fruity odor.

Honeydews are ripe when rind has creamy to yellowish color and velvety texture. Immature honeydews are whitish-green.

Ripe watermelons have some yellow color on one side. If melons are white or pale green on one side, they are not ripe.

Oranges, Grapefruit and Lemons: Choose those heavy for their size. Smoother, thinner skins usually indicate more juice. Most skin markings do not affect quality. Oranges with a slight greenish tinge may be just as ripe as fully colored ones. Light or greenish-yellow lemons are more tart than deep yellow ones. Avoid citrus fruits showing withered, sunken or soft areas.

NAPKIN FOLDING

FOR BEST RESULTS, use well-starched linen napkins if possible. For more complicated folds, 24-inch napkins work best. Practice the folds with newspapers. Children will have fun decorating the table once they learn these attractive folds!

SHIELD

Easy fold. Elegant with monogram in corner.

Instructions:

1. Fold into quarter size. If monogrammed, ornate corner should face down.
2. Turn up folded corner three-quarters.
3. Overlap right side and left side points.
4. Turn over; adjust sides so they are even, single point in center.
5. Place point up or down on plate, or left of plate.

1, 2

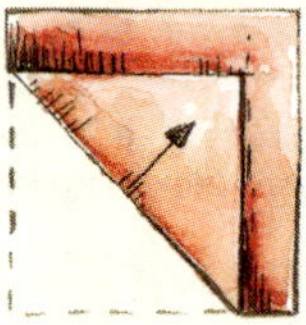

3

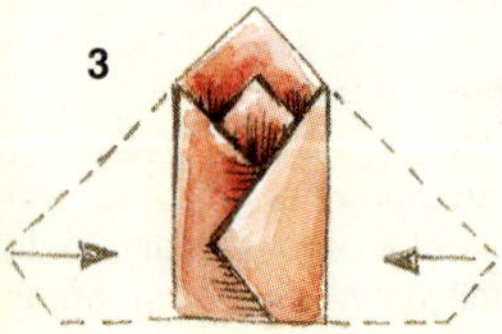

4

ROSETTE

Elegant on plate.

Instructions:

1. Fold left and right edges to center, leaving 1/2" opening along center.
2. Pleat firmly from top edge to bottom edge. Sharpen edges with hot iron.
3. Pinch center together. If necessary, use small piece of pipe cleaner to secure and top with single flower.
4. Spread out rosette.

1

2

3

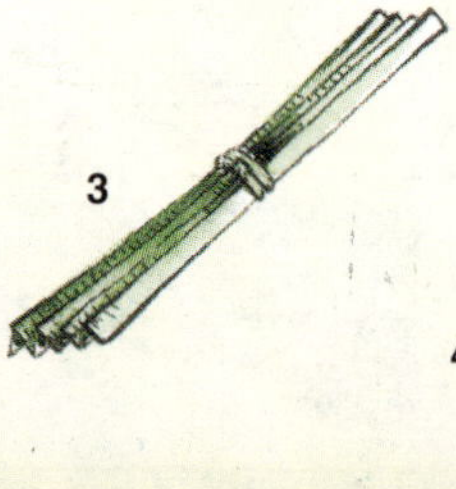

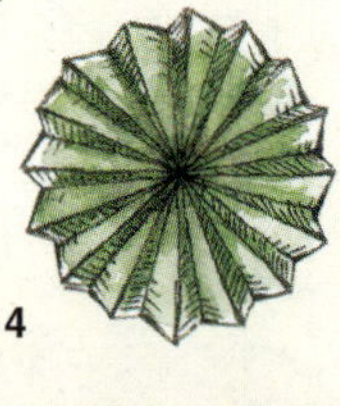

4

NAPKIN FOLDING

CANDLE

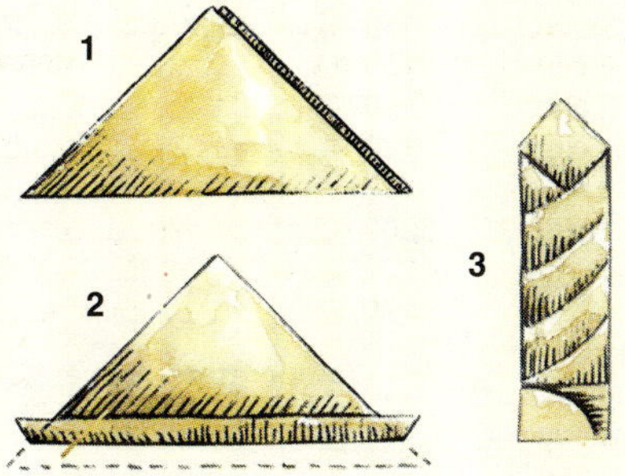

Easy to do; can be decorated.

Instructions:

1. Fold into triangle, point at top.
2. Turn lower edge up 1".
3. Turn over, folded edge down.
4. Roll tightly from left to right.
5. Tuck in corner. Stand upright.

FAN

Pretty in napkin ring or on plate.

Instructions:

1. Fold top and bottom edges to center.
2. Fold top and bottom edges to center a second time.
3. Pleat firmly from the left edge. Sharpen edges with hot iron.
4. Spread out fan. Balance flat folds of each side on table. Well-starched napkins will hold shape.

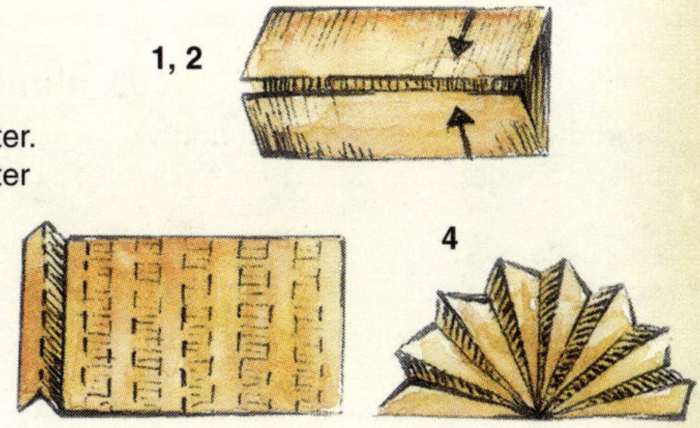

LILY

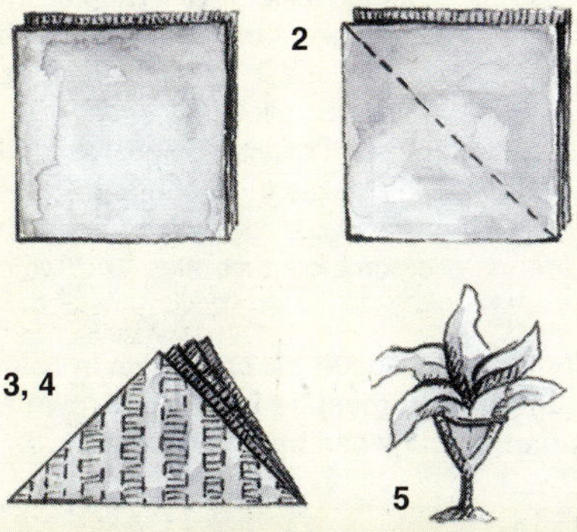

Effective and pretty on table.

Instructions:

1. Fold napkin into quarters.
2. Fold into triangle, closed corner to open points.
3. Turn two points over to other side. (Two points are on either side of closed point.)
4. Pleat.
5. Place closed end in glass. Pull down two points on each side and shape.

MEASUREMENTS & SUBSTITUTIONS

MEASUREMENTS

a pinch	1/8 teaspoon or less
3 teaspoons	1 tablespoon
4 tablespoons	1/4 cup
8 tablespoons	1/2 cup
12 tablespoons	3/4 cup
16 tablespoons	1 cup
2 cups	1 pint
4 cups	1 quart
4 quarts	1 gallon
8 quarts	1 peck
4 pecks	1 bushel
16 ounces	1 pound
32 ounces	1 quart
1 ounce liquid	2 tablespoons
8 ounces liquid	1 cup

Use standard measuring spoons and cups. All measurements are level.

C° TO F° CONVERSION

120° C	250° F
140° C	275° F
150° C	300° F
160° C	325° F
180° C	350° F
190° C	375° F
200° C	400° F
220° C	425° F
230° C	450° F

Temperature conversions are estimates.

SUBSTITUTIONS

Ingredient	Quantity	Substitute
baking powder	1 teaspoon	1/4 tsp. baking soda plus 1/2 tsp. cream of tartar
chocolate	1 square (1 oz.)	3 or 4 T. cocoa plus 1 T. butter
cornstarch	1 tablespoon	2 T. flour or 2 tsp. quick-cooking tapioca
cracker crumbs	3/4 cup	1 c. bread crumbs
dates	1 lb.	1 1/2 c. dates, pitted and cut
dry mustard	1 teaspoon	1 T. prepared mustard
flour, self-rising	1 cup	1 c. all-purpose flour, 1/2 tsp. salt, and 1 tsp. baking powder
herbs, fresh	1 tablespoon	1 tsp. dried herbs
ketchup or chili sauce	1 cup	1 c. tomato sauce plus 1/2 c. sugar and 2 T. vinegar (for use in cooking)
milk, sour	1 cup	1 T. lemon juice or vinegar plus sweet milk to make 1 c. (let stand 5 minutes)
whole	1 cup	1/2 c. evaporated milk plus 1/2 c. water
min. marshmallows	10	1 lg. marshmallow
onion, fresh	1 small	1 T. instant minced onion, rehydrated
sugar, brown	1/2 cup	2 T. molasses in 1/2 c. granulated sugar
powdered	1 cup	1 c. granulated sugar plus 1 tsp. cornstarch
tomato juice	1 cup	1/2 c. tomato sauce plus 1/2 c. water

When substituting cocoa for chocolate in cakes, the amount of flour must be reduced. Brown and white sugars usually can be interchanged.

EQUIVALENCY CHART

Food	Quantity	Yield
apple	1 medium	1 cup
banana, mashed	1 medium	1/3 cup
bread	1 1/2 slices	1 cup soft crumbs
bread	1 slice	1/4 cup fine, dry crumbs
butter	1 stick or 1/4 pound	1/2 cup
cheese, American, cubed	1 pound	2 2/3 cups
American, grated	1 pound	5 cups
cream cheese	3-ounce package	6 2/3 tablespoons
chocolate, bitter	1 square	1 ounce
cocoa	1 pound	4 cups
coconut	1 1/2 pound package	2 2/3 cups
coffee, ground	1 pound	5 cups
cornmeal	1 pound	3 cups
cornstarch	1 pound	3 cups
crackers, graham	14 squares	1 cup fine crumbs
saltine	28 crackers	1 cup fine crumbs
egg	4 - 5 whole	1 cup
whites	8 - 10	1 cup
yolks	10 - 12	1 cup
evaporated milk	1 cup	3 cups whipped
flour, cake, sifted	1 pound	4 1/2 cups
rye	1 pound	5 cups
white, sifted	1 pound	4 cups
white, unsifted	1 pound	3 3/4 cups
gelatin, flavored	3 1/4 ounces	1/2 cup
unflavored	1/4 ounce	1 tablespoon
lemon	1 medium	3 tablespoon juice
marshmallows	16	1/4 pound
noodles, cooked	8-ounce package	7 cups
uncooked	4 ounces (1 1/2 cups)	2 - 3 cups cooked
macaroni, cooked	8-ounce package	6 cups
macaroni, uncooked	4 ounces (1 1/4 cups)	2 1/4 cups cooked
spaghetti, uncooked	7 ounces	4 cups cooked
nuts, chopped	1/4 pound	1 cup
almonds	1 pound	3 1/2 cups
walnuts, broken	1 pound	3 cups
walnuts, unshelled	1 pound	1 1/2 to 1 3/4 cups
onion	1 medium	1/2 cup
orange	3 - 4 medium	1 cup juice
raisins	1 pound	3 1/2 cups
rice, brown	1 cup	4 cups cooked
converted	1 cup	3 1/2 cups cooked
regular	1 cup	3 cups cooked
wild	1 cup	4 cups cooked
sugar, brown	1 pound	2 1/2 cups
powdered	1 pound	3 1/2 cups
white	1 pound	2 cups
vanilla wafers	22	1 cup fine crumbs
zwieback, crumbled	4	1 cup

FOOD QUANTITIES

FOR LARGE SERVINGS

	25 Servings	50 Servings	100 Servings
Beverages:			
coffee	1/2 pound & 1 1/2 gallons water	1 pound & 3 gallons water	2 pounds & 6 gallons water
lemonade	10 - 15 lemons & 1 1/2 gallons water	20 - 30 lemons & 3 gallons water	40 - 60 lemons & 6 gallons water
tea	1/12 pound & 1 1/2 gallons water	1/6 pound & 3 gallons water	1/3 pound & 6 gallons water
Desserts:			
layered cake	1 12" cake	3 10" cakes	6 10" cakes
sheet cake	1 10" x 12" cake	1 12" x 20" cake	2 12" x 20" cakes
watermelon	37 1/2 pounds	75 pounds	150 pounds
whipping cream	3/4 pint	1 1/2 to 2 pints	3 - 4 pints
Ice cream:			
brick	3 1/4 quarts	6 1/2 quarts	13 quarts
bulk	2 1/4 quarts	4 1/2 quarts or 1 1/4 gallons	9 quarts or 2 1/2 gallons
Meat, poultry or fish:			
fish	13 pounds	25 pounds	50 pounds
fish, fillets or steak	7 1/2 pounds	15 pounds	30 pounds
hamburger	9 pounds	18 pounds	35 pounds
turkey or chicken	13 pounds	25 - 35 pounds	50 - 75 pounds
wieners (beef)	6 1/2 pounds	13 pounds	25 pounds
Salads, casseroles:			
baked beans	3/4 gallon	1 1/4 gallons	2 1/2 gallons
jello salad	3/4 gallon	1 1/4 gallons	2 1/2 gallons
potato salad	4 1/4 quarts	2 1/4 gallons	4 1/2 gallons
scalloped potatoes	4 1/2 quarts or 1 12" x 20" pan	9 quarts or 2 1/4 gallons	18 quarts 4 1/2 gallons
spaghetti	1 1/4 gallons	2 1/2 gallons	5 gallons
Sandwiches:			
bread	50 slices or 3 1-lb. loaves	100 slices or 6 1-lb. loaves	200 slices or 12 1-lb. loaves
butter	1/2 pound	1 pound	2 pounds
lettuce	1 1/2 heads	3 heads	6 heads
mayonnaise	1 cup	2 cups	4 cups
mixed filling			
meat, eggs, fish	1 1/2 quarts	3 quarts	6 quarts
jam, jelly	1 quart	2 quarts	4 quarts

QUICK FIXES

PRACTICALLY EVERYONE has experienced that dreadful moment in the kitchen when a recipe failed and dinner guests have arrived. Perhaps a failed timer, distraction or a missing or mismeasured ingredient is to blame. These handy tips can save the day!

Acidic foods – Sometimes a tomato-based sauce will become too acidic. Add baking soda, one teaspoon at a time, to the sauce. Use sugar as a sweeter alternative.

Burnt food on pots and pans – Allow the pan to cool on its own. Remove as much of the food as possible. Fill with hot water and add a capful of liquid fabric softener to the pot; let it stand for a few hours. You'll have an easier time removing the burnt food.

Chocolate seizes – Chocolate can seize (turn coarse and grainy) when it comes into contact with water. Place seized chocolate in a metal bowl over a large saucepan with an inch of simmering water in it. Over medium heat, slowly whisk in warm heavy cream. Use 1/4 cup cream to 4 ounces of chocolate. The chocolate will melt and become smooth.

Forgot to thaw whipped topping – Thaw in microwave for 1 minute on the defrost setting. Stir to blend well. Do not over thaw!

Hands smell like garlic or onion – Rinse hands under cold water while rubbing them with a large stainless steel spoon.

Hard brown sugar – Place in a paper bag and microwave for a few seconds, or place hard chunks in a food processor.

Jell-O too hard – Heat on a low microwave power setting for a very short time.

Lumpy gravy or sauce – Use a blender, food processor or simply strain.

No tomato juice – Mix 1/2 cup ketchup with 1/2 cup water.

Out of honey – Substitute 1 1/4 cups sugar dissolved in 1 cup water.

Overcooked sweet potatoes or carrots – Softened sweet potatoes and carrots make a wonderful soufflé with the addition of eggs and sugar. Consult your favorite cookbook for a good soufflé recipe. Overcooked sweet potatoes can also be used as pie filling.

Sandwich bread is stale – Toast or microwave bread briefly. Otherwise, turn it into bread crumbs. Bread exposed to light and heat will hasten its demise, so consider using a bread box. If the bread will not be eaten within a few days, store half in the freezer.

Soup, sauce, gravy too thin – Add 1 tablespoon of flour to hot soup, sauce or gravy. Whisk well (to avoid lumps) while the mixture is boiling. Repeat if necessary.

Sticky rice – Rinse rice with warm water.

Stew or soup is greasy – Refrigerate and remove grease once it congeals. Another trick is to lay cold lettuce leaves over the hot stew for about 10 seconds and then remove. Repeat as necessary.

Too salty – Add a little sugar and vinegar. For soups or sauces, add a raw peeled potato.

Too sweet – Add a little vinegar or lemon juice.

Undercooked cakes and cookies – Serve over vanilla ice cream. You can also layer pieces of cake or cookies with whipped cream and fresh fruit to form a dessert parfait. Crumbled cookies also make an excellent ice cream or cream pie topping.

COUNTING CALORIES

BEVERAGES

apple juice, 6 oz. 90
coffee (black) 0
cola, 12 oz. 115
cranberry juice, 6 oz. 115
ginger ale, 12 oz. 115
grape juice, (prepared from
    frozen concentrate), 6 oz. 142
lemonade, (prepared from
    frozen concentrate), 6 oz. 85
milk, protein fortified, 1 c. 105
    skim, 1 c. 90
    whole, 1 c. 160
orange juice, 6 oz. 85
pineapple juice, unsweetened, 6 oz. 95
root beer, 12 oz. 150
tonic (quinine water) 12 oz. 132

BREADS

cornbread, 1 sm. square 130
dumplings, 1 med. 70
French toast, 1 slice..........................135
melba toast, 1 slice 25
muffins, blueberry, 1 muffin 110
    bran, 1 muffin...............................106
    corn, 1 muffin...............................125
    English, 1 muffin 280
pancakes, 1 (4-in.) 60
pumpernickel, 1 slice 75
rye, 1 slice 60
waffle, 1 216
white, 1 slice ....60 - 70
whole wheat, 1 slice ....55 - 65

CEREALS

cornflakes, 1 c. 105
cream of wheat, 1 c. 120
oatmeal, 1 c. 148
rice flakes, 1 c. 105
shredded wheat, 1 biscuit 100
sugar krisps, 3/4 c. 110

CRACKERS

graham, 1 cracker ....15 - 30
rye crisp, 1 cracker..............................35
saltine, 1 cracker ....17 - 20
wheat thins, 1 cracker 9

DAIRY PRODUCTS

butter or margarine, 1 T. 100
cheese, American, 1 oz. 100
    camembert, 1 oz.............................85
    cheddar, 1 oz. 115
    cottage cheese, 1 oz. 30
    mozzarella, 1 oz. 90
    parmesan, 1 oz. 130
    ricotta, 1 oz. 50
    roquefort, 1 oz. 105
    Swiss, 1 oz. 105
cream, light, 1 T. 30
    heavy, 1 T. 55
    sour, 1 T. 45
hot chocolate, with milk, 1 c. 277
milk chocolate, 1 oz. ....145 - 155
yogurt
    made w/ whole milk, 1 c.......150 - 165
    made w/ skimmed milk, 1 c. 125

EGGS

fried, 1 lg. 100
poached or boiled, 1 lg. ....75 - 80
scrambled or in omelet, 1 lg. ....110 - 130

FISH & SEAFOOD

bass, 4 oz. 105
salmon, broiled or baked, 3 oz. 155
sardines, canned in oil, 3 oz. 170
trout, fried, 3 1/2 oz. 220
tuna, in oil, 3 oz. 170
    in water, 3 oz. 110

COUNTING CALORIES

FRUITS

apple, 1 med. ....80 - 100
applesauce, sweetened, 1/2 c. ....90 - 115
  unsweetened, 1/2 c. 50
banana, 1 med. 85
blueberries, 1/2 c. 45
cantaloupe, 1/2 c. 24
cherries (pitted), raw, 1/2 c. 40
grapefruit, 1/2 med. 55
grapes, 1/2 c. ....35 - 55
honeydew, 1/2 c. 55
mango, 1 med. 90
orange, 1 med. ....65 - 75
peach, 1 med. 35
pear, 1 med. ....60 - 100
pineapple, fresh, 1/2 c. 40
  canned in syrup, 1/2 c. 95
plum, 1 med. 30
strawberries, fresh, 1/2 c. 30
  frozen and sweetened, 1/2 c. ..120 - 140
tangerine, 1 lg. 39
watermelon, 1/2 c. 42

MEAT & POULTRY

beef, ground (lean), 3 oz. 185
  roast, 3 oz. 185
chicken, broiled, 3 oz. 115
lamb chop (lean), 3 oz. ....175 - 200
steak, sirloin, 3 oz. 175
  tenderloin, 3 oz. 174
  top round, 3 oz. 162
turkey, dark meat, 3 oz. 175
  white meat, 3 oz. 150
veal, cutlet, 3 oz. 156
  roast, 3 oz. 76

NUTS

almonds, 2 T. 105
cashews, 2 T. 100
peanuts, 2 T. 105
peanut butter, 1 T. 95
pecans, 2 T. 95
pistachios, 2 T. 92
walnuts, 2 T. 80

PASTA

macaroni or spaghetti,
  cooked, 3/4 c. 115

SALAD DRESSINGS

blue cheese, 1 T. 70
French, 1 T. 65
Italian, 1 T. 80
mayonnaise, 1 T. 100
olive oil, 1 T. 124
Russian, 1 T. 70
salad oil, 1 T. 120

SOUPS

bean, 1 c. ....130 - 180
beef noodle, 1 c. 70
bouillon and consomme, 1 c. 30
chicken noodle, 1 c. 65
chicken with rice, 1 c. 50
minestrone, 1 c. ....80 - 150
split pea, 1 c. ....145 - 170
tomato with milk, 1 c. 170
vegetable, 1 c. ....80 - 100

VEGETABLES

asparagus, 1 c. 35
broccoli, cooked, 1/2 c. 25
cabbage, cooked, 1/2 c. ....15 - 20
carrots, cooked, 1/2 c. ....25 - 30
cauliflower, 1/2 c. ....10 - 15
corn (kernels), 1/2 c. 70
green beans, 1 c. 30
lettuce, shredded, 1/2 c. 5
mushrooms, canned, 1/2 c. 20
onions, cooked, 1/2 c. 30
peas, cooked, 1/2 c. 60
potato, baked, 1 med. 90
  chips, 8-10 100
  mashed, w/milk & butter, 1 c. ..200 - 300
spinach, 1 c. 40
tomato, raw, 1 med. 25
  cooked, 1/2 c. 30

COOKING TERMS

Au gratin: Topped with crumbs and/or cheese and browned in oven or under broiler.

Au jus: Served in its own juices.

Baste: To moisten foods during cooking with pan drippings or special sauce in order to add flavor and prevent drying.

Bisque: A thick cream soup.

Blanch: To immerse in rapidly boiling water and allow to cook slightly.

Cream: To soften a fat, especially butter, by beating it at room temperature. Butter and sugar are often creamed together, making a smooth, soft paste.

Crimp: To seal the edges of a two-crust pie either by pinching them at intervals with the fingers or by pressing them together with the tines of a fork.

Crudités: An assortment of raw vegetables (i.e. carrots, broccoli, celery, mushrooms) that is served as an hors d'oeuvre, often accompanied by a dip.

Degrease: To remove fat from the surface of stews, soups or stock. Usually cooled in the refrigerator so that fat hardens and is easily removed.

Dredge: To coat lightly with flour, cornmeal, etc.

Entrée: The main course.

Fold: To incorporate a delicate substance, such as whipped cream or beaten egg whites, into another substance without releasing air bubbles. A spatula is used to gently bring part of the mixture from the bottom of the bowl to the top. The process is repeated, while slowly rotating the bowl, until the ingredients are thoroughly blended.

Glaze: To cover with a glossy coating, such as a melted and somewhat diluted jelly for fruit desserts.

Julienne: To cut or slice vegetables, fruits or cheeses into match-shaped slivers.

Marinate: To allow food to stand in a liquid in order to tenderize or to add flavor.

Meuniére: Dredged with flour and sautéed in butter.

Mince: To chop food into very small pieces.

Parboil: To boil until partially cooked; to blanch. Usually final cooking in a seasoned sauce follows this procedure.

Pare: To remove the outermost skin of a fruit or vegetable.

Poach: To cook gently in hot liquid kept just below the boiling point.

Purée: To mash foods by hand by rubbing through a sieve or food mill, or by whirling in a blender or food processor until perfectly smooth.

Refresh: To run cold water over food that has been parboiled in order to stop the cooking process quickly.

Sauté: To cook and/or brown food in a small quantity of hot shortening.

Scald: To heat to just below the boiling point, when tiny bubbles appear at the edge of the saucepan.

Simmer: To cook in liquid just below the boiling point. The surface of the liquid should be barely moving, broken from time to time by slowly rising bubbles.

Steep: To let food stand in hot liquid in order to extract or to enhance flavor, like tea in hot water or poached fruit in syrup.

Toss: To combine ingredients with a repeated lifting motion.

Whip: To beat rapidly in order to incorporate air and produce expansion, as in heavy cream or egg whites.